DISCOVERING THE ANCIENT PAST

DISCOVERING THE ANCIENT PAST

A LOOK AT THE EVIDENCE

Merry E. Wiesner
University of Wisconsin—Milwaukee

Julius R. Ruff
Marquette University

Franklin M. Doeringer
Lawrence University

William Bruce Wheeler
University of Tennessee

HOUGHTON MIFFLIN COMPANY   **Boston**   **New York**

Senior Sponsoring Editor: Nancy Blaine
Development Editor: Julie Dunn
Associate Project Editor: Reba Libby
Editorial Assistant: Rachel Zanders
Production/Design Coordinator: Sarah Ambrose
Manufacturing Manager: Florence Cadran
Senior Marketing Manager: Sandra McGuire

Cover image: The Art Archive/Archaeological Museum Naples/Dagli Orti, Ref. AA366178.

Printed in the U.S.A.

Library of Congress Catalog Card Number: 2002117268

ISBN: 0–618–37930–4

1 2 3 4 5 6 7 8 9–MP–08 07 06 05 04

CONTENTS

PREFACE

The title of this book begins with a verb, a choice that reflects our basic philosophy about history. History is not simply something one learns about; it is something one does. One discovers the past, and what makes this pursuit exciting is not only the past that is discovered but also the process of discovery itself. This process can be simultaneously exhilarating and frustrating, enlightening and confusing, but it is always challenging enough to convince those of us who are professional historians to spend our lives at it.

The recognition that history involves discovery as much as physics or astronomy does is often not shared by students, whose classroom experience of history frequently does not extend beyond listening to lectures and reading textbooks. This more passive approach may be particularly strong in courses focusing on eras far removed in time from our own. Providing the background that students need to make historical conclusions and discoveries on their own can be extremely time-consuming, especially in courses on ancient history that may be designed to cover a thousand years or more in fifteen weeks. *Discovering the Ancient Past: A Look at the Evidence* is thus designed with two goals in mind. The first is to allow students enrolled in ancient history courses to *do* history in the same way we as historians do—to examine a group of original sources in order to answer questions about the past. We feel that contact with original sources is an excellent means of communicating the excitement of doing history, especially for societies that may seem both exotic and familiar, such as the ancient world. The second goal is to provide students with sufficient background in each chapter to allow them to begin the process of interpretation on their own. This book differs from most source collections that cover the ancient world in that each chapter includes both sources and background information, and is organized around a question or questions that students can answer from material contained in that chapter.

For students to learn history the way we as historians do, they must not only be confronted with the evidence; they must also learn how to use that evidence to arrive at a conclusion. In other words, they must learn historical methodology. Too often methodology (or even the notion that historians *have* a methodology) is reserved for upper-level or graduate methods or historiography courses; students in chronologically—or topically—defined courses are simply presented with historical facts and interpretations without being shown how these were unearthed or formulated. Students may learn that historians hold different interpretations of the significance of an event or individual or different ideas about causation, but they are not informed about how historians come to such conclusions.

Thus, along with evidence and background material, we have provided explicit suggestions about how one might analyze that evidence, guiding students as they reach their own conclusions. As they work through the various chapters, students will discover not only that the sources of historical information are wide-ranging, but also that the methodologies appropriate to understanding and using them are equally diverse. By doing history themselves, students will learn how intellectual historians handle philosophical treatises, economic historians quantitative data, social historians court records, and political and diplomatic historians theoretical treatises and letters. They will also be asked to consider the limitations of their evidence, to explore what historical questions it cannot answer as well as those it can. Instead of passive observers, students become active participants.

Following an approach that we have found successful in many different classroom situations, we have divided each chapter into five parts: The Problem, Sources and Method, The Evidence, Questions to Consider, and Epilogue. The section called "The Problem" presents the general historical background and context for the evidence offered and concludes with the central question or questions explored in the chapter. The section titled "Sources and Method" provides specific information about the sources and suggests ways in which students might best study and analyze this primary evidence. It also discusses how previous historians have evaluated such sources and mentions any major disputes about methodology or interpretation. "The Evidence" forms the core of each chapter, presenting a variety of original sources for students to use in completing the central task. In "Questions to Consider," suggestions are offered about connections among the sources, and students are guided to draw deductions from the evidence. The final section, "Epilogue," traces both the immediate effects of the issue under discussion and its impact on later developments.

Along with its incorporation of methodology and focus on specific questions, this book differs from most source collections that cover the ancient world in two additional ways. One is the span of time and geography covered, from the river-valley civilizations of Mesopotamia and Egypt and the nomadic peoples of the steppes of western Asia in the third millennium B.C.E. to the eastern Roman Empire and the Germanic tribes in the time of Justinian. Thus students will be able to learn about long-term changes in technology, economic structures, and social systems, along with more rapid developments in politics and ideas. Chapter 1, for example, looks at the tools and institutions developed over many centuries in the ancient world to address the need for water, while Chapter 7 takes a very focused look at the achievements of one man, Caesar Augustus. The broader geographic scope will help them gain a sense of the interconnectedness of the ancient world, which has been such an important thrust in the scholarship of the last twenty years. Chapter 2, for example, asks students to compare the creation accounts in the Rig Veda, the I Ching, and the Torah, allowing them to test ideas about the differences and similarities between "Western" and "Eastern" cultures in the ancient world.

The second unusual feature of this book is the variety of evidence it presents. The use of archaeological materials has always been important in studying ancient history, and this book presents a range of these: coins, buildings, roads, grave markers, pottery. It also introduces students to ways in which modern technology has enhanced the study of the physical remains of the past through such methods as aerial photography and satellite imagery. We feel that visual material is particularly important in helping students understand an era when the vast majority of people could not read, and have included a large number of visual sources: paintings, sculpture, maps, architectural plans, textiles, bas reliefs. Two of the chapters, in fact, use nonwritten evidence exclusively; Chapter 4 asks students to analyze depictions of the human form, and Chapter 6 asks them to evaluate the impact of the horse on human development. In choosing written evidence, we again have tried to offer a broad sample—creation accounts, hymns, political treatises, Hebrew and Christian Scripture, law codes, proclamations, chronicles, histories, philosophical treatises, sermons, letters.

Within this broad framework in terms of chronology, geography, and source materials, we have tried to present a series of historical issues and events from the ancient Middle East, Mediterranean, and Europe of significance to the instructor as well as of interest to the students. We have also aimed to provide a balance among political, social, economic, intellectual, and cultural history. In other words, we have attempted to create a kind of historical sampler that we believe will help students learn about the ancient world as well as learn the methods and skills used by historians.

These skills—analyzing arguments, developing hypotheses, comparing evidence, testing conclusions, and reevaluating material—will not only enable students to master historical content; they will also provide the necessary foundation for critical thinking in other college courses and after college as well.

Discovering the Ancient Past is designed to accommodate any format of ancient history course, from the small lecture/discussion class of a liberal arts or community college to the large lecture with discussions led by teaching assistants at a sizable university. The chapters may be used for individual assignments, team projects, class discussions, papers, and exams. Each is self-contained, so that any combination may be assigned. The book is not intended to replace a standard textbook; it was written to accompany any ancient history text the instructor chooses.

Acknowledgments

In the completion of this book, the authors received assistance from a number of people. Our colleagues and students at the University of Wisconsin–Milwaukee, Lawrence University, Marquette University, and the University of Tennessee, Knoxville, have been generous with their ideas and time. The authors also wish to extend their thanks to the staff of Houghton Mifflin Company for their enthusiastic support.

M.E.W.
W.B.W.
J.R.R.
F.M.D.

CHAPTER ONE

THE NEED FOR WATER IN

ANCIENT SOCIETIES

THE PROBLEM

The title of the course for which you are using this book is probably a variant of "Ancient Civilization." Why do we use the term "civilization"? What distinguishes human cultures that are labeled civilizations from those that are not? Though great differences separate them, all civilizations share some basic characteristics. The most important of these similarities is the presence of cities; indeed, the word "civilization" comes from the Latin word *civilis* (meaning "civic"), which is also the root of "citizen" and "civil". Historians and archaeologists generally define a city as a place inhabited by more than 5,000 people, and they have discovered the remains of the earliest communities of this size in ancient Mesopotamia, which is present-day Iraq.

Why should the presence of cities be the distinguishing mark of cultural development? It is not the cities themselves but what they imply about a culture that makes them so important. Any society in which thousands of people live in close proximity to one another must have some sort of laws or rules governing human behavior. These may be either part of an oral tradition or, as in ancient Mesopotamia, written down. A city must provide its residents with a constant supply of food, which means developing ways to transport food into the city from the surrounding farmland, to store food throughout the year, and to save it for years marked by poor harvests. Not only does the presence of cities indicate that people could transport and store food effectively, but it also reveals that they were producing enough surplus food to allow for specialization of labor. If all work time had been devoted to farming, it would not have been possible to build roads, produce storage bins, or enforce laws on which the city depended. This specialization of labor, then, gave some members of society the opportunity and time to create and produce goods and artifacts that were not directly essential to daily survival. Urban residents in Mesopotamia began to construct large buildings and decorate them with sculptures, paintings, and mosaics; to write poetry and history; and to develop religious and philosophical ideas, all of which are pursuits we consider essential to a civilization. As the cities themselves grew, they required greater and greater amounts of food to feed their inhabitants, which led to further technological development.

Mesopotamia was in many ways an odd location for the beginning of a civilization. True, the soil is so rich that the region is called the Fertile Crescent, but it does not receive enough natural rainfall to grow crops steadily year after year. In fact, this region is not where agriculture began in the West; that happened closer to the Mediterranean, where the rainfall was more regular. Apparently, as techniques of planting and harvesting crops spread into Mesopotamia, the inhabitants realized that they would be able to use these techniques effectively only through irrigation. They needed to tap the waters flowing in the Tigris and Euphrates rivers, a project requiring the cooperation of a great many people. Thus, rather than proving a block to further development, the need for irrigation in ancient Mesopotamia may have been one of the reasons that cities first arose there. We may never be able to know this with certainty, because irrigation systems were already in place when written records began and because cities and irrigation expanded at the same time. We do

know, however, that in Mesopotamia, neither could have existed without the other; cities could survive only where irrigation had created a food surplus, and irrigation could survive only where enough people were available to create and maintain ditches and other parts of the system.

Building irrigation systems presented both technical and organizational problems. The Tigris and Euphrates were fast-flowing rivers that carried soil as well as water down from the highlands. This rich soil created new farmland where the rivers emptied into the Persian Gulf. (The ancient Persian Gulf ended more than 100 miles north of its present boundary; all that land was created as the rivers filled in the delta.) The soil also rapidly clogged up the irrigation ditches, which consequently required constant cleaning. Every year these deposits were excavated and piled on the banks until the sides of the ditches grew so tall that they could no longer be cleaned easily. At this point the old ditch was abandoned and a new ditch was cut, tasks that required a great deal of work and the cooperation of everyone whose land was watered by that ditch.

Mesopotamian farmers used several types of irrigation. One technique, known as basin irrigation, was to level large plots of land fronting the rivers and main canals and build up dikes around them. In the spring and other times during the year when the water was high, farmers knocked holes in the dikes to admit water and fresh soil. Once the sediment had settled, they let the water flow back into the channel. They also built small waterways between their fields to provide water throughout the year, thereby developing a system of perennial irrigation. In the hillier country of northern Mesopotamia, farmers built terraces with water channels running alongside them. The hillside terraces provided narrow strips of flat land to farm, and the waterways were dug to connect with brooks and streams.

Farmers could depend on gravity to bring water to their fields during spring and flood seasons, but at other times they needed water-raising machines. They devised numerous types of machines, some of which are still in use today in many parts of the world. These solved some problems but created others, as farmers with machines could drain an irrigation ditch during times of low water, leaving their neighbors with nothing. How were rights to water to be decided? Solving this problem was crucial to human social organization, and the first recorded laws regarding property rights in fact concern not rights to land but rights to water. In Mesopotamia, land was useless unless it was irrigated.

Many of the irrigation techniques developed in Mesopotamia either spread to Egypt or were developed independently there. Because it received even less rainfall than Mesopotamia, Egypt was totally dependent on the Nile for watering crops. Fortunately, the Nile was a much better source of water than the Tigris and Euphrates because it flooded regularly, allowing for easy basin irrigation. The rise and fall of the Nile was so regular, in fact, that the Egyptians based their 365-day calendar on its annual flooding. The Egyptians also constructed waterways and water-lifting machines to allow for perennial irrigation. As in Mesopotamia, irrigation in Egypt both caused and resulted from the growth of cities. It contributed as well to the power of the kings, whom the Egyptian people regarded as responsible for the flood of the Nile.

Irrigation was more difficult in places that did not have flood-prone rivers, including many parts of North Africa and the Near East. Here people adapted techniques to conserve water from sporadic heavy rainfalls. They dammed the temporary lakes (termed "wadis") created by these rainfalls and built ditches to convey the water to fields, rather than allowing it simply to flow off onto the desert. Sometimes this wadi irrigation involved a whole series of small dams down the course of rivers that ran only after storms. Besides providing water, wadi irrigation also built up terraces because the rivers carried soil with them.

The earliest water systems were for crop irrigation, but people also began to demand good drinking water. In many parts of the ancient world, the demand for drinking water led to the establishment of a second system because river water that is suitable for irrigation may be brackish, unpleasant, or even unhealthful to drink. In southern Europe, where lakes were often not far from growing cities, people solved the problem by building channels made of timber, stone, or clay earthenware to carry water from the lakes to the city. These channels might be open or closed, depending on the terrain and the level of technical development of the culture that built them. Generally they relied on gravity flow and fed into underground tanks or reservoirs in the city; the oldest known water channels are in Jerusalem and date from about 1000 B.C.E. The construction of such systems, which demanded even more technical expertise than the building of irrigation ditches, provoked additional legal problems about ownership of the right to this clean, cool water.

When lakes were not located close enough to make aboveground channels feasible, people had to rely on water from aquifers, underground water-bearing layers of gravel or porous rock. The water could be obtained from wells drilled in the ground, but wells could supply only a small amount of water at a time. Once an aquifer had been discovered, however, a horizontal channel could be dug to lead the water to an outside channel or reservoir. A horizontal channel worked only in hilly areas where the aquifer stood higher than a nearby valley, but such channels, dating back more than two thousand years and known as *qanats*, have been found in Iran, Syria, Egypt, and Turkey. If the amount of water it yielded was large enough, the qanat could be used for irrigation as well as drinking water.

When the Romans conquered the Middle East and North Africa in the second century B.C.E., they inherited irrigation systems that in some cases had already been in existence for more than 2,000 years. The Romans

carried many ideas to other parts of their empire and made innovations as the terrain or distance required. Most of the European territory in the Roman Empire received adequate rainfall for farming without irrigation, but many Roman cities, especially Rome itself, experienced a chronic shortage of drinking water. The Romans solved this problem by building aqueducts, covered or uncovered channels that brought water into the cities from lakes and springs. The first of these in Rome was built in 312 B.C.E., and the system expanded continuously up to about 150 C.E. Over 300 miles of aqueducts served the city of Rome alone, with extensive systems in the outlying provinces as well. Although Roman engineers went to great lengths to avoid valleys, they were occasionally forced to construct enormous bridges to carry the aqueducts over valleys. Some of these bridges were more than 150 feet high, and a few, such as the bridge-aqueduct in Segovia, Spain, still bring water to city residents. The Romans' sophisticated architectural and construction techniques—the arch and water-resistant cement, for example—enabled them to build water systems undreamed of in Mesopotamia and Egypt. Legal problems were not as easily solved, however, and disputes about water rights recur frequently throughout the long history of Rome.

Supplying cities with water was not simply a technological problem; it had economic, legal, and political implications. Through their solutions to these complex problems, ancient societies created what we call civilization. Your task in this chapter will be to use both visual and written evidence of ancient water systems

to answer the question, How did the need for a steady supply of water shape civilization?

SOURCES AND METHOD

Historians use a wide variety of sources when examining ancient irrigation and water supply systems. Since many of these systems were created before the development of writing, archaeological evidence is extremely important, especially in examining technological development. This evidence may be the actual remains of ancient ditches, machines, or aqueducts, but in many areas these have completely disappeared. This does not mean that they have left no trace, however, for the ancient uses of modern landscapes are often revealed through patterns of depressions and discoloration.

The best way to see these patterns is through aerial photography. Analyzing aerial photographs can be a difficult task, and learning how to read ancient land-use patterns through the overlay of modern development takes a great deal of training. Occasionally the older patterns can be quite clear, however, and only a small amount of additional information is necessary for you to begin to decode them. The first piece of evidence, Source 1, is an aerial photograph of the site of a pre-Roman city in Italy. Examine the picture carefully. Can you see the old grid pattern of irrigation ditches, which shows up as light and dark marsh grass? The

dark lines are the outlines of ancient irrigation ditches, the lighter squares are ancient fields, and the white parallel lines superimposed on the top are part of a modern drainage system. To examine the ancient system, you will need to strip away the modern system mentally. What do you think the broader black strip at the top left is? Does this system look like basin or perennial irrigation? Look at the flatness of the landscape. Would silting be a problem?

A more sophisticated type of aerial photography involves the use of satellites rather than airplanes. Satellites can take extremely detailed pictures of the earth's surface that reveal natural and artificially constructed features, both ancient and contemporary. The sharpest images are produced by high-resolution military satellites whose pictures are not available to the public. Low-power images produced by LANDSAT, the only U.S. commercial imaging satellite system, are adequate for most archaeological and historical purposes, however. Source 2 is a map of the major ancient irrigation ditches between the Tigris and Euphrates rivers that were identifiable in a recent LANDSAT image. What does the size of the system reveal about Mesopotamian technology? What does it imply about the political systems in this area—would you expect, for example, the cities in

Mesopotamia to be hostile to one another? New technologies such as LANDSAT imagery not only provide answers to questions, but also guide future research. How could you use this map to plan further investigations of irrigation systems?

Aerial photography provides visual evidence of entire irrigation systems but not of the specific tools and machines used to lift water to the fields. For these we must look to the remains of the tools themselves or to depictions of them in tomb paintings, mosaics, and pottery. Source 3 is the earliest depiction of irrigation ditches that has survived from ancient Egypt, carved on the head of a ceremonial mace dating from around 3100 B.C.E. The large figure in the middle is one of the early kings of Egypt, who is holding a hoe and who is flanked by two palm-fan bearers and a man holding a basket for the dirt dug up by the hoe. At the bottom are two other workmen, also with hoes, excavating or deepening the ditches. Based on what you already know about Egyptian society, would you expect the king himself to be digging ditches? Why might this mace, which signified royal authority, show the king involved in building irrigation ditches?

Some of the machines depicted in ancient paintings are still in use today, showing that many techniques for lifting water have not changed at all for thousands of years. Sources 4 through 7 show four different machines for raising water that we know were in use in ancient times and are still in use in many parts of the world today: the shaduf, saqiya,

Archimedes' screw,[1] and noria. To assess their role and importance, you must consider a number of different factors while carefully examining the four diagrams. Some of these factors are technical: How complicated is the machine to build? Does it have many moving parts that must all be in good repair? How much water can it lift? How high can it lift the water? Can it work with both flowing and stationary water? Some factors are economic: Does the machine require a person to operate it, thus taking that person away from other types of labor? Does it require a strong adult, or can it be operated by a child? Does it require an animal, which must be fed and cared for? Some factors are both economic and political: Does the machine require a variety of raw materials to build, more than one family might possess? Does it require any raw materials, like metal, that would have to be imported? (Such questions are political because someone has to decide which families get the raw materials necessary for their fields.) Some factors are legal: Does the machine raise so much water that laws about distribution would become necessary? At this point, you may want to make a chart summarizing your assessment of the advantages and disadvantages of each machine, which will help you in making your final conclusions.

We will now turn from visual to written sources. Because water is such a vital commodity, mention of water systems appears very early in

1. Archimedes (287–212 B.C.E.) was a Greek mathematician and inventor who is credited with inventing this machine.

recorded human history. The next five sources are written accounts of the construction or operation of water systems. Source 8 contains sections from the Code of Hammurabi, a Babylonian legal code dating from 1750 B.C.E., that refer to irrigation. Source 9 is a description of the Roman aqueduct system written by Vitruvius during the first century B.C.E., and Source 10 is a description of the water-system projects undertaken by Emperor Claudius during his reign (41–54 C.E.), written by the Roman historian Suetonius. The next selection is a discussion of some of the problems associated with Rome's water system written about 100 C.E. by Frontinus, who was commissioner of the water supply. The last is a proclamation issued by Emperor Theodosius in 438 as part of his code of laws, an edict that had probably been in effect for many earlier decades as well.

As you read these sources, notice first of all the technical issues that the authors are addressing. What problems in tapping, transportation, and storage of water do they discuss? What solutions do they suggest? Then look at legal problems, which you can find most clearly stated in the selection by Frontinus (Source 11) and the law codes of Hammurabi and Theodosius (Source 12). Keep in mind when you are reading the law codes that laws are generally written to address problems that already exist, not those the lawmakers are simply anticipating. The presence of a law, especially one that is frequently repeated, is often a good indication that the prohibited activity was probably happening, and happening often. How did people misuse or harm the water systems? What penalties were provided for those who did? Who controlled the legal use of water, and who decided how water was to be distributed?

The written sources also include information about political and economic factors in ancient water supply systems that is nearly impossible to gain from archaeological evidence. Careful reading can reveal who paid for the construction of such systems and who stood to gain financially from them once they were built. What reasons, other than the simple need for water, might rulers have had for building water systems? What political and economic factors entered into decisions about the ways in which water was to be distributed?

THE EVIDENCE

Source 1 from Leo Deuel, Flights into Yesterday: The Story of Aerial Archeology *(New York: St. Martin's Press, 1969), p. 236. Photo by Fotoaerea Valvassori, Ravenna.*

1. Aerial Photograph of Pre-Roman City in Italy

2. Major Ancient Levees Identifiable in LANDSAT Imagery

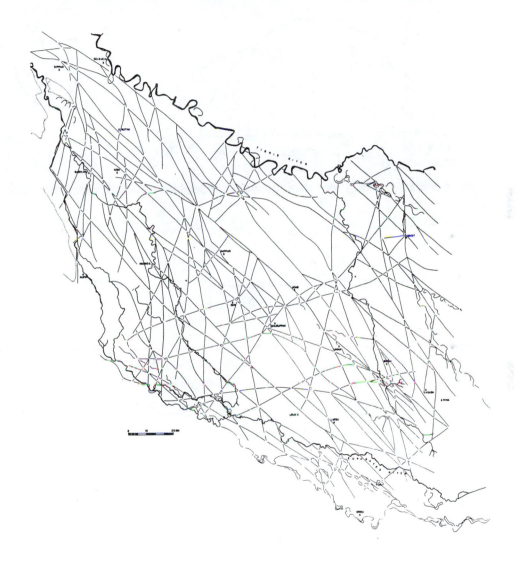

3. Early Egyptian King Cutting an Irrigation Ditch, Drawn from Mace-head Carving, 3100 B.C.E.

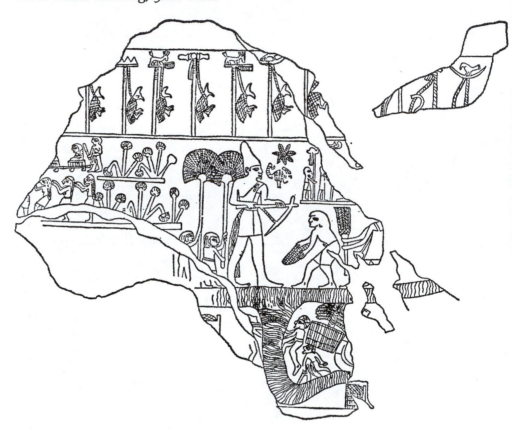

Sources 4 through 7 adapted from sketches by Merry E. Wiesner.

4. Shaduf

5. Saqiya

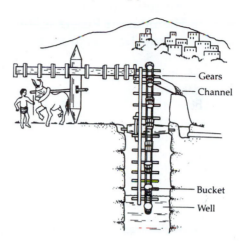

6. Archimedes' Screw

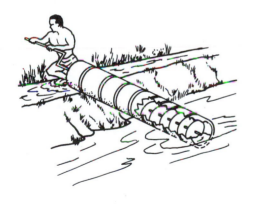

7. Noria

Source 8 from Robert F. Harper, The Code of Hammurabi *(Chicago: University of Chicago Press, 1904).*

8. Sections from the Code of Hammurabi Referring to Irrigation, 1750 B.C.E.

53. If a man neglects to maintain his dike and does not strengthen it, and a break is made in his dike and the water carries away the farmland, the man in whose dike the break has been made shall replace the grain which has been damaged.

54. If he is not able to replace the grain, they shall sell him and his goods and the farmers whose grain the water has carried away shall divide [the results of the sale].

55. If a man opens his canal for irrigation and neglects it and the water carries away an adjacent field, he shall pay out grain on the basis of the adjacent field.

56. If a man opens up the water and the water carries away the improvements of an adjacent field, he shall pay out ten gur of grain per bur [of damaged land]. . . .

66. If a man has stolen a watering-machine from the meadow, he shall pay five shekels of silver to the owner of the watering-machine.

Sources 9 and 10 from Naphtali Lewis and Meyer Reinhold, editors and translators, Roman Civilization *(New York: Columbia University Press, 1955), pp. 304–306; pp. 151–152. Reprinted with permission of the publisher.*

9. Vitruvius's Description of the Roman Aqueduct System, first century B.C.E.

The supply of water is made by three methods: by channels through walled conduits, or by lead pipes, or by earthenware pipes. And they are arranged as follows. In the case of conduits, the structure must be very solid; the bed of the channel must be leveled with a fall of not less than half a foot in 100 feet. The walled conduits are to be arched over so that the minimum amount of sun may strike the water. When it comes to the city walls, a reservoir is to be made. To this reservoir a triple distribution tank is to be joined to receive the water; and three pipes of equal size are to be placed in the reservoir, leading to the adjoining tanks, so that when there is an overflow from the two outer tanks, it may deliver into the middle tank. From the middle tank pipes will be laid to all basins and fountains; from the second tank to the baths, in order to furnish an annual revenue to the treasury; to avoid a deficiency in the public supply, private houses are to be supplied from the third, for private persons will not be able to divert the water, since they have their own limited supply from the distribution sources. Another reason why I have made these divisions is that those who take private supplies into their houses may by their taxes paid through tax farmers contribute to the maintenance of the water supply.

If, however, there are hills between the city and the source, we must proceed as follows: underground channels are to be dug and leveled to the fall mentioned above. If the bed is of tufa or stone, the channel may be cut in it; but if it is of soil or sand, the bed of the channel and the walls with the vaulting must be constructed, and the water should be thus conducted. Air shafts are to be so constructed that they are 120 feet apart.

But if the supply is to be by lead pipes, first of all a reservoir is to be built at the source. Then the opening of the pipe is to be determined in accordance with the amount of water, and these pipes are to be laid from the source reservoir to a reservoir which is inside the city.

When an aqueduct is to be made with lead pipes it is to have the following arrangement. If there is a fall from the source to the city and the intervening hills are not high enough to interrupt the supply, then if there are valleys, we must build substructures to bring it up to a level, as in the case of channels and conduits. If the way round the valley is not long, a circuit should be used; but if the valleys are expansive, the course will be directed down the hill, and when it reaches the bottom it is carried on a low substructure so that the level there may continue as far as possible. This will form a "belly," which the Greeks call *koilia*. When the "belly" comes to the hill opposite, and the long distance of the "belly" makes the water slow in welling up, the water is to be forced to the height of the top of the hill. . . .

Again, it is not without advantage to put reservoirs at intervals of 24,000 feet, so that if a break occurs anywhere neither the whole load of water nor the whole structure need be disturbed, and the place where it has occurred may be more easily found. But these reservoirs are to be neither in the descent nor on the level portion of the "belly," nor at risings, nor anywhere in a valley, but on unbroken level ground.

But if we wish to employ a less expensive method, we must proceed as follows. Earthenware pipes are to be made not less than two inches thick, but these pipes should be so tongued at one end that they can fit into and join one another. The joints are to be coated with quicklime mixed with oil. . . . Everything also is to be fixed as for lead pipes. Further, when the water is first let in from the source, ashes are to be put in beforehand, so that if any joints are not sufficiently coated they may be lined with the ashes.

Water supply by earthenware pipes has these advantages. First, in the construction: if a break occurs, anybody can repair it. Again, water is much more wholesome from earthenware pipes than from lead pipes. For it seems to

[13]

be made injurious by lead, because white lead is produced by it; and this is said to be harmful to the human body. So if what is produced by anything is injurious, there is no doubt that the thing itself is not wholesome. We can take an example from the workers in lead who have complexions affected by pallor. For when lead is smelted in casting, the fumes from it settle on the members of the body and, burning them, rob the limbs of the virtues of the blood. Therefore it seems that water should by no means be brought in lead pipes if we desire to have it wholesome. Everyday life can be used to show that the flavor from earthenware pipes is better, because everybody (even those who load their table with silver vessels) uses earthenware to preserve the purity of water.

But if we are to create springs from which the water supplies come, we must dig wells.

But if the soil is hard, or if the veins of water lie too deep, then supplies of water are to be collected from the roofs or higher ground in concrete cisterns. . . . If the cisterns are made double or triple, so that they can be changed by percolation, they will make the supply of water much more wholesome. For when the sediment has a place to settle in, the water will be more limpid and will keep its taste without any smell. If not, salt must be added to purify it.

10. Suetonius's Description of the Water Projects Undertaken by Emperor Claudius (r. 41–54 C.E.)

The public works which Claudius completed were great and essential rather than numerous; they were in particular the following: an aqueduct begun by Caligula; also the drainage channel of Lake Fucine and the harbor at Ostia, although in the case of the last two he knew that Augustus had refused the former to the Marsians in spite of their frequent requests, and that the latter had often been considered by the deified Julius but given up because of its difficulty. He brought to the city on stone arches the cool and abundant springs of the Claudian aqueduct . . . and at the same time the channel of the New Anio, distributing them into many beautifully ornamented fountains. He made the attempt on the Fucine Lake as much in the hope of gain as of glory, inasmuch as there were some who offered to drain it at their own cost provided the land that was drained be given them. He finished the drainage canal, which was three miles in length, partly by leveling and partly by tunneling a mountain, a work of great difficulty requiring eleven years, although he had 30,000 men at work all the time without interruption.

[14]

Source 11 from B. K. Workman, editor and translator, They Saw It Happen in Classical Times *(New York: Barnes & Noble, 1964), pp. 179–181. Reprinted by permission of Blackwell Publishing Ltd.*

11. Frontinus's Discussion of Rome's Water System, ca 100 C.E.

The New Anio[2] is drawn from the river in the district of Sinbrinum, at about the forty-second milestone along the Via Sublacensis. On either side of the river at this point are fields of rich soil which make the banks less firm, so that the water in the aqueduct is discoloured and muddy even without the damage done by storms. So a little way along from the inlet a cleansing basin was built where the water could settle and be purified between the river and the conduit. Even so, in the event of rain, the water reaches the city in a muddy state. The length of the New Anio is about 47 miles, of which over 39 are underground and more than 7 carried on structures above the ground. In the upper reaches a distance of about two miles in various sections is carried on low structures or arches. Nearer the city, from the seventh Roman milestone, is half a mile on substructures and five miles on arches. These arches are very high, rising in certain places to a height of 109 feet.

. . . All the aqueducts reach the city at different levels. So some serve the higher districts and some cannot reach loftier ground. For the hills of Rome have gradually increased in height because of the rubble from frequent fires. There are five aqueducts high enough at entrance to reach all the city, but they supply water at different pressures. . . .

Anyone who wants to tap water for private consumption must send in an application and take it, duly signed by the Emperor, to the Commissioner. The latter must take immediate action on Caesar's grant, and enroll one of the Imperial freedmen to help him in the business. . . . The right to water once granted cannot be inherited or bought, and does not go with the property, though long ago a privilege was extended to the public baths that their right should last in perpetuity. . . . When grants lapse, notice is given and record made in the ledgers, which are consulted so that future applicants can be given vacant supplies. The previous custom was to cut off these lapsed supplies at once, to make some profit by a temporary sale to the landowners or even to outsiders. Our Emperor felt that property should not suddenly be left without water, and that it would be fairer to give thirty days' notice for other arrangements to be made by the interested party. . . .

Now that I have explained the situation with regard to private supply, it will be pertinent to give some examples of the ways in which men have broken these very sound arrangements and have been caught red-handed. In some

2. An aqueduct completed under the emperor Claudius in 52 C.E.

reservoirs I have found larger valves in position than had been granted, and some have not even had the official stamp on them. When a stamped valve exceeds the legal dimensions, then the private advantage of the controller who stamped it is uncovered. When a valve is not even stamped, then both parties are clearly liable, chiefly the purchaser, but also the controller. Sometimes stamped valves of the correct dimensions open into pipes of a larger cross-section. The result is that the water is not kept in for the legal distance, but forced through a short, narrow pipe and easily fills the larger one which is joined to it. So care must be taken that, when a valve is stamped, the pipes connected to it should be stamped as of the correct length ordered by Senatorial decree. For then and only then will the controller be fully liable when he knows that only stamped pipes must be positioned.

When valves are sited, good care must be taken to see that they are placed in a horizontal line, not one above the other. A lower inlet gets a greater pressure of water, the upper one less, because the supply of water is taken by the lower. In some pipes no valves are positioned at all. These are called "free" pipes, and are opened and closed to suit the watermen.

Another of the watermen's intolerable practices is to make a new outlet from the cistern when a water-grant is transferred to a new owner, leaving the old one for themselves. I would say that it was one of the Commissioner's chief duties to put a stop to this. For it affects not only the proper protection of the supply, but also the upkeep of the reservoir which would be ruined if needlessly filled with outlets.

Another financial scheme of the watermen, which they call "puncturing," must also be abolished. There are long separate stretches all over the city through which the pipes pass hidden under the pavement. I found out that these pipes were being tapped everywhere by the "puncturers," from which water was supplied by private pipe to all the business premises in the area, with the result that only a meagre amount reached the public utilities. I can estimate the volume of water stolen in this way from the amount of lead piping which was removed when these branch pipes were dug up.

Source 12 from Naphtali Lewis and Meyer Reinhold, editors and translators, Roman Civilization *(New York: Columbia University Press, 1955), pp. 479–480. Reprinted with permission of the publisher.*

12. Proclamation of Emperor Theodosius, 438 C.E.

It is our will that the landholders over whose lands the courses of aqueducts pass shall be exempt from extraordinary burdens, so that by their work the aqueducts may be cleansed when they are choked with dirt. The said landholders shall not be subject to any other burden of a superindiction,[3] lest they be occupied in other matters and not be present to clean the aqueducts. If they neglect this duty, they shall be punished by the forfeiture of their landholdings; for the fisc[4] will take possession of the landed estate of any man whose negligence contributes to the damage of the aqueducts. Furthermore, persons through whose landed estates the aqueducts pass should know that they may have trees to the right and left at a distance of fifteen feet from the aqueducts, and your[5] office shall see to it that these trees are cut out if they grow too luxuriantly at any time, so that their roots may not injure the structure of the aqueduct.

QUESTIONS TO CONSIDER

Now that you have looked at both visual and written evidence, you will need to put together the information you have gathered from each type of source to achieve a more complete picture. Because sources for the earliest period of human development are so scanty, we need to use every shred of information available and use it somewhat creatively, making speculations where no specific evidence exists.

Take all the evidence about technical problems first. Keeping in mind that the ancient world had no power equipment and no tools more elaborate than axes, hammers, saws, and drills (the Romans also had planes and chisels), what would you judge to be the most difficult purely technical problem involved in constructing water systems? In keeping them operating? The four diagrams of the water-raising machines are arranged in chronological order of their development: The shaduf may be as old as 2500 B.C.E., and the other three did not appear until a thousand years later. Looking at your chart on the advantages and disadvantages of each machine, in what ways did the later machines improve on the shaduf? What additional problems might these improvements have produced? What types of technological experimentation did the need for water encourage?

Technological advance is not always an unmitigated blessing. For example, water standing in irrigation ditches can become brackish, providing a good breeding ground for mosquitoes and other carriers of disease. Cities that depend on irrigation suffer food shortages and famine when ditches cannot be kept clear or when river levels are low. The diversion of large quantities of water for irrigation makes rivers much smaller

3. That is, any special taxes.

4. **fisc**: the imperial treasury.

5. This proclamation was addressed to the administrator of the water supply, the same office that Frontinus held earlier.

when they finally reach their deltas, which means that the deltas become increasingly salty from seawater and unable to support the types of plant and animal life they originally fostered. Judging by the aerial photograph and the LANDSAT map, would you expect any of these problems in ancient Italy or Mesopotamia? Do you find evidence in the written sources for problems in the later Roman water systems that were caused by technical advances? Do the written sources offer suggestions for solving these problems?

Now consider what you have learned about the economic issues associated with water systems. You have doubtless noticed that tremendous numbers of people were needed to construct irrigation ditches and aqueducts. Some of the written sources, such as the extract from Suetonius, provide exact figures. The size and complexity of the systems in the other sources also imply a substantial work force, given the lack of elaborate equipment. The rulers of Egypt, Mesopotamia, and Rome saw the need for a large labor force as no problem; it was, rather, a solution to the greater problem of unemployment. According to a story told about the Roman emperor Vespasian, when he was offered a labor-saving machine, he refused to allow its use because that would put people out of work and lead to social problems in Rome. We might regard this concern for full employment as a positive social attitude, but it should also tell you something about the value of labor in ancient societies. What would you expect wages to be

for construction workers? What class of people would you expect to find working on these water systems?

Large numbers of workers were needed not only to build but also to maintain irrigation systems and to operate water-lifting machines. What does this fact tell you about the value of labor? What would happen with a sudden drop in the population, such as that caused by a famine or epidemic? How would a loss of workers affect the available food supply?

The sources also reveal information about political factors associated with water systems. What does the construction of these systems indicate about the power of rulers to coerce or hire labor? How do rulers control the building and maintenance of machines and ditches? How might their control affect the power and independence of local communities or of individual families? What does this tell you about the role of water in expanding centralized political power?

Finally, the sources provide evidence of alterations in the law made necessary by the search for water. Previously unrestricted and unregulated actions now came under the control of public authorities, which meant that the number of enforcement agents and courts had to increase. What would this do to taxation levels? In what ways would political concerns shape the regulations?

Political issues affect not only the types of laws to be passed, but also the stringency or selectivity with which those laws are enforced. We have very little information about how rigidly law codes were implemented in ancient societies, for few

[18]

legal documents have survived; law codes were frequently recopied and reissued, but the outcome of individual cases was not. It is therefore dangerous to assume that the prescribed penalties were actually levied or that the law was regularly obeyed. (Think for a minute the mistake a person 2,000 years from now would make in describing traffic patterns in twentieth-century America if he or she assumed that the posted speed limit described the actual speed at which traffic moved!) Looking again at the law codes of Hammurabi and Theodosius, would you expect the penalties to be carried out, or do they appear to serve more as a strong warning? How would the penalties differ in their effects on poor and rich people?

You are now ready to answer the question posed at the beginning of the chapter. How did the need for a steady supply of water affect the development of civilization in the West?

EPILOGUE

The irrigation and water supply systems of the ancient world not only required huge amounts of labor, but also made necessary a strong central authority to coerce or hire that labor and to enforce laws to keep the channels flowing. At first, each Mesopotamian city managed its own irrigation system, but the wealthy and advanced cities were attractive targets for foreign conquerors. The political history of ancient Mesopotamia was one of wave after wave of conquerors coming down from the north—the Akkadians, Babylonians, Assyrians, Persians, Greeks, and finally the Romans. Most of these conquerors realized the importance of irrigation and ordered the conquered residents to maintain or expand their systems. When the Muslims invaded the region in the seventh century, they also learned Mesopotamian techniques and spread these westward into North Africa and Spain, where Roman irrigation systems had in many places fallen apart.

Irrigation could also be overdone, however, and during periods of political centralization many areas were overirrigated, which led to salinization, making the land useless for farming. This, combined with the rivers of Mesopotamia changing their courses, meant that many cities could not survive. Centuries of irrigation combined with too little fertilization made even land that was not salinized less and less productive.

The benefits and problems produced by irrigation are not limited to the ancient world, however; they can be seen in many modern societies. One of the best modern examples comes from the same part of the world we have been studying in this chapter. Throughout the twentieth century, Egypt has expanded its irrigation system watered by the Nile with a series of dams, culminating in the Aswan High Dam; this dam, begun in 1960, was designed to provide hydroelectric power and limit the free flow of water at the height of the flood season. The enormous reservoir formed by the dam can also be tapped at low-water times to allow for perennial irrigation. The Aswan Dam serves all its intended purposes very well, but it has also created some unexpected problems. The river's regular flooding had brought new fertile soil to the Nile Valley and carried away the salts that resulted from evaporation. Once the dam stopped the flooding, Egyptian fields needed artificial fertilizer to remain productive, a commodity many farmers could not afford. The soil of the Nile Valley has a high clay content, rendering drainage difficult, and a steady supply of water makes many fields waterlogged and unusable. The large reservoir created by the dam sits in the middle of the Sahara, allowing a tremendous amount of evaporation and significantly decreasing the total flow of water in the Nile; it has also put many acres of farmland under water and forced the relocation of tens of thousands of people. The drought in North Africa has further lowered the Nile's level, decreasing the amount of hydroelectric power the river can produce. Ending the flooding also allowed snails carrying bilharzia or schistosomiasis—an intestinal parasite that makes people very weak—to proliferate in the fields and irrigation ditches. The high water table resulting from the dam is destroying many ancient monuments, such as the temples of Luxor and Karnak, that have survived for millennia. Thus, like the lead pipes that brought water to the Romans, the Aswan High Dam has proved a mixed blessing in modern Egypt.

As you reflect on what you have discovered in this chapter, you may want to think about problems associated with the distribution of water in your own region. How does the need for water affect the political and economic structures of your city or state? What technological solutions has your region devised, and how have these worked?

CHAPTER TWO

WRITING AND POWER: DEFINING

WORLD-VIEWS (1750–200 B.C.E.)

According to Islamic tradition, when the angel Gabriel first revealed himself to Muhammad around the year 610, among the first words he spoke to Muhammad were these:

> In the name of the Lord who created all things. He has taught us the use of the pen. He taught us that which we know not.[1]

Although there is no record that Muhammad himself could either read or write, there is little doubt that the man who ultimately would be revered by Muslims as the Prophet understood the power that literacy gave to those who could read and write, a power that literate people held over those who were not literate. Thoughts could be shaped, codified, and transmitted over both distance and time. Laws (whether political, economic, or religious) could be written down and interpreted or enforced by those who could record or read them. Perhaps more important, writing gave to some the power to bind a people together by giving them a shared history, a common literature, a united world-view, and even a shared *cosmology* (a branch of philosophy that deals with the origin, process, and structure of the universe). And while the oral traditions of nonliterate peoples could be powerful, effective, and in some ways even more "democratic" (in that all who heard could thereby participate in the carrying on of laws, religion, and history), writing possessed certain advantages over an oral tradition, not the least of which being that later historians from other cultures could gain access to the history, culture, and thought of peoples of the past.

Forms of "written" communication are nearly as old as humanity itself. Cave paintings and etchings[2] surely were intended to transmit simple

1. Qur'an (Koran) XCVI, 1–5.

2. Carvings or etchings on cave walls are referred to by archaeologists as petroglyphs; cave paintings are called petrograms.

messages as well as to provide means of self-expression. Message sticks (Australia), wampum belts (Native Americans), shell designs (Nigeria), knotted cords (Tibet, Polynesia, parts of Africa), bean patterns (pre-Inca Peru), and the like—all were used to communicate uncomplicated messages.

Beginning about six thousand years ago, however, people began to develop more complex and codified (systematic, with rules) forms of written communication. Evolving first among the Sumerians of the Fertile Crescent—the land between the Tigris and Euphrates rivers—in approximately 3500 B.C.E., various types of writing on stone, clay tablets, and papyrus[3] emerged independently in Egypt, China, the Near East, Crete, Cyprus, and (by about 1000 B.C.E.) Central America. Ultimately, various cultures developed over two hundred written scripts, approximately eighty of which are still in use today.[4]

Wherever writing developed and whatever particular form it took, all types of writing can be divided into two general systems: *ideographic* and *phonetic*. Ideographic writing, known

also as thought writing, evolved from using pictures to represent things or thoughts (Sumerian pictorials, Egyptian hieroglyphics, and Chinese pictographs, among others). The advantage of ideographic writing is that it is not tied to any particular spoken language and thus can be understood by people speaking a variety of tongues and dialects. The principal disadvantage of ideographic writing is that it requires the memorization of an immense number of different signs, or ideograms—four to six thousand, for example, for literate Chinese. On the other hand, in phonetic writing, each sign (or letter, in our writing) represents a particular sound, and signs are combined to make the sounds for particular words. For example, most Western Europeans employ a form of phonetic writing that uses the signs of the Roman alphabet. Regularized in the sixth century B.C.E., the Roman alphabet originally contained twenty-one signs (letters); the number was later expanded to twenty-six.[5] The chief advantages of phonetic writing are that only a few signs need to be memorized and that these signs can be grouped in an almost endless number of sound combinations to make words and to create new words.[6]

Wherever writing developed, those who mastered this skill often wielded great power and commanded enormous respect. In Egypt, scribes were

---

3. **papyrus:** a type of paper, developed by the Egyptians around 3100 B.C.E., that was made from the inner stems of the papyrus plant, which were pressed together with some form of adhesive; after being written on, the papyrus then was rolled into scrolls.

4. Of all the written scripts known to have existed, over twenty still are undecipherable. People who decipher ancient inscriptions or writings are known as epigraphers. For more on this exciting profession, see John Chadwick, *The Decipherment of Linear B* (Cambridge, England, 1958); Carol Andrews, *The Rosetta Stone* (London, 1981); Michael D. Coe, *Breaking the Maya Code* (New York, 1992).

5. The letters *W, J, Y, Z,* and *U* were added later.

6. An unabridged English dictionary contains approximately 500,000 words, and hundreds of new words are added to the language each decade.

exempt from physical labor, taxation, and military service. As one scribe wrote, "Put writing in your heart that you protect yourself from hard labor of any kind." Scribes were likewise respected in Mesopotamia, among the Aztecs of Central America, and later in the nations of Islam. Most societies founded schools to teach royalty, nobility, and scribes the craft of writing, but in no early culture was universal literacy considered either necessary or desirable. This was because those in power quickly realized that those who could write possessed the capacity to shape the thoughts of those who could not. The illiterate would gather (or would be forcibly gathered) to listen to the readings of edicts, proclamations, laws, or religious texts and liturgies.[7]

Along with commercial agreements and legal codes, one of the first things a people committed to writing was their own explanation of the creation of the universe, the world, and human beings. Such creation accounts often bound a people together and formed a philosophical foundation for their thoughts and actions.

By studying these written explanations of creation, historians can come to understand a particular people's value system, its view of itself, and the relationship of the people to the world, to the universe, and to a god or gods. In addition, historians can gain an understanding of a people's own view of history. To a particular people, is history linear (resembling a straight line, from event to event), cyclical (circular, with patterns recurring), of another form, or formless (with events occurring purely at random, by chance)? In sum, by studying a people's accounts of creation, historians can learn a remarkable amount about how the people thought and even why they behaved as they did.

In this chapter, you will be analyzing the creation accounts of the Babylonians of the Fertile Crescent (written down sometime between 1750 and 1400 B.C.E.), the Indo-Aryans of ancient India (Rig Veda, written down in ca 600 B.C.E.), the Zhou dynasty of ancient China (Yijing, parts of which can be dated roughly at 1000 B.C.E., although the section you will be reading dates from around the third century B.C.E.), and the Israelites of ancient Israel (the Torah, traditionally first read publicly by the scribe Ezra in Jerusalem in 444 B.C.E.).[8]

Historians generally agree that Mesopotamia,[9] the area between the Tigris and Euphrates rivers (in modern-day Iraq), was the scene of the earliest civilization. It was here that a people known as Sumerians domesticated plants and animals; devised an irrigation system; constructed cities such as Ur, Uruk, and Lagash; established trade routes to lands as far away as Egypt; and developed what was probably the world's first writing system, at first pictographic but ultimately evolving into a phonetic system. Later conquerors of the

7. **liturgy:** a prescribed form for a public religious service; many religions have written down their liturgies in prayer books or missals.

8. See Nehemiah 8:1–8.

9. **Mesopotamia:** a Greek word meaning "land between the rivers."

Sumerians, such as the Babylonians,[10] adopted much of Sumerian culture, including its writing and its cosmology. Atra-hasis (Source 1), the Babylonian creation account, borrowed heavily from the Sumerians.

The Indo-Aryans migrated to present-day India from the northwest around 1500 B.C.E., either conquering the earlier Indus civilization or moving in after its fall. Originally a warlike and pastoral people, the Aryans quickly adapted themselves to a sedentary, food-producing life. Politically, their Vedic society was divided into a strict caste system of priests (Brahman), warriors (Kshatriya), peasants (Vaishya), and serfs (Shudra). Although the original Aryan conquerors were illiterate, the preceding Indus Valley civilization had developed a writing system that was a mixture of ideographic and phonetic forms.[11] By roughly 700 B.C.E., however, Vedic society had developed its own form of writing known as Brahmi, apparently derived from a North Semitic script.

In Vedic society, writing apparently was first used in political contexts, but soon was adopted by the Brahman to systematically collect songs, hymns, histories, and other materials that had been passed orally from generation to generation. The oldest of those collections was the Rig Veda (Source 2),[12] a collection of 1,017 hymns or songs divided into ten chapters or books. Some of these songs had been present in Vedic society at least since the Indo-Aryan migration to northern India in roughly 1500 B.C.E. It is here that the society's creation accounts can be found.

In China, the Shang dynasty (ca 1523–1027 B.C.E.) was overthrown by the Zhou (Chou), once-loyal dependents of the Shang whose military technology (including horse-drawn chariots) gave them the upper hand over their former masters. But the Zhou were wise enough to retain much of Shang culture, including its system of writing and its religious beliefs. A major part of those beliefs had to do with divination, the art of foretelling the future. Priests would take the bottom shell of a tortoise, pierce the shell with a small hole, ask a question, and then apply heat to the hole in the shell. The resulting cracks in the shell formed various patterns that the priests could then interpret in order to predict future events. By around 200 B.C.E., the Yijing (or Book of Changes) had been completed and served as an interpretive guide that substituted eight trigrams (sets of three parallel lines) and sixty-four hexagrams (six parallel lines) for the cracks in the tortoise shell. The Yijing is less a religious book than it is a volume of philosophy and ethics, and it was considered important enough to escape the great book burning of 213 B.C.E. It is in the Yijing (Source 4) that the Chinese creation account can be found.

About the time that the Indo-Aryans were moving into India and

10. The Babylonians were known as Amorites, a Semitic people who invaded Sumer from the west and built the city of Babylon. Their most famous ruler was Hammurabi, the author of a comprehensive law code for Babylon.

11. The Indus script is one of those that is still a mystery.

12. **Veda:** "wisdom, or the path to wisdom."

the Shang dynasty was in the process of controlling the eastern half of the Yellow River valley, in Mesopotamia and the Arabian peninsula groups of homeless nomads (referred to in Mesopotamian and Egyptian sources as "Habiru") wandered across the semiarid landscape grazing their herds. One of these groups came to be known as "Hebrews," or "Israelites" or "Jews."[13] Sometime after 1550 B.C.E., the Jews voluntarily migrated to Egypt to escape a drought, but soon were enslaved by the Egyptians. Around 1200 B.C.E., the Jews either abandoned or escaped from Egypt. The decline of both the Egyptian and Hittite empires had left a power vacuum along the eastern coast of the Mediterranean Sea, and it was here that the Israelites ultimately settled, fighting off Philistines and other peoples in order to seize and hold the land. Sometime after 925 B.C.E. (the traditional death of King Solomon), the Israelites broke into two kingdoms. The northern kingdom was destroyed by Assyrian invaders, while the southern kingdom (Judah) survived for another century and a half, until the Babylonian captivity.

Written Hebrew was one of the several offshoots of North Semitic script (another, as we have seen, was Brahmi) and was in use as early as ca 800 B.C.E. The form of Hebrew writing known as Square Hebrew (for the rectangular shaping of the letters) traditionally owed its adoption to the scribe Ezra in the fifth century B.C.E. Like all Semitic scripts, Hebrew is consonantal—that is, phonetic with consonant letters or sounds (in the case of Hebrew, twenty-two), but no vowels.

Similar to the early writings of other peoples, the Torah contains the Jews' creation account, history, and laws. Traditionally, authorship is credited to Moses, although a majority of biblical scholars assert that the Torah comes from more than a single source. According to ancient tradition, Joshua had the Torah "engraved upon the stones of the altar" of the tabernacle sometime before 1100 B.C.E., a claim that most scholars dispute as much too early (the fifth century B.C.E. is more likely). Like those of other peoples, the Israelites' explanation of creation (Source 3, from the book of Genesis, which began to be stabilized around 720 B.C.E.) tells historians a great deal about the Jewish people themselves.

Your tasks in this chapter will require you to use all your analytical reading skills plus a good deal of historical imagination.

First, you must read each account to learn how each of these peoples sought to explain the creation of the world. Then, using your historical imagination, show what each creation account tells us about the people who thought it critical enough to write it down.

What does the creation account of each of the peoples excerpted in the Evidence section tell us about the people themselves? What can we

13. At the time, "Hebrew" referred to a social category, whereas "Israelite" was used to describe all the people of the group; "Jews" derived from the southern kingdom's surviving tribe of Judah.

discover about how they viewed the universe, themselves, the role of a god or gods, and the unfolding of history itself?

SOURCES AND METHOD

When people today consult the Rig Veda, the Torah, or the Yijing, most do so either as part of their religious worship or as an inspirational guide.[14] Each of these writings, however, also is a historical document that can be examined and analyzed for what that document tells us about those who created it and those who preserved and venerated it.

As you might expect, historians approach such a document in quite different ways from members of a group for which the document is an important part of their creed or philosophy. To begin with, whenever it is possible, historians prefer to read the document in its oldest version and in its original language. In that way, mistakes made in copying or translating, as well as purposeful additions to or deletions from the original text, will not lead the historians into errors of judgment. Second, it is important to historians to know as closely as possible the date (or dates) of the document's creation. This information is valuable to historians because it enables them to study the context and understand more about the people who were living during that period, the events taking place, and the ideas in circulation.

Historians call this process learning about the "climate of opinion" of a particular time period. Unfortunately, very early documents (such as the ones you will be working with in this chapter) cannot be dated very precisely because they were written down only after a long period of oral transmission.

After completing these early steps, historians then are prepared to examine the document itself. When dealing with creation accounts, historians ask of each written account a series of questions: How does the account explain the creation of the universe, the world, and human beings? Is the creation divinely inspired—in other words, did a god or gods play an active role in the creation process, and for what purpose? Are human beings merely one among many objects of creation, or are human beings the pinnacle of the creation process? In return for creation and care, do human beings have any obligation to their creator? Finally, is the creation process in the account lineal (proceeding sequentially along a line from one event to another), cyclical (circular), of another pattern, or without pattern (formless)?

Having subjected each creation account to this series of questions, historians then are ready to ask what each document reveals about the people who created it. This will take some reading in your text about the people under scrutiny, as well as a

14. Atra-hasis was lost for centuries and began to be discovered only in the mid-1800s (large parts are still missing). No contemporary people venerate it as a religious text.

considerable amount of historical imagination. For example, if each creation account can be seen as a life guide for those who venerate it, what does the account encourage or compel (or forbid) the true believers to do? Is the creation process *reproduced* in the lives of true believers (from birth to death)? What does that process tell you about the people who created the account?

Finally, you are ready to compare the four creation accounts and the people who committed them to memory and later to writing. Historians call this process *comparative textual analysis*, and it is one of the most basic methods of investigation used throughout all the humanities (literature, philosophy, linguistics, history, and the like). As you compare these accounts and their creators, using the questions above as initial guides, be careful *not* to fall into the habit of thinking of certain cultures or peoples as "inferior" or "superior" on the basis of how far or near a particular group's beliefs are to your own beliefs or philosophy. This is a common trap, and you must make every effort to avoid it. After all, each of the creation accounts you will be examining and analyzing was preserved by a people or peoples for thousands of years. All except Atra-hasis have become the foundation for one or more current religions or philosophies, and as such have been deemed

satisfying by a group or groups for many, many generations. Historians, therefore, approach these sources with great sensitivity and respect.

Atra-hasis (Source 1), as noted above, was lost for two millennia, surviving only in some Hebrew traditions that became part of the Book of Genesis (Atra-hasis was a man who was warned of a flood by the god Enki and was urged to build a boat and escape with his family and a selection of animals). The Rig Veda (Source 2) is the oldest of the sacred texts of modern Hinduism (733 million followers in 1992). The Torah (Source 3) is considered sacred to Jews (18 million), Christians (1.8 billion), and Muslims (971 million), all of whom are referred to by Muslims as People of the Book. The Yijing (Source 4) is one of the bases of Confucianism (195 million adherents is only a guess), a westernization of the name of the great teacher K'ung Fu-tze (551–479 B.C.E.).

As you read the Evidence, be sure to take notes. One effective way of organizing your thoughts is to divide your note pages into two parts. On the left side of the page, summarize the creation account you are reading. Then, on the right side, summarize your thoughts (and questions) about the value system, the view of history, and the relationship between beings that you are able to infer from the creation account.

Source 1 from W. G. Lambert and A. R. Millard, Atra-hasis: The Babylonian Story of the Flood (Oxford: Oxford University Press, 1969; reprinted Winona Lake, Ind.: Eisenbrauns, 1999), pp. 57, 59, 61. Reprinted by permission.

1. Excerpts from Atra-hasis

[The account begins with a universe that contained only the gods. The three senior gods (Anu, Enlil, and Enki) agree to divide the universe into three spheres of influence, with Anu in charge of heaven, Enlil of earth, and Enki of the water beneath the earth. The junior gods, required by Enlil to work, revolt against the senior gods. Thus the three senior gods call on Belet-ili,[15] the birth goddess, to create workers to serve the gods.]

While [Belet-ili, the birth-goddess], is present,
Let the birth-goddess create offspring
And let man bear the toil of the gods.
They summoned and asked the goddess,
The midwife of the gods, wise Mami,
'You are the birth-goddess, creatress of mankind,
Create Lullu[16] that he may bear the yoke,
Let him bear the yoke assigned by Enlil,
Let man carry the toil of the gods.'
Nintu opened her mouth
And addressed the great gods,
'It is not possible for me to make things,
Skill lies with Enki.
Since he can cleanse everything
Let him give me the clay so that I can make it.'
Enki opened his mouth
And addressed the great gods,
'On the first, seventh, and fifteenth day of the month
I will make a purifying bath.
Let one god be slaughtered
So that all the gods may be cleansed in a dipping...
So that we may hear the drum for the rest of time
Let there be a spirit from the god's flesh.
Let it proclaim living (man) as its sign,
So that this be not forgotten let there be a spirit.'
In the assembly answered 'Yes'
The great Anunnaki, who administer destinies.

15. Interestingly, Belet-ili, the birth goddess, is also referred to as Mami or Mama.
16. **Lullu:** man.

On the first, seventh, and fifteenth day of the month
He made a purifying bath.
We-ila, who had personality,
They slaughtered in their assembly.
From his flesh and blood
Nintu mixed clay.
For the rest [of time they heard the drum],
From the flesh of the god [there was] a spirit.
It proclaimed living (man) as its sign,
And so that this was not forgotten [there was] a spirit.
After she had mixed that clay

She summoned the Anunnaki, the great gods.
The Igigi, the great gods,
Spat upon the clay.
Mami opened her mouth
And addressed the great gods,
'You commanded me a task, I have completed it;
You have slaughtered a god together with his personality.
I have removed your heavy work,
I have imposed your toil on man.
You raised a cry for mankind,
I have loosed the yoke, I have established freedom.'
They heard this speech of hers,
They ran together and kissed her feet (saying),
'Formerly we used to call you Mami,
Now let your name be Mistress-of-All-the-Gods (Belet-kala-ili) . . .

[*As the number of humans increased, their noise bothered the gods. Therefore Enlil tried to reduce the human population through plagues and other devices. It was in this context that he summoned up the flood, from which Atra-hasis and his family escaped. It is likely that, while in captivity in Babylon, the Hebrew people heard this account.*]

Source 2 from Franklin Edgerton, trans., The Beginnings of Indian Philosophy *(Cambridge, Mass.: Harvard University Press, 1965), pp. 60–61, 67–68, 73, 74.*

2. Excerpts from Book 10 of the Rig Veda

10.72[17]

1. We will now proclaim the origins of the gods to win applause (from any) who shall behold them in a later age, as the hymns are chanted.

2. Brahmanaspati (the Lord of the Holy Word) smelted them together, as a smith. In the primal age of the gods the Existent was born from the Non-existent.

3. In the first age of the gods the Existent was born from the Non-existent. After it (the Existent) the regions were born—(after) it, from the (World-mother) in labour.

4. The world was born from the (World-mother) in labour; from the world the regions were born. From Aditi Daksa was born, from Daksa likewise Aditi (was born).[18]

5. Aditi, verily, was born, who is thy daughter, O Daksa. After her the gods were born, the blessed ones, companions of immortality.

6. When, O gods, there in the flood you stood, holding fast to one another, then from you, as from dancers, thick dust arose.

7. When, O gods, like wizard-priests, you made the worlds to swell, then you brought forth the sun that had been hidden in the sea.

8. There were eight sons of Aditi, which were born of her body. She went to the gods with seven; the (Sun-)bird she cast away.

9. With seven sons Aditi went to the primal generation (of gods). She brought back the (Sun-)bird for alternate procreation and death.

17. The Rig Veda is organized into ten books totaling 1,017 hymns. The number 10.72 means hymn #72 of book #10.

18. Aditi "is Mother, is Father, is Son...is all that is born, that will be born" (Rig Veda, 1.89). Normally, however, Aditi is taken to mean the Great Mother from whom the world was born, as well as the mother of the gods themselves. Daksa is masculine and often referred to as the "primordial cause," the original power of wisdom. Daksa's personification fluctuates throughout the Vedas.

10.81

1. The seer who, in sacrificing all these worlds, took his seat as hotar-priest, our father—he, with prayer seeking wealth (i.e., sacrificing), concealing that which was first, entered into the later beings.

2. What, verily, was that resting-place (support)? What manner of thing did he begin from, and how vast was it, that from which the All-maker, the all-seeing, creating the earth, unfolded the heaven by his might?

3. With eyes and face in all directions, likewise with arms and feet in all directions, he welded (as a smith) them together with his arms, with fan-bellows, creating heaven and earth, the sole god.

4. What, verily, was the wood, what the lumber, from which they carpentered out heaven and earth? You wise ones, with your wisdom inquire into that, upon what base he rested, establishing the worlds.

5. These your highest places, your lowest also, and these that are your midmost, All-maker, teach to (your) friends at the oblation, O Self-mighty One. Yourself offer sacrifice, prospering your own self (thereby).

6. O All-maker, thriving on sacrifice, do you sacrifice for yourself (i.e., create, by the cosmic "sacrifice" of creation) earth and heaven. Let other people round about stray helplessly; for us here let there be a generous patron.

7. Let us summon today for aid at the (sacrificial) contest the Lord of Holy Utterance,[19] the All-maker, who inspires the intellect. Let him take pleasure in our offerings, being helpful to all, working surely unto our support.

10.90

1. The Purusa[20] has a thousand heads, a thousand eyes, and a thousand feet. He, encompassing the world on all sides, stood out ten fingers' lengths beyond.

2. The Purusa alone is all this universe, what has been, and what is to be. He rules likewise over (the world of) immortality (viz. the gods), which he grows beyond, by (sacrificial?) food.

3. Such is the extent of his greatness; and the Purusa is still greater than this. A quarter of him is all beings, three quarters are (the world of) the immortal in heaven.

4. In his three-quarters the Purusa arose to the upper regions; a quarter of him, on the other hand, came to be here below. From this (quarter) he

---

19. **Lord of Holy Utterance:** the feminine version of the Lord of the Holy Word (see 10.72, verse 2), which were hymns composed by the Brahman (priests); the Brahman held contests to see who could compose the best hymns.

20. **Purusa:** man as a cosmic being, a sort of world-giant.

expanded manifoldly into the things that eat and those that do not eat (animate and inanimate beings).

5. From him the Shining One (the cosmic waters) was born, from the Shining One (was born likewise) the Purusa. Being born (from the Shining One) he extended beyond the world, behind and also before.

6. When the gods, with the Purusa as oblation,[21] extended (performed) the (cosmic) sacrifice, Spring became the butter for it, Summer the firewood, Autumn the oblation.

7. They consecrated on the sacred grass this sacrifice, (namely) the Purusa, born in the beginning. With him the gods sacrificed, the Sadhyas,[22] and the Seers.

8. From this sacrifice, offered as whole-offering, the ghee-mixture[23] (the juice that flowed off) was collected; it made these animals—those of the air, of the jungle, and of the village.

9. From this sacrifice, offered as whole-offering, the stanzas of praise (the Rigveda) and the melodies (Samaveda) were produced; the meters were produced therefrom, the sacrificial formulas (Yajurveda) were produced therefrom.

10. Therefrom were produced horses, and whatever animals have (cutting-) teeth on both jaws. Cattle were produced therefrom, therefrom were born goats and sheep.

11. When they divided the Purusa (as the victim at the cosmic sacrifice), into how many parts did they separate him? What did his mouth become? What his two arms? What are declared to be his two thighs, his two feet?

12. The Brahman (priestly caste) was his mouth, his two arms became the Rajanya (warrior caste); his two thighs are the Vaisya (artisan caste), from his two feet the Sudra (serf caste) was produced.

13. The moon sprang from his thought-organ, the sun was produced from his eye; from his mouth Indra (war-god and soma-drinker) and Agni (the Fire-god), from his breath Vayu (the wind) was produced.

14. From his navel arose the atmosphere, from his head the heaven evolved; from his two feet the earth, from his ear the directions. Thus they fashioned the worlds.

21. **oblation:** offering (to a deity).
22. **Sadhyas:** ancient gods or demigods.
23. **ghee:** a clarified butter, used in religious rituals.

15. Seven were his surrounding sticks (at the burnt-offering), thrice seven were made the pieces of kindling wood, when the gods, extending (performing) the (cosmic) sacrifice, bound the Purusa as the victim.

16. With offering the gods offered the offering; these were the first (holy) institutions. Verily these powers have followed up to heaven, where are the Sadhya-gods of old.

10.129

1. Non-existent there was not, existent there was not then. There was not the atmospheric space, nor the vault beyond. What stirred, where, and in whose control? Was there water, a deep abyss?

2. Nor death nor immortality (mortals nor immortals) was there then; there was no distinction of night or day. That One breathed without breath by inner power; than it verily there was nothing else further.

3. Darkness there was, hidden by darkness, in the beginning; an undistinguished ocean was This All. What generative principle was enveloped by emptiness—by the might of (its own) fervour That One was born.

4. Desire (creative, or perhaps sacrificial, impulse) arose then in the beginning, which was the first seed of thought. The (causal) connection (bandhu) of the existent the sages found in the non-existent, searching with devotion in their hearts.

5. Straight across was stretched the (dividing-)cord of them (i.e., of the following); below (what) was there? above (what) was there? Seed-bearers (male forces) there were, strengths (female forces) there were; (female) innate power below, (male) impellent force above.[24]

6. Who truly knows? Who shall here proclaim it—whence they were produced, whence this creation? The gods (arose) on this side (later), by the creation of this (empiric world, to which the gods belong); then who knows whence it came into being?

7. This creation, whence it came into being, whether it was established, or whether not—he who is its overseer in the highest heaven, he verily knows, or perchance he knows not.

---

24. A suggestion that the world was created by some sort of cosmic intercourse between male powers and female powers. But, as Edgerton suggests, verses 6 and 7 strongly imply that the poet feels that he has gone too far. See *Beginnings of Indian Philosophy*, p. 73. See also Abinash Chandra Bose, *Hymns from the Vedas* (New York: Asia Publishing House, 1966), pp. 303–305.

3. From the First Book of
Moses, called Genesis

CHAPTER 1

1] When God began to create the heaven and the earth—2] the earth being
unformed and void, with darkness over the surface of the deep[25] and a wind[26]
from God sweeping over the water—3] God said, "Let there be light"; and
there was light. 4] God saw that the light was good, and God separated the
light from the darkness. 5] God called the light Day, and the darkness He
called Night. And there was evening and there was morning, a first day.

6] God said, "Let there be an expanse in the midst of the water, that it may
separate water from water." 7] God made the expanse, and it separated the
water which was below the expanse from the water which was above the
expanse. And it was so. 8] God called the expanse Sky. And there was evening,
and there was morning, a second day.

9] God said, "Let the water below the sky be gathered into one area, that the
dry land may appear." And it was so. 10] God called the dry land Earth, and
the gathering of waters He called Seas. And God saw that this was good.
11] And God said, "Let the earth sprout vegetation: seed-bearing plants, fruit
trees of every kind on earth that bear fruit with the seed in it." And it was so.
12] The earth brought forth vegetation: seed-bearing plants of every kind, and
trees of every kind bearing fruit with the seed in it. And God saw that this was
good. 13] And there was evening and there was morning, a third day.

14] God said, "Let there be lights in the expanse of the sky to separate day
from night; they shall serve as signs for the set times—the days and the years;
15] and they shall serve as lights in the expanse of the sky to shine upon the
earth." And it was so. 16] God made the two great lights, the greater light
to dominate the day and the lesser light to dominate the night, and the stars.
17] And God set them in the expanse of the sky to shine upon the earth, 18] to
dominate the day and the night, and to separate light from darkness. And God
saw that this was good. 19] And there was evening and there was morning, a
fourth day.

25. Some Hebraic scholars point out that this phrase ("surface of the deep") echoes a
"Mesopotamian creation story where it is told that heaven and earth were formed from the
carcass of the sea dragon, Tiamat." *The Torah: A Modern Commentary*, p. 18.

26. **wind:** also translated as "spirit."

20] God said, "Let the waters bring forth swarms of living creatures, and birds that fly above the earth across the expanse of the sky." 21] God created the great sea monsters, and all the living creatures of every kind that creep, which the waters brought forth in swarms; and all the winged birds of every kind. And God saw that this was good. 22] God blessed them, saying, "Be fertile and increase, fill the waters in the seas, and let the birds increase on the earth." 23] And there was evening and there was morning, a fifth day.

24] God said, "Let the earth bring forth every kind of living creature: cattle, creeping things, and wild beasts of every kind." And it was so. 25] God made wild beasts of every kind and cattle of every kind, and all kinds of creeping things of the earth. And God saw that this was good. 26] And God said, "Let us make man in our image, after our likeness. They shall rule the fish of the sea, the birds of the sky, the cattle, the whole earth, and all the creeping things that creep on earth." 27] And God created man in His image, in the image of God He created him; male and female He created them. 28] God blessed them and God said to them, "Be fertile and increase, fill the earth and master it; and rule the fish of the sea, the birds of the sky, and all the living things that creep on earth."

29] God said, "See, I give you every seed-bearing plant that is upon all the earth, and every tree that has seed-bearing fruit; they shall be yours for food. 30] And to all the animals on land, to all the birds of the sky, and to everything that creeps on earth, in which there is the breath of life, [I give] all the green plants for food." And it was so.[27] 31] And God saw all that He had made, and found it very good. And there was evening and there was morning, the sixth day.

CHAPTER 2

1] The heaven and the earth were finished, and all their array. 2] On the seventh day God finished the work which He had been doing, and He ceased on the seventh day from all the work which He had done. 3] And God blessed the seventh day and declared it holy, because on it God ceased from all the work of creation which He had done.

4] Such is the story of heaven and earth when they were created.

When the LORD God made earth and heaven—5] when no shrub of the field was yet on earth and no grasses of the field had yet sprouted, because the LORD God had not sent rain upon the earth and there was no man to till the soil, 6] but a flow would well up from the ground and water the whole surface

---

27. Many biblical scholars assert that humans and other animals were herbivores (exclusively vegetarian) until after the Flood, when they became omnivores (eating all kinds of food, including the flesh of other animals). See Genesis 9:3 and Isaiah 11:7.

of the earth—7] the LORD God formed man from the dust of the earth. He blew into his nostrils the breath of life, and man became a living being.

8] The LORD God planted a garden in Eden, in the east, and placed there the man whom He had formed. 9] And from the ground the LORD God caused to grow every tree that was pleasing to the sight and good for food, with the tree of life in the middle of the garden, and the tree of knowledge of good and bad. . . .

15] The LORD God took the man and placed him in the garden of Eden, to till it and tend it. 16] And the LORD God commanded the man, saying, "Of every tree of the garden you are free to eat; 17] but as for the tree of knowledge of good and bad, you must not eat of it; for as soon as you eat of it, you shall die."[28]

18] The LORD God said, "It is not good for man to be alone; I will make a fitting helper for him." 19] And the LORD God formed out of the earth all the wild beasts and all the birds of the sky, and brought them to the man to see what he would call them; and whatever the man called each living creature, that would be its name. 20] And the man gave names to all the cattle and to the birds of the sky and to all the wild beasts; but for Adam no fitting helper was found. 21] So the LORD God cast a deep sleep upon the man; and, while he slept, He took one of his ribs and closed up the flesh at that spot. 22] And the LORD God fashioned the rib that He had taken from the man into a woman; and He brought her to the man. 23] Then the man said, "This one at last / Is bone of my bones / And flesh of my flesh. / This one shall be called Woman, / For from man was she taken." 24] Hence a man leaves his father and mother and clings to his wife, so that they become one flesh.

[*Disobeying God's command, Adam and Eve ate the forbidden fruit, were cursed by God, and were banished from the Garden. Their first two children were Cain and Abel. Out of jealousy, Cain murdered Abel and was even further banished. Adam and Eve had many more children. After several generations, humans had become corrupt, and God determined to punish them by flooding the land. He warned righteous Noah, who gathered his family and all species in an ark, which survived the flood. Many generations later, people attempted to build a tower to reach heaven, but were confounded by God, who caused them to begin speaking different languages. Many generations later, God appeared to Abram, offering to make a covenant (contract) with him.*]

CHAPTER 17

1] When Abram was ninety-nine years old, the Lord appeared to Abram and said to him, "I am El Shaddai.[29] Walk in My ways and be blameless. 2] I will

28. Given the fact that Adam did not die immediately upon eating the forbidden fruit, perhaps a better translation might be "you shall lose your immortality."
29. **El Shaddai:** God Almighty.

establish My covenant between Me and you, and I will make you exceedingly numerous."

3] Abram threw himself on his face, as God spoke to him further, 4] "As for Me, this is My covenant with you: You shall be the father of a multitude of nations. 5] And you shall no longer be called Abram, but your name shall be Abraham, for I make you the father of a multitude of nations. 6] I will make you exceedingly fertile, and make nations of you; and kings shall come forth from you. 7] I will maintain My covenant between Me and you, and your offspring to come, as an everlasting covenant throughout the ages, to be God to you and to your offspring to come. 8] I give the land you sojourn in to you and your offspring to come, all the land of Canaan, as an everlasting possession. I will be their God."

9] God further said to Abraham, "As for you, you and your offspring to come throughout the ages shall keep My covenant. 10] Such shall be the covenant between Me and you and your offspring to follow which you shall keep: every male among you shall be circumcised. 11] You shall circumcise the flesh of your foreskin, and that shall be the sign of the covenant between Me and you. 12] And throughout the generations, every male among you shall be circumcised at the age of eight days. As for the homeborn slave and the one bought from an outsider who is not of your offspring, 13] they must be circumcised, homeborn and purchased alike. Thus shall My covenant be marked in your flesh as an everlasting pact. 14] And if any male who is uncircumcised fails to circumcise the flesh of his foreskin, that person shall be cut off from his kin; he has broken My covenant."

15] And God said to Abraham, "As for your wife Sarai, you shall not call her Sarai, but her name shall be Sarah. 16] I will bless her; indeed, I will give you a son by her. I will bless her so that she shall give rise to nations; rulers of peoples shall issue from her." 17] Abraham threw himself on his face and laughed, as he said to himself, "Can a child be born to a man a hundred years old, or can Sarah bear a child at ninety?" 18] And Abraham said to God, "Oh that Ishmael might live by Your favor!" 19] God said, "Nevertheless, Sarah your wife shall bear you a son, and you shall name him Isaac; and I will maintain My covenant with him as an everlasting covenant for his offspring to come. 20] As for Ishmael, I have heeded you. I hereby bless him. I will make him fertile and exceedingly numerous. He shall be the father of twelve chieftains, and I will make of him a great nation. 21] But My covenant I will maintain with Isaac, whom Sarah shall bear to you at this season next year." 22] And when He was done speaking with him, God was gone from Abraham.

23] Then Abraham took his son Ishmael, and all his homeborn slaves and all those he had bought, every male in Abraham's household, and he circumcised the flesh of their foreskins on that very day, as God had spoken to him. 24] Abraham was ninety-nine years old when he circumcised the flesh of his foreskin, 25] and his son Ishmael was thirteen years old when he was circumcised in the flesh of his foreskin. 26] Thus Abraham and his son Ishmael were circumcised on that very day; 27] and all his household, his homeborn slaves and those that had been bought from outsiders, were circumcised with him. . . .

Source 4 from Cary F. Baynes, trans., The I Ching [Yijing], or Book of Changes, 3d ed. (Princeton: Princeton University Press, 1967), pp. 280, 283–287, 293–296, 328–335. Copyright © 1967 by Princeton University Press. Reprinted by permission of Princeton University Press.

4. From Yijing, Commentary on the Appended Judgments

Heaven is high, the earth is low; thus the Creative and the Receptive are determined. In correspondence with this difference between low and high, inferior and superior places are established.

Movement and rest have their definite laws;[30] according to these, firm and yielding lines are differentiated.

Events follow definite trends, each according to its nature. Things are distinguished from one another in definite classes. In this way good fortune and misfortune come about. In the heavens phenomena take form; on earth shapes take form. In this way change and transformation become manifest.

Therefore the eight trigrams succeed one another by turns, as the firm and the yielding displace each other.[31]

Things are aroused by thunder and lightning; they are fertilized by wind and rain. Sun and moon follow their courses and it is now hot, now cold.

The way of the Creative brings about the male.

The way of the Receptive brings about the female.

The Creative knows the great beginnings.

The Receptive completes the finished things.

The Creative knows through the easy.

The Receptive can do things through the simple.

What is easy, is easy to know; what is simple, is easy to follow. He who is easy to know attains fealty. He who is easy to follow attains works. He who possesses attachment can endure for long; he who possesses works can become great. To endure is the disposition of the sage; greatness is the field of action of the sage.

By means of the easy and the simple we grasp the laws of the whole world. When the laws of the whole world are grasped, therein lies perfection. . . .

30. The *Book of Changes* is concerned primarily with understanding and predicting what appears to be constant and random change. ("Everything flows on and on like this river, without pause, day and night."—K'ung Fu-tze)

31. **displace each other:** an example of cyclical change.

The Book of Changes contains the measure of heaven and earth; therefore it enables us to comprehend the tao[32] of heaven and earth and its order.

Looking upward, we contemplate with its help the signs in the heavens; looking down, we examine the lines of the earth. Thus we come to know the circumstances of the dark and the light. Going back to the beginnings of things and pursuing them to the end, we come to know the lessons of birth and of death. The union of seed and power produces all things; the escape of the soul brings about change. Through this we come to know the conditions of outgoing and returning spirits.

Since in this way man comes to resemble heaven and earth, he is not in conflict with them. His wisdom embraces all things, and his tao brings order into the whole world; therefore he does not err. He is active everywhere but does not let himself be carried away. He rejoices in heaven and has knowledge of fate, therefore he is free of care. He is content with his circumstances and genuine in his kindness, therefore he can practice love.

In it are included the forms and the scope of everything in the heavens and on earth, so that nothing escapes it. In it all things everywhere are completed, so that none is missing. Therefore by means of it we can penetrate the tao of day and night, and so understand it. Therefore the spirit is bound to no one place, nor the Book of Changes to any one form. . . .

When in early antiquity Pao Hsi [Baoxi][33] ruled the world, he looked upward and contemplated the images in the heavens; he looked downward and contemplated the patterns on earth. He contemplated the markings of birds and beasts and the adaptations to the regions. He proceeded directly from himself and indirectly from objects. Thus he invented the eight trigrams in order to enter into connection with the virtues of the light of the gods and to regulate the conditions of all beings.

He made knotted cords and used them for nets and baskets in hunting and fishing. He probably took this from the hexagram of THE CLINGING.

When Pao Hsi's clan was gone, there sprang up the clan of the Divine Husbandman.[34] He split a piece of wood for a plowshare and bent a piece of wood for the plow handle, and taught the whole world the advantage of laying open the earth with a plow. He probably took this from the hexagram of INCREASE.

When the sun stood at midday, he held a market. He caused the people of the earth to come together and collected the wares of the earth. They exchanged these with one another, then returned home, and each thing found its place. Probably he took this from the hexagram of BITING THROUGH.

32. **tao:** the way.

33. More commonly known as Fuxi (ca 2953–2838 B.C.E.), who is credited with constructing the eight trigrams based on cracks in a tortoise shell, from which was developed the system of Yijing.

34. **Shennong:** the teacher of agriculture to humans.

When the clan of the Divine Husbandman was gone, there sprang up the clans of the Yellow Emperor, of Yao, and of Shun. They brought continuity into their alterations, so that the people did not grow weary. They were divine in the transformations they wrought, so that the people were content. When one change had run its course, they altered. (Through alteration they achieved continuity.) Through continuity they achieved duration. Therefore: "They were blessed by heaven. Good fortune. Nothing that does not further."

The Yellow Emperor, Yao, and Shun allowed the upper and lower garments to hang down, and the world was in order. They probably took this from the hexagrams of THE CREATIVE and THE RECEPTIVE.

They scooped out tree trunks for boats and they hardened wood in the fire to make oars. The advantage of boats and oars lay in providing means of communication. (They reached distant parts, in order to benefit the whole world.) They probably took this from the hexagram of DISPERSION.

They tamed the ox and yoked the horse. Thus heavy loads could be transported and distant regions reached, for the benefit of the world. They probably took this from the hexagram of FOLLOWING.

They introduced double gates and night watchmen with clappers, in order to deal with robbers. They probably took this from the hexagram of ENTHUSIASM.

They split wood and made a pestle of it. They made a hollow in the ground for a mortar. The use of the mortar and pestle was of benefit to all mankind. They probably took this from the hexagram of PREPONDERANCE OF THE SMALL.

They strung a piece of wood for a bow and hardened pieces of wood in the fire for arrows. The use of bow and arrow is to keep the world in fear. They probably took this from the hexagram of OPPOSITION.

In primitive times people dwelt in caves and lived in forests. The holy men of a later time made the change to buildings. At the top was a ridgepole, and sloping down from it there was a roof, to keep off wind and rain. They probably took this from the hexagram of THE POWER OF THE GREAT.

In primitive times the dead were buried by covering them thickly with brushwood and placing them in the open country, without burial mound or grove of trees. The period of mourning had no definite duration. The holy men of a later time introduced inner and outer coffins instead. They probably took this from the hexagram of PREPONDERANCE OF THE GREAT.

In primitive times people knotted cords in order to govern. The holy men of a later age introduced written documents instead, as a means of governing the various officials and supervising the people. They probably took this from the hexagram of BREAKTHROUGH.

QUESTIONS TO CONSIDER

One of the first truths that historians come to appreciate is that people from different cultures not only think differently about various subjects (such as life, death, and cosmology) but also use different thought patterns when attempting to solve a problem. Thus we must determine not only what people of the past think, but also how they think.[35] Accounts or interpretations of creation are excellent sources from which to deduce not only how a particular culture thinks about creation, but how it thinks in general.

Sumero-Babylonian traditions had more than one account of the creation and of the early history of human beings, of which Atra-hasis probably is the oldest. Written in cuneiform script using a stylus on soft clay that later was baked to harden it, the Atra-hasis creation epic is still fragmentary, and parts of the broken tablets are still being discovered in excavations.

Why did the gods decide to create human beings? What, therefore, is the purpose of humans? How were the first humans constructed by Belet-ili? What materials were used? Why was it necessary to kill the junior god

35. The same can be said about the study of writing itself. For example, fewer than half of the systems of writing that exist (or are known to have existed) begin at the top left of a page and move from left to right, then drop down one line and repeat the process. Some peoples' systems require writing right to left, some vertically (either top to bottom or bottom to top), and some circularly, and a few (like the Aztec script of Central America) have no particular form at all.

We-ila? What was We-ila's "contribution" to humans? In your opinion, what does this tell about the Babylonians' concept of human beings? Of their gods?

The first thing that we discover about Vedic culture is that it has not one creation account but several. In Rig Veda 10.72, the creation of the universe is compared to the birth of a human child. Who is Aditi, and what function does she perform? But how was Aditi created (see verses 2–5)? Note that these verses have a cyclical pattern: Aditi is born and gives birth and in turn is born. This cyclical thought pattern would become a key component of Hindu philosophy (Westerners are most familiar with it in the Hindu doctrines of *karma* and reincarnation—see R.V. 10.81, verse 1).

R.V. 10.81 is interesting for two reasons. First, this creation account, unlike that in 10.72, is quasi-monotheistic (monotheism is belief in one god), in this case called the All-maker. But might that All-maker in fact be Aditi herself (both are feminine)? More interesting are the questions asked in verses 2 and 4. If originally there was nothing (10.72 called it the "Non-existent"), then where did the materials to make the world come from? Does the hymn's composer answer those questions?

In R.V. 10.90, the universe itself (Purusa) is masculine and encompasses everything, including the gods. Note, however, the cyclical thinking again in verse 5, and in verse 6, in which Purusa (the universe) is himself sacrificed by the gods to create all other things. What is the implication about how humans are to honor this creation process? How does this creation account support and justify the Vedic caste system?

In R.V. 10.129, the author begins by emphasizing the nothingness that preceded creation. And then, mysteriously, That One was born. But what role (if any) did That One play in creation? What about the male forces and female forces? Where did those forces come from? What feelings does the author convey in verses 6 and 7?

The narrative of creation in the Torah is a familiar one to Jews, Christians, and Muslims, and is quite different from the accounts in the Rig Veda. Almost immediately, however, we see that we are confronted not with *one* creation account in the Torah, but with *two*. Notice that Genesis 1:1 through 2:4 contains one account and, immediately following, Genesis 2:5–24 is *another* account, in some ways markedly different. In your view, what are the principal differences between the two creation accounts in Genesis? Can you explain why there are two accounts? Why do you think that both accounts were included and have remained stable fixtures in Genesis for over 2,700 years?

In the Torah, it is extremely clear that the Israelites (and the later Christians and Muslims) were strict monotheists. Moreover, the one god of the Torah exhibits human traits—intent, desire, love, satisfaction, anger, and other emotions—and is given a voice that speaks to many people. And even more important, God has made some specific pro-mises to and demands on the humans He created, most especially the ancient Israelites (the "Chosen People," as explicitly stated in Genesis 17:2). What were those demands? What was the covenant?

In contrast to the Torah, the Yijing not only lacks an account of a divinely inspired or god-caused creation, but also seems almost unconcerned about these questions at all. Gods do appear (Heaven, the high god, is most prominent), but more as abstract models for humans to emulate than as powers to worship or obey. Instead, the Yijing is a search for order, for patterns that can be discovered in the heavens and then later on earth—the patterns of birth and of life and of death.

How can the Creative and the Receptive be seen in the universe? Can any patterns be discerned and applied to the world? In this way, "man comes to resemble heavens and earth, he is not in conflict with them." One can see day and night (and day again) in the heavens. To what could you compare that cycle on earth?

How is Pao Hsi (Baoxi) treated in the Yijing? Obviously, he was not a god, but he was nicknamed "the inventor" by millions in later years. What did Pao Hsi "invent"? The remainder of the excerpt traces a line of creative leaders or sages. What were their contributions? How did they "discover" these things? What was the final (the highest) gift of the holy men? Finally, how did those who venerated the Yijing think about creation?

EPILOGUE

The development of writing held out many advantages for a culture. Important commercial agreements (water rights, real estate titles, merchant contracts, bills of sale) could be recorded and handed down with considerably more precision, often giving the ownership of property and goods more security and status. Laws and proclamations also could be codified, read in public, and enforced with more regularity. Finally, works of religion, philosophy, and literature could bind a people together, give them a sense of their past and of mission, and shape and mold their collective thought.

For these reasons, a people's written accounts of creation were never merely interpretations of the origins of the universe, the world, and human beings. The Torah revealed the Jews' (and later Christians' and Muslims') belief in a purposeful deity who created humans for a specific purpose and made a covenantal agreement with Abraham and his descendants that required worship and obedience to God's laws in return for God's blessing and protection. Not only did the Rig Veda strengthen Indian thinking about the cyclical laws that governed birth, life, and death, but it also legitimized the Aryan caste system of priests, warriors, peasants, and serfs. The Yijing called the Chinese to meditation about the interrelationships of all things—past, present, and future. Indeed, these creation accounts as well as all others (and there are

literally dozens) contain much more than a simple relating of origins.

Just as writing offered cultures that possessed it certain advantages, so also the ability to read and write elevated certain individuals, elite groups, and classes *within* a culture. To begin with, it was these people who had the power to make and enforce laws, to mold and sanction beliefs, and to exercise authority over the illiterate. As soon as a particular group had established a political or religious canon,[36] its next step often was to punish those who violated or opposed the established orthodoxy.

There is little doubt that literate elites tried to limit the spread of writing. But ultimately such restraint was almost impossible. The invention of the printing press in the mid-fifteenth century in Mainz (Germany) made it possible for writing to reach an almost limitless audience.[37] As a result, literacy in western Europe increased dramatically. Once political and religious canons could be read by many, however, disputes erupted, often over the "proper" interpretation of these canons. Yet once Pandora's box had been opened, it was nearly impossible to close it again.

Ultimately, widespread literacy strengthened the cultures in which it occurred and gave them great advantages over those in which literacy was more limited or confined. In the long run, near-universal literacy tended to support political stability and continuity, in part because of earlier

36. **canon:** code of law.

37. In fact, printing, movable type, and paper all had been invented in China over five hundred years earlier.

political revolts and changes that, ironically, literacy often had instigated, and in part because literate cultures could develop and disseminate technology and economic systems that more often led toward economic abundance. It may be no accident that in the world's most prosperous economies (Germany, Japan, the United States, the Scandinavian nations, the United Kingdom, France, and the like), illiteracy is negligible and political stability is prevalent, whereas in the world's poorest nations (such as Niger, Mali, and Bangladesh), illiteracy rates are high and political systems are often unstable.[38]

It would take centuries before the relationship between widespread literacy, economic abundance, and political stability would be fully understood. And yet as early as the prophet Muhammad, people appreciated the fact that writing meant power, and that the pen (or carving tool or stylus or quill or brush or whatever writing instrument) could be mightier than the sword.

38. United Nations statistics from 2003 of literacy rates for those aged 15–24 show Niger with 65 percent illiteracy in men and 85 percent in women, Mali with 50 percent illiteracy in men and 58 percent in women (milleniumindicators.org).

CHAPTER THREE

POLYTHEISM AND MONOTHEISM IN THE

FERTILE CRESCENT, ca 3000–500 B.C.E.

THE PROBLEM

Ancient men and women, like all peoples, struggled with answering basic questions about their existence. What were the origins of human beings and their world? What was the purpose of human existence? How could they explain the events that occurred in their lives? How could they establish order in their societies? In a prescientific age, ancient men and women answered such questions in religious terms, and indeed spiritual thought and institutions largely defined their cultures. Thus an understanding of religious thought and practice is essential to the study of ancient civilization.

Especially significant in the study of ancient civilization is the region of the Fertile Crescent, the relatively well-watered band of arable soil in southwestern Asia extending through modern Israel, Lebanon, and Syria along the shore of the Mediterranean Sea to the Tigris and Euphrates river

valleys in Iraq. In this zone ancient men and women first abandoned hunting and gathering and turned to domesticating animals and farming. They established the urban centers in which the first civilizations of the West were founded. In this region they also propounded some of the first formal religious answers to the existential questions with which they struggled. Indeed, these ancient men and women developed two very different religious traditions. One tradition typified ancient religious thought in many ways; the other, as we will see, established the theological foundation for the three great religions of the modern West: Judaism, Christianity, and Islam.

The first of these religious traditions chronologically was polytheism, the worship of many gods and goddesses. It was virtually the universal fashion in which ancient men and women in the Fertile Crescent answered questions about their existence and the world around them. They associated deities with every

Chapter 3

Polytheism and

Monotheism in

the Fertile

Crescent, ca

3000–500 B.C.E.

conceivable physical phenomenon, human emotion, event, or even their cities, clans, or trades. Thus ancients might have prayed to the sea god for a safe voyage, or to the fertility god for a good harvest or a fecund herd. Individuals worshiped personal gods, too. All such worship was anthropomorphic; that is, its practitioners envisioned their gods and goddesses as living beings and portrayed them in human or animal form, and they believed that their deities, although immortal, ate, drank, married, reproduced, and experienced a full range of emotions just like humans. Although the followers of such beliefs frequently venerated one deity above others as a sort of supreme god in their pantheon of gods and goddesses, they almost never worshiped one god, a practice called monotheism.

The oldest formal religious practices of which scholars have any significant knowledge are the polytheistic rites of the peoples of ancient Mesopotamia, the area that forms the eastern portion of the Fertile Crescent between the Tigris and Euphrates rivers in Iraq. The search for reliable water supplies was central to the existence of ancient communities, and scholars long have assumed that the waters of these two rivers drew the earliest inhabitants to Mesopotamia. Indeed, the region's water, and its lack of great natural barriers to human movement, drew a number of different peoples to the region.

The first significant inhabitants of early Mesopotamia were the Sumerians, a people of uncertain origins whose language was unrelated to any known today, including those of the Semitic language groups native to Mesopotamia. Settling in southern Mesopotamia sometime in the fourth millennium B.C.E., the Sumerians created flourishing cities like Uruk, Ur, and Nippur and traded widely throughout the Fertile Crescent. The cultural life that they created in their cities constituted the first civilization of the West and shaped the culture of Mesopotamia for three millennia. Central to this cultural life was the Sumerians' invention of a writing system, *cuneiform*, with which they kept their business records and created their literature. Cuneiform was a complicated system of wedge-shaped characters (*cuneus* is Latin for "wedge") that were typically inscribed on clay tablets with reed styli by scribes specially schooled in its intricacies. It constituted the universal writing system of scholars, theologians, and diplomats of the Fertile Crescent for several millennia; indeed, Alexander the Great and his soldiers found scribes of the region still using cuneiform in the fourth century B.C.E. The polytheistic religious beliefs of the Sumerians also became universal in Mesopotamia and much of the Fertile Crescent. Thus, even though the Sumerians eventually disappeared from the region as a distinct people, subsumed by successive conquerors and the Semitic-language natives of the region, their achievements formed the basis for a common ancient Mesopotamian culture. Among the peoples sharing this culture were the Akkadians from northern Mesopotamia, who conquered the Sumerian cities

[46]

and merged them into an empire ruled by Sargon I about 2350 B.C.E.; the Babylonians, who, under Hammurabi (r. ca 1792–1750 B.C.E.), created a major state centered on their capital of Babylon; the Elamites, who built a large Mesopotamian realm in the late second and early first millennia with its capital at Susa in modern Iran; and the Assyrians, who created a large, warlike state that conquered much of the region in the first millennium B.C.E.

The first Sumerian settlers of the region and their successors found that they had to cope with a difficult environment. They had to drain marshland for cultivation along the rivers' banks, and they could expand their area of arable land only by building irrigation systems. They found, too, that the Tigris and Euphrates flooded unpredictably and that their waters might quickly kill large numbers of inhabitants along with their livestock and destroy the irrigation works so vital to those who survived inundations. Weather was difficult, too, for early men and women. Today the sun parches the region, producing temperatures as high as 125 degrees Fahrenheit in the warmer months, while heavy winter rains can turn much of the area into mud. Human action also rendered the region dangerous for early men and women. Ancient Mesopotamians fought each other for water supplies at the same time that they had to struggle with invaders of this region, which had few natural barriers to attack.

The grim realities of life in ancient Mesopotamia shaped the religious outlook of its inhabitants. Ancient Mesopotamians could not assume that order, stability, and personal safety would be their lot, and in their quest to explain the difficulties that surrounded them and to ward off imminent dangers they devised a polytheistic belief system. They saw individual human beings as having little consequence in the cosmic order, and one Mesopotamian author wrote: "Mere man—his days are numbered; whatever he may do, he is but the wind."[1] Indeed, Mesopotamians saw themselves as pawns in the hands of capricious gods whose needs they were created to serve and whose ways they were incapable of knowing. One Babylonian text conveys the dilemma of these ancient peoples in their relations with such gods:

What seems good to oneself, is a
   crime before a god.
What to one's heart seems bad, is
   good before one's god.
Who may comprehend the minds of
   gods in heaven's depth?
The thoughts of (those) divine deep
   waters, who could fathom them?
How could mankind, beclouded, comprehend the ways of the gods?[2]

Ancient Mesopotamians believed in the existence of a pantheon of literally thousands of deities, whom they

1. Gilgamesh Epic, Old Babylonian version, Yale Tablet IV, 7–8, quoted in Thorkild Jacobsen and William A. Irwin, *The Intellectual Adventure of Ancient Man: An Essay on Speculative Thought in the Ancient Near East* (Chicago: University of Chicago Press, 1946), p. 125.
2. W. G. Lambert, ed., *Babylonian Wisdom Literature* (Oxford: Clarendon Press, 1960), p. 40, lines 34–38.

Chapter 3

Polytheism and

Monotheism in

the Fertile

Crescent, ca

3000–500 B.C.E.

arranged in a hierarchy. There were, however, four especially significant deities in this Mesopotamian pantheon, although their names changed somewhat over the centuries. (We will provide the Sumerian name of each with the Babylonian equivalent in parentheses.) An (Anu or Anum), whose name is the Sumerian word for "sky," was the god of the heavens, and may have been venerated as the chief god in the period prior to the invention of writing. By the time written religious records came into use, however, this deity, though important, was not the chief god. The second important deity for the Sumerians, Enlil, whose name means "Lord Storm," was a god of great power, a kind of chief executive who executed the will of the gods. The Babylonians ascribed many of Enlil's powers to a god they called Marduk. The third significant god was Enki (Ea), god of wisdom and organizer of the earth under Enlil's direction, and the fourth key deity was Ninhursaga (Ninmah, Nintur, and other names), the mother of all living things. In addition to these four central gods and goddesses, Mesopotamians also particularly worshiped three astral deities: Nanna (Sîn), the moon god; Nanna's son, the sun god Utu (Shamash), whose dispelling of darkness made him the deity associated with equity and justice; and Nanna's daughter, Inanna (Ishtar), the goddess of love and fertility, but also war.

Mesopotamians believed that these gods and numerous other deities controlled the fate of the world and mankind in an assembly in which An and Enlil proposed action that the other deities deliberated. When the deities reached a decision, Enlil, or a god or demon designated by him, carried it out. Mesopotamians sought to influence the outcomes of these divine deliberations in several ways. Most individuals had personal gods, deities often long venerated by their families, who they hoped might intercede with the main deities in their behalf. Indeed, the Sumerian word for "good luck" means "to acquire a god," that is, a personal deity who would work for the earthly success of an individual.

The main fashion in which Mesopotamians attempted to influence their deities, however, was in the elaborate cultic activities of their temples, and each deity enjoyed particular veneration in certain locations. Mesopotamians believed that each city was the possession of an individual deity who was entitled to all of its wealth and the labor and devotion of its inhabitants. Thus Uruk was the possession of An, while Nippur was the city of Enlil, and Babylon that of Marduk. To adequately fund the worship of these divinities, Mesopotamian temples owned considerable land, employed tenant farmers to work it, and ran business enterprises, but we now know that they did not own all property, as scholars once thought. Nevertheless, Mesopotamians, anxious to find favor in the eyes of their gods, turned over considerable wealth to the temples, which scribes carefully recorded on clay tablets. This wealth supported a virtual household for the deity in each temple. Priests dressed the god's image in rich clothing, prepared ritual meals for him, and entertained him with music. Such wealth also supported elaborate public festivals honoring the gods with ceremonies and parades. Eventually, too, the priesthood devised an elaborate system to interpret natural omens that they alleged predicted the gods' intentions toward humans.

These practices represent a belief system, dominated by a professional priesthood, which established little direct relationship between the individual and the divine, beyond the prayers and offerings that the individual rendered to his or her personal god. Reward for service to the gods, and obedience to the kings whom Mesopotamians saw as deputies of their deities, came in the form of divine protection from the dangers of this life and was measured in good health, long life, and material success. But death, in the end, overtook all, and while Mesopotamian notions of the afterlife still remain vague to modern scholars, they seem to have offered the individual little prospect of a reward for a virtuous life on earth. The Mesopotamian view was that all of the dead seem to share a miserable afterlife, even the greatest of heroes.

The second religious tradition of the ancient Fertile Crescent, monotheism, is inextricably linked with the history of the Hebrews, who were originally nomadic herdsmen. Their recorded history began in the second millennium B.C.E. as they left Mesopotamia led by the patriarch Abraham and settled first in Canaan, a region along the eastern shore of the Mediterranean Sea that partially included the territory of the modern state of Israel. Further migration, possibly because of a drought in Canaan, led the Hebrews to Egypt, where the government eventually reduced them to doing forced labor on its building projects in the Nile Delta.

In approximately 1250 B.C.E., a remarkable leader named Moses led the Hebrews' escape from Egypt, an event remembered as the Exodus. Received by the Hebrews as a messenger of God, Moses spiritually unified them in the midst of their Exodus by committing them to the worship of one deity, referred to as *YHWH* in ancient Hebrew texts (ancient Hebrew employed no vowels) and *Yahweh* in much of modern scholarship. The Hebrews' vision of their deity was unique in the second millennium B.C.E. For them, Yahweh was the all-powerful creator of the world, and, unlike Mesopotamian deities, he alone controlled every aspect of the universe. He was invisible and omnipresent, too, and because the Hebrews believed him to be eternal, they never envisioned him as being born or having physical needs like Mesopotamian gods and goddesses. Most importantly in the Hebrews' religious vision, Yahweh was kind, merciful, and slow to anger, and he chiefly demanded that his followers exhibit their devotion to him through their obedience to the ethical code revealed in laws associated with him.

Committed to following the laws and teachings of Yahweh, the Hebrews returned to Canaan, which

Chapter 3

Polytheism and

Monotheism in

the Fertile

Crescent, ca

3000–500 B.C.E.

they believed Yahweh had promised to them, and conquered the land with military force. Their first-millennium B.C.E. sojourn in this land was often difficult. Organized first as a tribal federation, the Hebrews had to defend their conquests. Indeed, their military needs required them to abandon tribal government for a monarchy under King Saul (r. ca 1024–1000 B.C.E.). Following Saul's death in battle, the throne passed first to King David (r. ca 1000–961 B.C.E.) and then to King Solomon (r. ca 961–922 B.C.E.). Under the latter monarch, the Hebrew state grew to its greatest extent, and a great spiritual center arose in the temple built in the royal capital, Jerusalem.

At Solomon's death, however, the Hebrew state divided. The northern part of the state, resentful of Solomon's high taxes and the favoritism he showed the south, established itself as the kingdom of Israel, with its capital at Samaria. The south, the kingdom of Judah, retained Jerusalem as its capital. This division of the Hebrew state occurred at a most unfortunate time, just as dangerous and powerful new states were emerging in the Fertile Crescent. Thus Israel fell to the Assyrians in 722 B.C.E., and these conquerors transported the Hebrews of the north to other parts of their growing empire. There, the Hebrew tribes of northern Canaan lost their religious identity as other Middle Eastern peoples culturally subsumed them.

The kingdom of Judah survived to 586 B.C.E. when the forces of a new Babylonian empire captured Jerusalem and carried the Hebrews of the south off into captivity in Babylon. There was a real risk that the captives would lose their religious identity in such an exile, just as had their northern kinsmen, but remarkably their religious culture survived. Priests and scholars undertook to preserve religious tradition by drawing together the laws and oral traditions of the Hebrews into texts that would become the Old Testament, and preachers rekindled religious belief with predictions that Yahweh would restore the Hebrews to their homeland. Indeed, such a prediction bore fruit when the Persians conquered Babylon and allowed the Hebrews to return to Judah, by that time a Persian province. There, the Hebrews, henceforth usually called Jews because of their residence in Judah, rebuilt the temple destroyed by the Babylonians.

Although Persian and Babylonian conquests—followed by those of Alexander the Great and the Romans—ended ancient Hebrew political independence, Judaism survived as a distinct faith. Indeed, it survived even as Roman conquerors in the first century C.E. scattered Jews around the West in a diaspora that left many of them living far from their traditional homeland. They often survived as a religious minority among peoples who shared little of their religious culture. In part, this survival was the result of the distinctiveness of that culture. The Jews' adherence to the traditional laws of Yahweh gave them an identity that made their assimilation into other religious traditions difficult and that bound the individual to the religious tradition.

Your goal in this chapter is to analyze the ways in which the polytheism of ancient Mesopotamia and the monotheism of the Hebrews proposed answers to the basic questions posed at the opening of this chapter. What were the origins of human beings and their world? How did they explain the events that occurred in their lives? How could they establish order in their societies? As you develop answers to these questions, you should better understand ancient religion and the societies that produced it.

SOURCES AND METHOD

Archaeology is an essential tool in reconstructing the life of the ancient world. Archaeological excavations, systematically carried on by modern scholars, are recovering increasing evidence of the art, architecture, and learning of the ancient world, and in recent years their discoveries have dramatically increased historians' knowledge of the Fertile Crescent and its religious life. Indeed, modern scholars have amassed virtually all of their knowledge of ancient Mesopotamia in the past two centuries. Their systematic recovery of the physical remains of the region's ancient civilization commenced only in the 1830s when the French scholar Paul Émile Botta (1805–1870) began to excavate the mysterious mounds, called *tells* in Arabic, that dotted the otherwise flat Mesopotamian landscape. Formed by centuries of drifting sand accumulating around the ruins of ancient cities and temples, these mounds yielded ancient artifacts and architecture to archaeologists. Scholars' efforts to interpret the significance of their findings advanced considerably when the German philologist Georg Friedrich Grotefend (1775–1853) successfully deciphered the cuneiform writing of ancient scribes. Equipped with such linguistic skills, archaeologists have been able to exploit dramatic discoveries to increase their knowledge of Mesopotamian civilization. One such discovery was the excavation of the library of the Assyrian king Ashurbanipal (r. 668–627 B.C.E.) in Nineveh. That monarch had attempted to assemble all of the region's learning in his library, and the 22,000 tablets that archaeologists discovered there have proven to be a remarkable source for the study of Mesopotamian civilization.

Sources 1 and 2 offer pictorial evidence of archaeologists' work and provide us with an introduction to the physical remains of ancient Mesopotamian religious life. Both sources illustrate the ziggurat constructed by King Ur-Nammu at Ur about 2100 B.C.E., a time when that Sumerian city was the capital of a considerable empire. Ziggurats were stepped pyramids, as Source 1 shows, that were characteristic features of Mesopotamian temple sites. Source 1 is a sketch based on the work of Sir Leonard Wooley, a twentieth-century archaeologist who led some of the most important digs at Ur. The ziggurat illustrated in the sketch was

Chapter 3

Polytheism and

Monotheism in

the Fertile

Crescent, ca

3000–500 B.C.E.

part of the shrine of the moon god, Nanna, who was the patron god of Ur, and it was the center of a massive temple complex including shrines to Nanna and his wife Ningal, offices for the priests, and storehouses for the temple's wealth. Many scholars think that the Mesopotamians believed that the god dwelt atop the ziggurat in a shrine that was open only to priests, who reached it by mounting staircases like those illustrated in Source 1.

Source 2, a photograph of this ziggurat after archaeologists removed the tell that had concealed the structure for centuries, shows this religious site as it looks today. Its two top terraces have been lost to the ravages of time, but the scale of the structure may be gauged by comparing it to the automobile in the foreground. Constructed in the sun-baked mud brick of the region and faced with harder, fired bricks, the ziggurat measures about 200 feet by 150 feet at its base and today stands about 50 feet high. Four millennia ago, temple attendants planted the terraces with trees and green plants, which must have made the ziggurat look like a mountain. What impression do you think that the ziggurat made on ancient residents of Ur? If you combine this impression with the closure of the inner sanctum of the ziggurat to laypeople, and recall the riches that Mesopotamians offered to their temples, what sort of religious sentiments do you suppose worshipers at such a shrine might have experienced? Why might you agree with a modern scholar who has written that the divine in ancient Mesopotamia "was

above all something grandiose, inaccessible, dominating, and to be feared"?[3] Why can you find little connection between the individual and the deity in this architectural expression of ancient polytheism?

Mesopotamian religious thinkers produced no systematic theological treatises yet discovered by archaeologists. Thus modern students of the region must reconstruct Mesopotamian religion from the texts of actual religious rites that archaeologists have uncovered. The precise ancient purpose of the text in Source 3 is unclear; its words come from an early-second-millennium column found near Babylon on the Euphrates River that is in a poor state of preservation. Perhaps the words originally were a prayer or incantation, but scholars do know that they present us with a vision of human origins that was widespread in Mesopotamia. What does this text tell us about the position of mankind in the Mesopotamian cosmos? Why did the gods create humans? Why do you suppose the gods created the first man from a mixture of divine blood and clay? Given this vision of human origins, what do you suppose Mesopotamians believed that they owed their deities?

Source 4 reminds us that the various linguistic groups of Mesopotamia shared a common cultural heritage. It is a prayer found on a tablet at King Ashurbanipal's palace in Nineveh, with a text in both Sumerian and the Akkadian language of northern Mesopotamia. Impossible

3. Jean Bottéro, *Religion in Ancient Mesopotamia*, translated by Teresa Lavender Fagan (Chicago: University of Chicago Press, 2001), p.37.

to date precisely, this was a prayer to the moon god known as Nannar (or Nanna) to the Sumerians and Sîn to the Babylonians. Why does the prayer exalt the moon god as "supreme" when, in the Sumerian pantheon, Enlil largely occupied that position, while among Babylonians the supreme deity was Marduk? Assessing the text, why might you conclude that this attribution of superior status was an attempt to win the favor of the god? What are the alleged powers of this moon god? Is this god loved by his worshipers or feared by them?

Source 5 presents four excerpts from the oldest work of Western literature yet identified by scholars, the *Epic of Gilgamesh*, a poem of more than three thousand lines. Archaeologists discovered the first, partial text of this great epic in the ruins of King Ashurbanipal's palace library in Nineveh. That first discovery, however, yielded only part of the epic, and only slowly have scholars pieced the rest of it together with discoveries of additional portions of the text at archaeological digs elsewhere in Mesopotamia. Indeed, their task is still under way. Nevertheless, the result of their labors is an ancient text that gives us further insight into Mesopotamian religion, even though the epic itself is not a religious work.

The hero of the epic, Gilgamesh, was king of Uruk about 2600 B.C.E., and according to tradition he built the city's walls. Poetry recounting his legendary exploits dates from at least 2000 B.C.E. and was written in cuneiform in the major languages of the region. The epic presents Gilgamesh as part god, a vigorous ruler who embellished his city and who had many adventures with his friend, Enkidu. Together, however, they ran afoul of the gods. They slew Huwawa, a monster assigned by Enlil to guard a forest, and they felled the cedar trees in it. Gilgamesh insulted the goddess Ishtar when she sought his hand in marriage, and he and Enkidu slew the bull of heaven that the goddess sent to Uruk to punish him. Divine punishment, envisioned in a dream, caused Enkidu's death, as the first lines of Source 5 show. Gilgamesh deeply mourned the loss of his friend, but the king resolved to avoid the fate of Enkidu, and all mortals, and set off on a quest to find the secret of immortality. That quest set Gilgamesh searching for the sole survivor of the all-killing flood that was part of Mesopotamian mythology. The gods had granted immortality to that survivor, Utnapishtim, and Gilgamesh sought to learn from him the secret of eternal life.

In undertaking his search for Utnapishtim, Gilgamesh ignored the prescient warnings of a tavern-keeper, referred to as an alewife in the translation in Source 5, that he was disregarding mankind's proper relationship with the cosmos. When Gilgamesh finally managed to meet Utnapishtim by crossing the waters that separated the realm of death from that of the living, the latter gave Gilgamesh a test requiring that he remain awake for seven days and nights. The king promptly went to sleep, however, losing his chance to learn the secret of immortality, and Utnapishtim ordered Gilgamesh to return to the land of the living, where

Chapter 3

Polytheism and
Monotheism in
the Fertile
Crescent, ca
3000–500 B.C.E.

he, of course, would face eventual death. But thanks to the intervention of the wife of Utnapishtim, Gilgamesh got one more chance to avoid early death with a magical plant that offered rejuvenation. How did he lose this opportunity, too? What does the epic tell us about Mesopotamians' belief in their gods' control of their destinies? How did Mesopotamians view the afterlife? Did the powerful and wealthy fare any better there than commoners? Is there any sense here that the gods even cared about man's fate? What was Gilgamesh's fate? Why do you think that this part of the epic ends with Gilgamesh taking the boatman who had conveyed him back and forth across the waters on a tour of the walls and sights of Uruk?

Source 6 presents us with the Mesopotamians' quest to establish earthly order. Ancient Mesopotamians viewed their world as an extension of the divine world. The gods simply delegated their authority on earth to kings, and ancient authors often used the words "the Enlil functions" to designate the power of these kings, which, in their view, reflected the almighty power of the god Enlil. Thus, just as that chief god kept order in the divine world, the king kept order on earth. And, indeed, there was considerable need for an authority figure to keep order in the ancient Tigris and Euphrates River valleys. Mesopotamians lived in densely populated cities and engaged in competitive commercial and agricultural activities that created ample opportunity for human conflict. Moreover, there was little in the

way of social control in Mesopotamian religion; the ancient polytheism of Mesopotamia seems not to have obligated its followers to adhere to an ethical code as part of their spiritual devotion. Thus, archaeologists have found evidence that Mesopotamian rulers began attempting to regulate human behavior with detailed law codes by 2400 B.C.E., if not earlier.

Source 6 presents the most famous Mesopotamian law code, that of Hammurabi, the ruler of Babylon (r. ca 1792–1750 B.C.E.). First discovered by French archaeologists in 1901 carved in cuneiform characters on a stele, or upright stone slab, the laws of Hammurabi have now been found at a number of Mesopotamian sites. What does the prologue of the law code suggest that Mesopotamians saw as the source of law and order in their earthly realm? The code itself represents what legal scholars call case law; that is, it describes specific actions and circumstances and then posits their legal consequences. Why do you think Babylonian society required such a detailed law code? What aspects of life did the code regulate? Did its scope exceed the bounds of modern law? Did Hammurabi's code regulate a society in which all citizens were equal? Why might you characterize the sections dealing with criminal law as harsh by modern standards?

If the sources of ancient Mesopotamian polytheism have been known to Western scholars for only about two centuries, the sources of the religion of the ancient Hebrews have been the object of serious scholarly study for two millennia. Those sources are the texts that constitute the Hebrew Bible, what Jews call *Tanak* (an acronym based on the first letters of the three divisions of the Hebrew Bible: Torah ["Law"], Nebi'im ["Prophets"], and Kethubim ["Writings"]), and the first part of the Christian Bible, the Old Testament. Traditionally scholars have studied these works through intense textual analyses in which they apply their theological, linguistic, and historical knowledge to better understand the origins and development of these biblical texts, which are the essential foundations for the religious beliefs of many in the West.

Such study has allowed modern scholars to identify differences in textual authorships and actually to date the books of the Old Testament. They know, for example, that they have yet to find a single biblical text dating to the traditional second-millennium B.C.E. origins of Hebrew monotheism. Instead, they have found that much of the Old Testament commentary on the origins of Hebrew monotheism was written considerably later. The first Old Testament books, including Genesis and Exodus, which recount the Creation story and the early history of the Hebrews through about 1200 B.C.E., were written later, perhaps between about 950 and 800 B.C.E. Thus these and other Old Testament texts were not the work of authors who actually witnessed the events that they recounted. Instead, these were the work of extremely talented, later authors who wove Hebrew oral traditions, songs, prayers, and laws into coherent texts of often beautiful literary quality.

Scholars' knowledge of this evolution of the Old Testament text caused some among them in the early and mid-twentieth century to question the traditional second-millennium B.C.E. origins of Hebrew monotheism in the time of Abraham and Moses. They reasoned that the authors of the Old Testament books who recounted the earliest Hebrew history probably projected their own monotheism onto their ancestors. These scholars placed the origin of true monotheism later, at the time of the prophetic writings of the eighth and ninth centuries B.C.E., in part because their textual analyses suggested that the authors of the prophetic texts indeed described events that they witnessed.

More recently, however, Old Testament scholarship has been powerfully affected by the results of archaeological excavations in the western Fertile Crescent. These excavations at non-Hebrew sites are now providing important verification of much found in the Old Testament accounts of the earliest Hebrew experiences. The most important of these sites is that of Ugarit (modern Ras Shamra) on the Mediterranean coast of Syria. There, archaeological digs under way since 1928 have uncovered the remains of a port city and cultural center that flourished at the time of the Hebrews' flight from Egypt. Texts discovered at Ugarit, written in the local language that was closely related to Hebrew, contain the poetry and myths of the Hebrews' close neighbors and confirm many of the stories and practices of the Old Testament books like Genesis and Exodus. As a result,

Chapter 3

Polytheism and

Monotheism in

the Fertile

Crescent, ca

3000–500 B.C.E.

recent scholars have been better able to place Hebrew monotheism into the cultural context of the ancient Middle East as well as to better understand its earliest origins.

It is clear that Hebrew monotheism and Mesopotamian polytheism shared certain geographic and cultural roots. The Old Testament places the origin of Abraham and his kin squarely in southern Mesopotamia at Ur, and they also dwelt at Haran in northern Mesopotamia before moving on to Canaan. Thus Mesopotamian and Hebrew cultures share certain elements; both have very similar Creation accounts, and both traditions recall an all-destroying flood. But despite these similarities, we can discern marked differences in the religious thought of the two groups in even the earliest Hebrew texts.

Source 7 presents the Creation account from Genesis 2:1–24. Biblical scholars know that this account is one of three originally distinct Creation stories that eventually became part of Genesis, and on the basis of close textual analysis they identify this as the oldest of the three. In Genesis it follows another, relatively more recent, Creation account that opens the book and that presents Yahweh creating the universe in seven days. The opening lines of the selection in Source 7 refer to that process. Compare this account with the Creation story in Source 3. What similarities do you note? How, for example, was the first man formed in each story? What location do you suspect for the Garden of Eden based on two of the rivers identified in the selection? Why do such similarities in the two ac-

counts suggest that they, or their authors, had similar origins? Next examine the text of Source 7 for its differences from the Mesopotamian account. For what reason did Mesopotamian deities form human beings? What did Yahweh intend for his human creations? What do you conclude from the fact that Yahweh permitted humans to name the animals that he had created? Why might you determine that the Hebrew account portrays a more benevolent deity than does the Mesopotamian story?

Source 8 describes the central event of the Hebrews' religious experience, their acceptance of the covenant with Yahweh that established them as his chosen people. The event described here occurred in the wilderness of Sinai, after the Hebrews' exodus from Egypt, when Yahweh descended to Mount Sinai and enunciated the covenant to Moses. In return for obeying Yahweh's law, the Hebrews would enjoy divine protection. The laws that form the covenant are known as the Ten Commandments, and Source 8A presents these from Exodus 20:1–17. Following the laws, in Source 8B, is the Hebrews' acceptance, described in Exodus 24:3, of Yahweh's terms for the covenant.

The laws contained in Source 8 are part of a broad general statement of law contained in the first five books of the Old Testament—Genesis, Exodus, Leviticus, Numbers, and Deuteronomy—that for Jews constitute the Torah or law. The Ten Commandments are quite different from the case law that we observed in Hammurabi's Code; they are what legal scholars call absolute, or apodictic, law. Such law states broad, absolute principles that cannot be violated, and it can be extremely important in ordering the lives of those subject to it, although it is essential that case law provide concrete applications of its principles. Although some biblical scholars have questioned whether this covenant truly established monotheism since it acknowledges the existence of "other gods," many others accept it as clearly establishing a special relationship between Yahweh and the Hebrews defined by a monotheistic faith. What did Yahweh expect of his people in the Ten Commandments? When you consider the commandments, why will you probably conclude that they established definite behavioral responsibilities for the individual within the covenanting group? What does Yahweh expect of his followers that Mesopotamian deities did not require of those who worshiped them? Why might you conclude that the phrase "ethical monotheism" is an apt description of the faith established by this covenant?

Source 9 presents sources from some of the books of the Torah that offer case law. Like Hammurabi's Code, they give us a fuller vision of the behavior that Yahweh expected of his followers. What is the source of the law in Source 9, and, ultimately, who is the guarantor of the peace that the law seeks to protect? Contrast your answers with those that you would give to the same questions posed about Hammurabi's Code. Who is the protector of the marginal members of Hebrew society: resident aliens, widows, orphans, and the poor?

In Leviticus 19:17, what do you find demanded of Yahweh's followers that goes well beyond simple adherence to the "law" in our modern sense of that word? Why might you conclude that these selections also spell out a code of personal ethics? Why might you probably conclude that the Hebrew laws demanded far more of those subject to them than did the laws of Hammurabi?

In return for their adherence to the Ten Commandments, the Old Testament tells us that Yahweh promised to deliver the land of Canaan into the possession of the Hebrews. The Hebrews' subsequent conquest and settlement of this region were fraught with problems. Traditionally nomadic herdsmen, the Hebrews had to adjust to a sedentary, agricultural life in Canaan, and they had to deal with dangerous neighbors like the warlike Philistines. But the greatest danger that they faced, according to the Old Testament, was a spiritual one. They had settled among Canaanite neighbors who, archaeological evidence shows, were more materially advanced than their Hebrew conquerors, and Canaanite culture must have tempted many Hebrews. But embracing aspects of that culture risked the cultural distinctiveness of the Hebrews, particularly in the area of religion. The Canaanites were polytheists, much of whose religious life centered on fertility cults that included ritualized sexual acts. These acts were fiercely condemned by Hebrew religious leaders, known as prophets.

The prophets represented a Hebrew manifestation of a long-standing

Chapter 3

Polytheism and

Monotheism in

the Fertile

Crescent, ca

3000–500 B.C.E.

Middle Eastern tradition in which religious figures prophesized the future and tried to shape human behavior. The Hebrew prophets of the first millennium B.C.E.—men like Elijah, Elisha, Isaiah, Hosea, and Amos—proclaimed that they were messengers of Yahweh and that they spoke his words. Thus biblical passages often start the words of the prophets with phrases like "Thus says the Lord. . . ." The words that followed such phrases typically condemned the kings of Israel and Judah who did not provide proper leadership to their people, the moral failings of Hebrew society, and most particularly the tendency of the Hebrews to adopt Canaanite religious practices. Usually, too, the prophets threatened divine action against Hebrews who did not change their ways, and they portrayed the conquests of Israel and Judah as acts of divine retribution.

Source 10 offers the words of several prophets as examples of the Hebrews' relationship with Yahweh and the struggle of the prophets to uphold the religious beliefs and practices of the covenant. Source 10A is from the book of Isaiah, a prophet active in the eighth century B.C.E. His writings suggest that Isaiah was a man of considerable culture and learning, and he warned of the moral and ethical failings of the Hebrews as well as of the growing threat from the Assyrians. Scholars believe that the later part of the book of Isaiah, including the selection in 10A, was the work of one of the great prophet's disciples. What does the author of these verses remind his readers about Yahweh's power? What does he say

that Yahweh values in his followers? How are such expectations consistent with Hebrew ethical monotheism?

Source 10B is a selection from the book of Hosea. His book includes an account of his marriage to Gomer, a woman who bore him three children and then was unfaithful to her marital vows. Hosea divorced her for this unfaithfulness and she became a prostitute, but he subsequently forgave Gomer and remarried her. Biblical scholars generally see Hosea's story as an allegory that represents the Hebrews' unfaithfulness to Yahweh and his ultimate mercy and forgiveness. What does Hosea condemn? Why might you conclude that he condemns religious syncretism, that is, the Hebrews' adoption of Canaanite rites? Source 10B also gives an eloquent account of Yahweh's relationship with the Hebrews. Why would you characterize that relationship as a parental one? Why do you think that Yahweh, like many parents, punished with extreme reluctance? Why do you conclude that Hosea saw Yahweh as a merciful god?

Despite the personal relationship between Yahweh and the individual Hebrew, there remained a certain distance between him and mortals, and his ways often remained inscrutable to them. This is evident even in Old Testament books written relatively late in time. One such book is that of Job, which may have been written as late as the fourth century B.C.E. Stylistically, it is one of the Old Testament's most remarkable books, comprising, in part, poetry of exceptional beauty. Its story, however, is its most compelling aspect, that of a righteous man who, despite his virtues and religious devotion, is afflicted by evil. This theme appears in Mesopotamian and Egyptian literature, too, but in the book of Job, excerpted in Source 11, the main theme is not the incidence of evil but the individual's relationship with Yahweh.

In the book, Yahweh tests Job, depriving him of his children and his property and afflicting him with illness. What is Job's response to these afflictions? How does he despair in an age that assumed that virtue would be rewarded not in the next life but with material success and good health in this life? How does Job even despair of ever getting a fair hearing from Yahweh? How does Yahweh respond to Job? Why might you find Yahweh's questions of Job almost mocking the weakness of mortals? What vision of Yahweh's power do you detect in his response to Job? Why can Job not know Yahweh's ways? What sort of profession of faith from Job led to the restoration of what he had lost?

Using this background information on ancient polytheism and monotheism in the Fertile Crescent, now turn to the sources themselves. As you read them, reflect on how the ancient followers of each religious tradition answered the basic existential questions with which we opened this chapter. What were the origins of human beings and their world? How did they explain events that occurred in their lives? How could they establish order in their societies?

Chapter 3
Polytheism and
Monotheism in
the Fertile
Crescent, ca
3000–500 B.C.E.

THE EVIDENCE

Source 1 from P.R.S. Moorey, Ur of the Chaldese: A Revised and Updated Edition of Sir Leonard Wooley's Excavations at Ur *(Ithaca: Cornell University Press, 1982), p. 148, which cites the Ur Excavation Report (Copyright, Trustees of the British Museum) as source of all drawings, unless otherwise noted.*

1. The Ziggurat of Ur-Nammu, King of Ur, ca 2100 B.C.E.

Source 2 from Hirmer Fotoarchiv, Munich.

2. The Ziggurat of Ur-Nammu, King of Ur, ca 2100 B.C.E., As It Looked After Twentieth-Century Archaeological Excavation Work

Source 3 from James B. Pritchard, ed., Ancient Near Eastern Texts Relating to the Old Testament, *3rd ed. with supplement (Princeton: Princeton University Press, 1969), pp. 99–100. Copyright © 1969 by Princeton University Press. Reprinted by permission of Princeton University Press.*

3. Creation of Man by the Mother Goddess

"That which is slight he shall raise to abundance;
The work of god man shall bear!"
The goddess they called to enquire,
The midwife of the gods, the wise Mami:[4]
"Thou art the mother-womb,
The one who creates mankind.
Create, then, Lullu[5] and let him bear the yoke!
The yoke he shall bear, . . . [. . .];
The work of god man shall bear!"

4. **Mami:** one of a series of names Mesopotamians applied to the mother goddess. They also included, among others, Nihursaga and Nintur, as well as the name Nintu that appears later in this text.
5. **Lullu:** literally, "the savage first man," really a figure akin to Adam of the Old Testament.

[61]

Chapter 3

Polytheism and

Monotheism in

the Fertile

Crescent, ca

3000–500 B.C.E.

Nintu opened her mouth,
Saying to the great gods:
"With me is the doing of (this) not suitable;
With Enki is (this) work (proper)!
He purifies everything,
Let him give me the clay, then I will do (it)"
Enki opened his mouth,
Saying to the great gods:
"On the first of the month, the seventh and fifteenth days,
I will prepare a purification, a bath.
Let one god be slain,
And let the gods be purified by immersion
In his flesh and his blood.
Let Nintu mix clay,
God and man,
Let them together be smeared with clay.
Unto eternity let us hear the drum."

Source 4 from R. F. Harper, ed., Assyrian and Babylonian Literature: Selected Translations *(New York: D. Appleton and Co., 1900), pp. 430–431.*

4. Prayer to the Moon God, Nannar or Sîn

O Lord, chief of the gods, who in heaven and on earth alone is supreme!
Father Nannar, lord of increase, chief of the gods!
Father Nannar, lord of heaven, great one, chief of the gods!
Father Nannar, lord of the moon, chief of the gods!
Father Nannar, lord of Ur, chief of the gods!
Father Nannar, lord of E-gis-sir-gal,[6] chief of the gods!
Father Nannar, lord of the moon-disk, brilliant one, chief of the gods!
Father Nannar, who rules with pomp, chief of the gods!
Father Nannar, who goes about in princely garb, chief of the gods!
O strong bull, with terrible horns, well-developed muscles,
    with a flowing beard of the colour of lapis lazuli,[7] full of
    vigour and life!
O fruit, which grows of itself, developed in appearance, beautiful
    to look upon, but whose luxuriance does not produce fruit!

6. **E-gis-sir-gal:** the name of the moon god's temple at Ur.

7. **lapis lazuli:** a semiprecious stone of deep blue color used by the ancients for beads and other ornaments.

O merciful one, begetter of everything, who has taken up his
   illustrious abode among living creatures!
O merciful and forgiving father, who holds in his hand the
   life of the whole country!
O Lord, thy divinity is full of fear, like the far-off heavens
   and the broad sea! . . .

. . . .

O Father, begetter of everything . . .
O Lord, who determines the decisions of heaven and earth,
   whose command no one [can set aside]!
O thou who holdest fire and water, who rulest over all creatures!
   What god can attain thy position?
In heaven who is exalted? Thou alone art exalted!
On earth who is exalted? Thou alone art exalted!

Source 5 from James B. Pritchard, ed., Ancient Near Eastern Texts Relating to the Old
Testament, *3rd ed. with supplement (Princeton: Princeton University Press, 1969), pp. 85–90,
96. Gilgamesh Epic translated in Pritchard by E. A. Speiser. Copyright © 1969 by Princeton
University Press. Reprinted by permission of Princeton University Press.*

5. The Epic of Gilgamesh

[*The Death of Enkidu*]

Gilgamesh in his palace holds a celebration.
Down lie the heroes on their beds of night
Also Enkidu lies down, a dream beholding.
Up rose Enkidu to relate his dream,
Saying to his friend:
"My friend, why are the great gods in council?"
[And] Enkidu answered Gilgamesh:
"[He]*ar* the dream which I had last night:
Anu, Enlil, Ea, and heavenly Shamash
   [Were in council].
And Anu said to Enlil:
'Because the Bull of Heaven they have slain, and Huwawa
They have slain, therefore'—said Anu—'the one of them
Who stripped the mountains of the cedar
   [Must die!]'
But Enlil said: 'Enkidu must die;
Gilgamesh, however, shall not die!'. . .

That night [he pours out] his feelings to his friend:
". . . My friend, I saw a dream last night:
The heavens shouted, the earth responded;

[63]

Chapter 3

Polytheism and

Monotheism in

the Fertile

Crescent, ca

3000–500 B.C.E.

While I was standing between them
(There was) a young man whose face was dark, . . .
Looking at me, he leads me to the House of Darkness,
    The abode of Irkalla,[8]
To the house which none leave who have entered it,
On the road from which there is no way back,
To the house wherein the dwellers are bereft of light,
Where dust is their fare and clay their food.
They are clothed like birds, with wings for garments,
And see no light, residing in darkness.
In the House of Dust, which I entered,
I looked at [rulers], their crowns put away;
I [saw princes], those (born to) the crown,
    Who had ruled the land from the days of yore.
[These *doubl*]es of Anu and Enlil were serving meat roasts;
They were serving bake[meats] and pouring
    Cool water from the waterskins.
In the House of Dust, which I entered,
Reside High Priest and acolyte,
Reside incantatory and ecstatic,
Reside the laver-anointers of the great gods,
Resides Etana,[9] resides Sumuqan . . .[10]

[*Gilgamesh Mourns Enkidu*]

For Enkidu, his friend, Gilgamesh
Weeps bitterly, as he ranges over the steppe:
When I die, shall I not be like Enkidu?
Woe has entered my belly.
Fearing death, I roam over the steppe.
To Utnapishtim, Ubar-Tutu's son,
I have taken the road to proceed in all haste . . .

[*Gilgamesh Meets the Tavern-Keeper*]

"Gilgamesh, whither rovest thou?
The life thou pursuest thou shalt not find.
When the gods created mankind,
Death for mankind they set aside,
Life in their own hands retaining.
Thou, Gilgamesh, let full be thy belly,

---

8. **Irkalla:** in Mesopotamian mythology, the queen of the underworld.
9. **Etana:** a legendary king carried to heaven by an eagle.
10. **Sumuqan:** the god of cattle.

[64]

Make thou merry by day and by night.
Of each day make thou a feast of rejoicing,
Day and night dance thou and play!
Let thy garments be sparkling fresh,
Thy head be washed; bathe thou in water.
Pay heed to the little one that holds on to thy hand,
Let thy spouse delight in thy bosom!
For this is the task of [mankind]!" . . .

[*Gilgamesh Leaves Utnapishtim and Returns to Uruk*]

His spouse says to him, to Utnapishtim the Faraway:
"Gilgamesh has come hither, toiling and straining.
What wilt thou give (him) that he may return to his land?"
At that he, Gilgamesh, raised up (his) pole,
To bring the boat nigh to the shore.
Utnapishtim [says] to him, [to] Gilgamesh:
"Gilgamesh, thou hast come hither, toiling and straining.
What shall I give thee that thou mayest return to thy land?
I will disclose, O Gilgamesh, a hidden thing,
And [*a secret of the gods* I will] tell thee:
This plant, like the buckthorn is [its . . .].
Its thorns will pr[ick thy hands] just as does the *rose*.
If thy hands obtain the plant, [thou wilt find new life]."
No sooner had Gilgamesh heard this,
     Than he opened the *wa*[*ter-pipe*],[11]
He tied heavy stones [to his feet],
They pulled him down into the deep [and he saw the plant].
He took the plant, though it pr[icked his hands].
He cut the heavy stones [from his feet].
The [s]ea cast him up upon its shore.

Gilgamesh says to him, to Urshanabi, the boatman:
"Urshanabi, this plant is a plant *apart*,
Whereby a man may regain his *life's breath*.
I will take it to ramparted Uruk,
     Will cause [. . .] to eat the plant . . . !
Its name shall be 'Man Becomes Young in Old Age.'
I myself shall eat (it)
     And thus return to the state of my youth."
After twenty leagues they broke off a morsel,
After thirty (further) leagues they prepared for the night.
Gilgamesh saw a well whose water was cool.

11. **water-pipe:** meaning unclear because of the incomplete state of the original text. The pipe is in some way related to Gilgamesh's dive.

[65]

Chapter 3

Polytheism and

Monotheism in

the Fertile

Crescent, ca

3000–500 B.C.E.

He went down into it to bathe in the water.
A serpent snuffed the fragrance of the plant;
It came up [from the water] and carried off the plant.
Going back it shed [its] slough.[12]

Thereupon Gilgamesh sits down and weeps,
His tears running down over his face.
[He took the hand] of Urshanabi, the boatman:
"[For] whom, Urshanabi, have my hands toiled?
For whom is being spent the blood of my heart?
I have not obtained a boon for myself.
For the earth-lion[13] have I effected a boon!
And now the tide will bear (it) twenty leagues away!
When I opened the *water-pipe* and [. . .] the gear,
I found that which has been placed as a sign for me:
    I shall withdraw,
And leave the boat on the shore!"
    After twenty leagues they broke off a morsel,
After thirty (further) leagues they prepared for the night.
    When they arrived in ramparted Uruk,
Gilgamesh says to him, to Urshanabi, the boatman:
"Go up. Urshanabi, walk on the ramparts of Uruk . . ."

Source 6 from James B. Pritchard, ed., Ancient Near Eastern Texts Relating to the Old Testament, *3rd ed. with supplement (Princeton: Princeton University Press, 1969), pp. 164–167, 169, 170, 172, 175, 178. This text in Pritchard translated by Theophile J. Meek. Copyright © 1969 by Princeton University Press. Reprinted by permission of Princeton University Press.*

6. The Code of Hammurabi

The Prologue

When lofty Anum, king of the Anunnaki,[14]
(and) Enlil, lord of heaven and earth,
the determiner of the destinies of the land,
determined for Marduk, the first-born of Enki,
the Enlil functions over all mankind,
made him great among the Igigi,[15]
called Babylon by its exalted name,

12. **slough:** the outer skin that a snake periodically sheds.
13. **earth-lion:** the serpent.
14. **Annunaki:** the lesser gods attending Annum.
15. **Igigi:** the lesser gods attending Enlil.

[66]

made it supreme in the world,
established for him in its midst an enduring kingship,
whose foundations are as firm as heaven and earth—
at that time Anum and Enlil named me
to promote the welfare of the people,
me, Hammurabi, the devout, god-fearing prince,
to cause justice to prevail in the land,
to destroy the wicked and the evil,
that the strong might not oppress the weak,
to rise like the sun over the black-headed (people),[16]
and to light up the land. . .

When Marduk commissioned me to guide the people aright,
to direct the land,
I established law and justice in the language of the land,
thereby promoting the welfare of the people.
At that time I decreed):

THE LAWS

1: If a seignior[17] accused a(nother) seignior and brought a charge of murder against him, but has not proved it, his accuser shall be put to death. . . .

3: If a seignior came forward with false testimony in a case, and has not proved the word which he spoke, if that case was a case involving life, that seignior shall be put to death.

4: If he came forward with (false) testimony concerning grain or money, he shall bear the penalty of that case.

5: If a judge gave a judgment, rendered a decision, deposited a sealed document, but later has altered his judgment, they shall prove that that judge altered the judgment which he gave and he shall pay twelvefold the claim which holds in that case; furthermore, they shall expel him in the assembly from his seat of judgment and he shall never again sit with the judges in a case.

6: If a seignior stole the property of church or state, that seignior shall be put to death; also the one who received the stolen goods from his hand shall be put to death.

7: If a seignior has purchased or he received for safekeeping either silver or gold or a male slave or a female slave or an ox or a sheep or an ass or any sort of thing from the hand of a seignior's son or a seignior's slave without witnesses and contracts, since that seignior is a thief, he shall be put to death.

---

16. **black-headed people:** a late Sumerian expression for mankind in general.
17. **seignior:** a free man of some standing in the community.

Chapter 3

Polytheism and

Monotheism in

the Fertile

Crescent, ca

3000–500 B.C.E.

8: If a seignior stole either an ox or a sheep or an ass or a pig or a boat, if it belonged to the church (or) if it belonged to the state, he shall make thirtyfold restitution; if it belonged to a private citizen, he shall make good tenfold. If the thief does not have sufficient to make restitution, he shall be put to death.

9: When a seignior, (some of) whose property was lost, has found his lost property in the possession of a(nother) seignior, if the seignior in whose possession the lost (property) was found has declared, "A seller sold (it) to me; I made the purchase in the presence of witnesses," and the owner of the lost (property) in turn has declared, "I will produce witnesses attesting to my lost (property)"; the purchaser having then produced the seller who made the sale to him and the witnesses in whose presence he made the purchase, and the owner of the lost (property) having also produced the witnesses attesting to his lost (property), the judges shall consider their evidence, and the witnesses in whose presence the purchase was made, along with the witnesses attesting to the lost (property), shall declare what they know in the presence of god, and since the seller was the thief, he shall be put to death, while the owner of the lost (property) shall take his lost (property), with the purchaser obtaining from the estate of the seller the money that he paid out.

10: If the (professed) purchaser has not produced the seller who made the sale to him and the witnesses in whose presence he made the purchase, but the owner of the lost property has produced witnesses attesting to his lost property, since the (professed) purchaser was the thief, he shall be put to death, while the owner of the lost property shall take his lost property.

11: If the (professed) owner of the lost property has not produced witnesses attesting to his lost property, since he was a cheat and started a false report, he shall be put to death. . . .

22: If a seignior committed robbery and has been caught, that seignior shall be put to death.

23: If the robber has not been caught, the robbed seignior shall set forth the particulars regarding his lost property in the presence of god, and the city and governor, in whose territory and district the robbery was committed, shall make good to him his lost property.

24: If it was a life (that was lost), the city and governor shall pay one mina[18] of silver to his people.

25: If fire broke out in a seignior's house and a seignior, who went to extinguish (it), cast his eye on the goods of the owner of the house and has appropriated the goods of the owner of the house, that seignior shall be thrown into that fire. . . .

18. **mina:** a weight of 500 grams.

88: If a merchant [lent] grain at interest, he shall receive sixty *qu* of grain per *kur* as interest.[19] If he lent money at interest, he shall receive one-sixth (shekel) six še (i.e. one-fifth shekel) per shekel of silver as interest.[20]

89: If a seignior, who [incurred] a debt, does not have the money to pay (it) back, but has the grain, [the merchant] shall take grain for his money [with its interest] in accordance with the ratio fixed by the king.

90: If the merchant increased the interest beyond [sixty *qu*] per *kur* [of grain] (or) one-sixth (shekel) six še [per shekel of money] and has collected (it), he shall forfeit whatever he lent. . . .

104: If a merchant lent grain, wool, oil, or any goods at all to a trader to retail, the trader shall write down the value and pay (it) back to the merchant, with the trader obtaining a sealed receipt for the money which he pays to the merchant.

105: If the trader has been careless and so has not obtained a sealed receipt for the money which he paid to the merchant, the money with no sealed receipt may not be credited to the account. . . .

195: If a son has struck his father, they shall cut off his hand.

196: If a seignior has destroyed the eye of a member of the aristocracy, they shall destroy his eye.

197: If he has broken a(nother) seignior's bone, they shall break his bone.

198: If he has destroyed the eye of a commoner or broken the bone of a commoner, he shall pay one mina of silver.

199: If he has destroyed the eye of a seignior's slave or broken the bone of a seignior's slave, he shall pay one-half his value.

200: If a seignior has knocked out a tooth of a seignior of his own rank, they shall knock out his tooth.

201: If he has knocked out a commoner's tooth, he shall pay one-third mina of silver.

202: If a seignior has struck the cheek of a seignior who is superior to him, he shall be beaten sixty (times) with an oxtail whip in the assembly.

203: If a member of the aristocracy has struck the cheek of a(nother) member of the aristocracy who is of the same rank as himself, he shall pay one mina of silver.

---

19. *qu, kur:* There were 300 *qu* in a *kur*. Thus, the interest rate was 20 percent.
20. *še:* There were 180 *še* in a shekel. Thus, the interest rate, again, was 20 percent.

Chapter 3
Polytheism and
Monotheism in
the Fertile
Crescent, ca
3000–500 B.C.E.

204: If a commoner has struck the cheek of a(nother) commoner, he shall pay ten shekels of silver.

205: If a seignior's slave has struck the cheek of a member of the aristocracy, they shall cut off his ear.

206: If a seignior has struck a(nother) seignior in a brawl and has inflicted an injury on him, that seignior shall swear, "I did not strike him deliberately"; and he shall also pay for the physician.

207: If he has died because of his blow, he shall swear (as before), and if it was a member of the aristocracy, he shall pay one-half mina of silver. . . .

Sources 7 through 11 from The Revised Standard Version of the Bible, *copyright © 1946, 1952, and 1971 by the Division of Christian Education of the National Council of the Churches of Christ in the USA. Used by permission. All rights reserved.*

7. The Creation, from Genesis 2:1–24

2 Thus the heavens and the earth were finished, and all their multitude, ²And on the seventh day God finished the work that he had done, and he rested on the seventh day from all the work that he had done. ³So God blessed the seventh day and hallowed it, because on it God rested from all the work that he had done in creation.

⁴These are the generations of the heavens and the earth when they were created.

In the day that the Lord God made the earth and the heavens, ⁵when no plant of the field was yet in the earth and no herb of the field had yet sprung up—for the Lord God had not caused it to rain upon the earth, and there was no one to till the ground; ⁶but a stream would rise from the earth, and water the whole face of the ground—⁷then the Lord God formed man from the dust of the ground, and breathed into his nostrils the breath of life; and the man became a living being. ⁸And the Lord God planted a garden in Eden, in the east; and there he put the man whom he had formed. ⁹Out of the ground the Lord God made to grow every tree that is pleasant to the sight and good for food, the tree of life also in the midst of the garden, and the tree of the knowledge of good and evil.

¹⁰A river flows out of Eden to water the garden, and from there it divides and becomes four branches. ¹¹The name of the first is Pishon;²¹ it is the one

21. **Pishon:** Biblical scholars have been unable to locate this river.

that flows around the whole land of Havilah,²² where there is gold; ¹²and the gold of that land is good; bdellium²³ and onyx stone are there. ¹³The name of the second river is Gihon;²⁴ it is the one that flows around the whole land of Cush.²⁵ ¹⁴The name of the third river is Tigris, which flows east of Assyria. And the fourth river is the Euphrates.

¹⁵The Lord God took the man and put him in the garden of Eden to till it and keep it. ¹⁶And the Lord God commanded the man, "You may freely eat of every tree of the garden; ¹⁷but of the tree of the knowledge of good and evil you shall not eat, for in the day that you eat of it you shall die."

¹⁸Then the Lord God said, "It is not good that the man should be alone; I will make him a helper as his partner." ¹⁹So out of the ground the Lord God formed every animal of the field and every bird of the air, and brought them to the man to see what he would call them; and whatever the man called every living creature, that was its name. ²⁰The man gave names to all cattle, and to the birds of the air, and to every animal of the field; but for the man there was not found a helper as his partner. ²¹So the Lord God caused a deep sleep to fall upon the man, and he slept; then he took one of his ribs and closed up its place with flesh. ²²And the rib that the Lord God had taken from the man he made into a woman and brought her to the man. ²³Then the man said,

"This at last is bone of my bones and flesh of my flesh; this one shall be called Woman, for out of Man this one was taken."

²⁴ Therefore a man leaves his father and his mother and clings to his wife, and they become one flesh.

8. The Ten Commandments

A. Exodus 20:1–17

2O Then God spoke all these words: ²I am the Lord your God, who brought you out of the land of Egypt, out of the house of slavery; ³you shall have no other gods before me.

⁴You shall not make for yourself an idol, whether in the form of anything that is in heaven above, or that is on the earth beneath, or that is in the water under the earth. ⁵You shall not bow down to them or worship them; for I the Lord your God am a jealous God, punishing children for the iniquity of

22. **Havilah:** a region of northern Arabia.

23. **bdellium:** an aromatic gum from trees of the incense tree family found in northeastern Africa. It was used for perfumes and medicines.

24. **Gihon:** a stream that flows from a spring on Mount Zion in Jerusalem.

25. **Cush:** a name that appears in ancient sources to identify two different states, one in eastern Mesopotamia, the other in northeast Africa in the region of the modern nation of Sudan.

Chapter 3

Polytheism and

Monotheism in

the Fertile

Crescent, ca

3000–500 B.C.E.

parents, to the third and the fourth generation of those who reject me, ⁶but showing steadfast love to the thousandth generation of those who love me and keep my commandments.

⁷You shall not make wrongful use of the name of the Lord your God, for the Lord will not acquit anyone who misuses his name.

⁸Remember the sabbath day, and keep it holy. ⁹Six days you shall labor and do all your work. ¹⁰But the seventh day is a sabbath to the Lord your God; you shall not do any work—you, your son or your daughter, your male or female slave, your livestock, or the alien resident in your towns. ¹¹For in six days the Lord made heaven and earth, the sea, and all that is in them, but rested the seventh day; therefore the Lord blessed the sabbath day and consecrated it.

¹²Honor your father and your mother, so that your days may be long in the land that the Lord your God is giving you.

¹³You shall not murder.

¹⁴You shall not commit adultery.

¹⁵You shall not steal.

¹⁶You shall not bear false witness against your neighbor.

¹⁷You shall not covet your neighbor's house; you shall not covet your neighbor's wife, or male or female slave, or ox, or donkey, or anything that belongs to your neighbor.

B. Exodus 24:3

³Moses came and told the people all the words of the Lord and all the ordinances; and all the people answered with one voice, and said, "All the words that the Lord has spoken we will do."

9. Selections from the Torah

A. Exodus 21:12–18, 26–34

¹²Whoever strikes a person mortally shall be put to death. ¹³If it was not premeditated, but came about by an act of God, then I will appoint for you a place to which the killer may flee. ¹⁴But if someone willfully attacks and kills another by treachery, you shall take the killer from my altar for execution.

¹⁵Whoever strikes father or mother shall be put to death.

¹⁶Whoever kidnaps a person, whether that person has been sold or is still held in possession, shall be put to death.

¹⁷Whoever curses father or mother shall be put to death.

¹⁸When individuals quarrel and one strikes the other with a stone or fist so that the injured party, though not dead, is confined to bed, ¹⁹but recovers and walks around outside with the help of a staff, then the assailant shall be free of liability, except to pay for the loss of time, and to arrange for full recovery. . . .

²⁶When a slaveowner strikes the eye of a male or female slave, destroying it, the owner shall let the slave go, a free person, to compensate for the eye. ²⁷If the owner knocks out a tooth of a male or female slave, the slave shall be let go, a free person, to compensate for the tooth.

²⁸When an ox gores a man or a woman to death, the ox shall be stoned, and its flesh shall not be eaten; but the owner of the ox shall not be liable. ²⁹If the ox has been accustomed to gore in the past, and its owner has been warned but has not restrained it, and it kills a man or a woman, the ox shall be stoned, and its owner also shall be put to death. ³⁰If a ransom is imposed on the owner, then the owner shall pay whatever is imposed for the redemption of the victim's life. ³¹If it gores a boy or a girl, the owner shall be dealt with according to this same rule. ³²If the ox gores a male or female slave, the owner shall pay to the slaveowner thirty shekels of silver, and the ox shall be stoned.

³³If someone leaves a pit open, or digs a pit and does not cover it, and an ox or a donkey falls into it, ³⁴the owner of the pit shall make restitution, giving money to its owner, but keeping the dead animal.

B. Exodus 22:1–7, 21–25

22 When someone steals an ox or a sheep, and slaughters it or sells it, the thief shall pay five oxen for an ox, and four sheep for a sheep. The thief shall make restitution, but if unable to do so, shall be sold for the theft. ⁴When the animal, whether ox or donkey or sheep, is found alive in the thief's possession, the thief shall pay double.

²If a thief is found breaking in, and is beaten to death, no bloodguilt is incurred; ³but if it happens after sunrise, bloodguilt is incurred.

⁵When someone causes a field or vineyard to be grazed over, or lets livestock loose to graze in someone else's field, restitution shall be made from the best in the owner's field or vineyard.

⁶When fire breaks out and catches in thorns so that the stacked grain or the standing grain or the field is consumed, the one who started the fire shall make full restitution.

⁷When someone delivers to a neighbor money or goods for safekeeping, and they are stolen from the neighbor's house, then the thief, if caught, shall pay double. ⁸If the thief is not caught, the owner of the house shall be brought before God, to determine whether or not the owner had laid hands on the neighbor's goods. . . .

²¹You shall not wrong or oppress a resident alien, for you were aliens in the land of Egypt. ²²You shall not abuse any widow or orphan. ²³If you do abuse them, when they cry out to me, I will surely heed their cry; ²⁴my wrath will burn, and I will kill you with the sword, and your wives shall become widows and your children orphans.

²⁵If you lend money to my people, to the poor among you, you shall not deal with them as a creditor; you shall not exact interest from them.

Chapter 3
Polytheism and
Monotheism in
the Fertile
Crescent, ca
3000–500 B.C.E.

C. Leviticus 19:9–17

⁹When you reap the harvest of your land, you shall not reap to the very edges of your field, or gather the gleanings of your harvest. ¹⁰You shall not strip your vineyard bare, or gather the fallen grapes of your vineyard; you shall leave them for the poor and the alien: I am the Lord your God.

¹¹You shall not steal; you shall not deal falsely; and you shall not lie to one another. ¹²And you shall not swear falsely by my name, profaning the name of your God: I am the Lord.

¹³You shall not defraud your neighbor; you shall not steal; and you shall not keep for yourself the wages of a laborer until morning. ¹⁴You shall not revile the deaf or put a stumbling block before the blind; you shall fear your God: I am the Lord.

¹⁵You shall not render an unjust judgment; you shall not be partial to the poor or defer to the great: with justice you shall judge your neighbor. ¹⁶You shall not go around as a slanderer among your people, and you shall not profit by the blood of your neighbor: I am the Lord.

¹⁷You shall not hate in your heart anyone of your kin; you shall reprove your neighbor, or you will incur guilt yourself. . . .

10. Selections from the Prophets

A. Isaiah 66:1–2

66Thus says the Lord: Heaven is my throne and the earth is my footstool; what is the house that you would build for me, and what is my resting place?

²All these things my hand has made, and so all these things are mine, says the Lord. But this is the one to whom I will look, to the humble and contrite in spirit, who trembles at my word.

B. Hosea 11:1–4, 8–9; 14:4

11When Israel was a child, I loved him, and out of Egypt I called my son. ²The more I called them, the more they went from me; they kept sacrificing to the Baals²⁶ and offering incense to idols.

³Yet it was I who taught Ephraim²⁷ to walk, I took them up in my arms; but they did not know that I healed them.

⁴I led them with cords of human kindness, with bands of love. I was to them like those who lift infants to their cheeks. I bent down to them and fed them. . . .

26. **Baals:** The chief deity in the Canaanite pantheon was called Baal.
27. **Ephraim:** one of the twelve tribes of the Hebrews.

[8]How can I give you up, Ephraim? How can I hand you over, O Israel? How can I make you like Admah? How can I treat you like Zeboiim?[28] My heart recoils within me; my compassion grows warm and tender.

[9]I will not execute my fierce anger; I will not again destroy Ephraim; for I am God and no mortal, the Holy One in your midst, and I will not come in wrath. . . .

14 [4]I will heal their disloyalty; I will love them freely, for my anger has turned from them.

11. The Book of Job

Job 1–3:3

1 There was once a man in the land of Uz[29] whose name was Job. That man was blameless and upright, one who feared God and turned away from evil. [2]There were born to him seven sons and three daughters. [3]He had seven thousand sheep, three thousand camels, five hundred yoke of oxen, five hundred donkeys, and very many servants; so that this man was the greatest of all the people of the east. [4]His sons used to go and hold feasts in one another's houses in turn; and they would send and invite their three sisters to eat and drink with them. [5]And when the feast days had run their course, Job would send and sanctify them, and he would rise early in the morning and offer burnt offerings according to the number of them all; for Job said, "It may be that my children have sinned, and cursed God in their hearts." This is what Job always did.

[6]One day the heavenly beings came to present themselves before the Lord, and Satan[30] also came among them. [7]The Lord said to Satan, "Where have you come from?" Satan answered the Lord, "From going to and fro on the earth, and, from walking up and down on it." [8]The Lord said to Satan, "Have you considered my servant Job? There is no one like him on the earth, a blameless and upright man who fears God and turns away from evil." [9]Then Satan answered the Lord, "Does Job fear God for nothing? [10]Have you not put a fence around him and his house and all that he has, on every side? You have blessed the work of his hands, and his possessions have increased in the land. [11]But stretch out your hand now, and touch all that he has, and he will curse you to your face." [12]The Lord said to Satan, "Very well, all that he has is in

---

28. **Admah, Zeboiim:** cities destroyed by Yahweh because of their wickedness along with Sodom and Gomorrah.

29. **Uz:** a region that modern scholars believe to have been in northern Arabia.

30. **Satan:** The name used in the original Hebrew text for this figure means "accuser." It does not refer to the devil figure that appeared later in both Jewish and Christian thought. Rather, the figure called "Satan" apparently was an angel charged with investigating conditions on earth.

Chapter 3

Polytheism and

Monotheism in

the Fertile

Crescent, ca

3000–500 B.C.E.

your power; only do not stretch out your hand against him!" So Satan went out from the presence of the Lord.

¹³One day when his sons and daughters were eating and drinking wine in the eldest brother's house, ¹⁴a messenger came to Job and said, "The oxen were plowing and the donkeys were feeding beside them, ¹⁵and the Sabeans[31] fell on them and carried them off, and killed the servants with the edge of the sword; I alone have escaped to tell you." ¹⁶While he was still speaking, another came and said, "The fire of God fell from heaven and burned up the sheep and the servants, and consumed them; I alone have escaped to tell you." ¹⁷While he was still speaking, another came and said, "The Chaldeans[32] formed three columns, made a raid on the camels and carried them off, and killed the servants with the edge of the sword; I alone have escaped to tell you."

¹⁸While he was still speaking, another came and said, "Your sons and daughters were eating and drinking wine in their eldest brother's house, ¹⁹and suddenly a great wind came across the desert, struck the four corners of the house, and it fell on the young people, and they are dead; I alone have escaped to tell you."

²⁰Then Job arose, tore his robe, shaved his head, and fell on the ground and worshiped. ²¹He said, "Naked I came from my mother's womb, and naked shall I return there; the Lord gave, and the Lord has taken away; blessed be the name of the Lord."

²²In all this Job did not sin or charge God with wrongdoing.

2 One day the heavenly beings came to present themselves before the Lord, and Satan also came among them to present himself before the Lord. ²The Lord said to Satan, "Where have you come from?" Satan answered the Lord, "From going to and fro on the earth, and from walking up and down on it." ³The Lord said to Satan, "Have you considered my servant Job? There is no one like him on the earth, a blameless and upright man who fears God and turns away from evil. He still persists in his integrity, although you incited me against him, to destroy him for no reason." ⁴Then Satan answered the Lord, "Skin for skin! All that people have they will give to save their lives. ⁵But stretch out your hand now and touch his bone and his flesh, and he will curse you to your face." ⁶The Lord said to Satan, "Very well, he is in your power; only spare his life."

⁷So Satan went out from the presence of the Lord, and inflicted loathsome sores on Job from the sole of his foot to the crown of his head. ⁸Job took a potsherd with which to scrape himself, and sat among the ashes.

⁹Then his wife said to him, "Do you still persist in your integrity? Curse God, and die." ¹⁰But he said to her, "You speak as any foolish woman would

31. **Sabeans:** a nomadic people of Arabia.

32. **Chaldeans:** a people of southern Mesopotamia in the region of Babylon.

speak. Shall we receive the good at the hand of God, and not receive the bad?" In all this Job did not sin with his lips.

¹¹Now when Job's three friends heard of all these troubles that had come upon him, each of them set out from his home—Eliphaz the Temanite, Bildad the Shuhite, and Zophar the Naamathite.³³ They met together to go and console and comfort him. ¹²When they saw him from a distance, they did not recognize him, and they raised their voices and wept aloud; they tore their robes and threw dust in the air upon their heads. ¹³They sat with him on the ground seven days and seven nights, and no one spoke a word to him, for they saw that his suffering was very great.

3 After this Job opened his mouth and cursed the day of his birth. ²Job said: ³"Let the day perish in which I was born, and the night that said, 'A man-child is conceived.' . . .

Job 9:1–4, 14–18, 22–24

9 Then Job answered: ²"Indeed I know that this is so; but how can a mortal be just before God?

³If one wished to contend with him, one could not answer him once in a thousand.

⁴He is wise in heart, and mighty in strength—who has resisted him, and succeeded? . . .

¹⁴How then can I answer him, choosing my words with him?

¹⁵Though I am innocent, I cannot answer him; I must appeal for mercy to my accuser.

¹⁶If I summoned him and he answered me, I do not believe that he would listen to my voice.

¹⁷For he crushes me with a tempest, and multiplies my wounds without cause;

¹⁸he will not let me get my breath, but fills me with bitterness . . .

²²It is all one; therefore I say, he destroys both the blameless and the wicked.

²³When disaster brings sudden death, he mocks at the calamity of the innocent.

²⁴The earth is given into the hand of the wicked; he covers the eyes of its judges—if it is not he, who then is it? . . .

Job 38:1–7

38 Then the Lord answered Job out of the whirlwind: ²"Who is this that darkens counsel by words without knowledge?

³Gird up your loins like a man, I will question you, and you shall declare to me.

---

33. **Temanite, Shuhite, Naamathite:** ethnic labels that identify Job's friends as residents of Arabia.

Chapter 3
Polytheism and
Monotheism in
the Fertile
Crescent, ca
3000–500 B.C.E.

[4]Where were you when I laid the foundation of the earth? Tell me, if you have understanding.
[5]Who determined its measurements—surely you know! Or who stretched the line upon it?
[6]On what were its bases sunk, or who laid its cornerstone
[7]when the morning stars sang together and all the heavenly beings shouted for joy? . . .

Job 42:1–2,10–17

42 Then Job answered the Lord: [2]"I know that you can do all things, and that no purpose of yours can be thwarted." . . .

[10]And the Lord restored the fortunes of Joband the Lord gave Job twice as much as he had before. [11]Then there came to him all his brothers and sisters and all who had known him before, and they ate bread with him in his house; they showed him sympathy and comforted him for all the evil that the Lord had brought upon him; and each of them gave him a piece of money and a gold ring. [12]The Lord blessed the latter days of Job more than his beginning; and he had fourteen thousand sheep, six thousand camels, a thousand yoke of oxen, and a thousand donkeys. [13]He also had seven sons and three daughters. [14]He named the first Jemimah, the second Keziah, and the third Keren-happuch. [15]In all the land there were no women so beautiful as Job's daughters; and their father gave them an inheritance along with their brothers. [16]After this Job lived one hundred and forty years, and saw his children, and his children's children, four generations. [17]And Job died, old and full of days.

QUESTIONS TO CONSIDER

One of the most important skills of the historian is the ability to think comparatively. Only by constantly comparing his or her data with those amassed by other students of historic societies can the historian fully understand the significance of his or her findings. Our sources on the religious history of the ancient Fertile Crescent offer us an opportunity for such comparative thought because, as we suggested at the outset of this chapter, both Mesopotamian polytheism and Hebrew monotheism were concerned with answering the same questions.

The first of those question involved human origins. Consider again the Creation accounts that you have read in both Mesopotamian and Hebrew texts. In what ways are the accounts similar? Why do you suspect that the accounts shared similar roots? How do they differ as to the purpose of human existence? How would you explain that difference in terms of the religious vision of the ancient Hebrews?

Both ancient peoples believed that divine action shaped their lives. Did the Mesopotamians and the Hebrews believe that they could understand fully why their respective deities behaved the way they did in shaping the lives of mortals? Why do the Mesopotamian gods and goddesses emerge from our sources as capricious and rather uncaring entities? How did the Hebrews envision Yahweh? If not always predictable, why did they find him just and merciful?

Religious thought played a key role, both in Mesopotamia and among the Hebrews, in ancients' efforts to give order to their societies by controlling human behavior. Did ancient Mesopotamian polytheism include anything resembling a code of personal behavior in its religious practices and teachings? Why, then, was the gods' delegation of the "Enlil functions" to kings so important in giving order to their society? How was the religious thought of the Hebrews grounded in a code of behavior right from the first? How did this allow them to order their society? Most scholars of world religions identify Hebrew monotheism as the first personal religion. Why do you find that the Hebrews' covenant with Yahweh had profound implications for the individual believer?

Finally, if we consider Mesopotamian polytheism as generally characteristic of the ancient religions of the West, what strikes you as unique about the religious life of the ancient Hebrews? Why might you think that the essential aspects of their belief system might attract others?

EPILOGUE

The relevance of the religious practices that we have examined in this chapter is not confined solely to the study of the ancient world. The religious ideas and rites that we have examined also have considerable relevance to the modern world in which we live.

The ancient polytheism of the Mesopotamians may not survive in the form it assumed for over two millennia in the eastern Fertile Crescent, but its salient features persist in parts of the globe today. Primitive peoples still conceive of their deities as the embodiment of great natural forces, envision them in anthropomorphic forms, and attempt to appease their capriciousness through elaborate rites.

The monotheism of the ancient Hebrews has had great long-term global influence. Indeed, the ethical monotheism that was at its core constitutes the foundation of the three great Western religions, Judaism, Christianity, and Islam, faiths that claim the spiritual allegiance of approximately four billion people worldwide, representing the majority of the human race. As their foundation, all three Western religions emphasize adherence to broad ethical principles enunciated first by the ancient Hebrews. The ancient Hebrew texts that we have examined form not only the Hebrew Bible, but

Chapter 3

Polytheism and

Monotheism in

the Fertile

Crescent, ca

3000–500 B.C.E.

also the Old Testament of the Christian Bible, and early Christian leaders from the first recognized their spiritual debt to the ancient Hebrews, even as they sought to distinguish early Christianity from Judaism. Thus, Saint Paul, the apostle to the Gentiles, lauded "the faith of our ancestor Abraham" in his first-century C.E. Letter to the Romans (Romans 4:12).

In Islam, the words of the Prophet Muhammad also acknowledge a spiritual inheritance from the ancient Hebrews. Ethical monotheism is the fundamental core of Islam, too, and we find the following words in the Qur'an, the sacred book of Islam:

Who will turn away from the creed of Abraham but one dull of soul? . . . We believe in God and what has been sent down to us, and what has been revealed to Abraham and Ishmael and Isaac and Jacob and their progeny, and that which was given to Moses and Jesus and all other prophets by the Lord. We make no distinction among them, and we submit to Him. (Qur'an, 2:130, 136)

In short, the religious ideas of the ancient world still play a great role in our modern world.

CHAPTER FOUR

REPRESENTING THE HUMAN FORM

(2600 B.C.E.–600 C.E.)

You have explored the role that writing and written texts played in shaping the world-views of several early civilizations. As important as they are, however, written texts are only one of the types of sources available for learning about early cultures. We can also use artistic and archaeological evidence, in the same way that we use such sources for information about preliterate cultures. Because so few people in early cultures were able to read, artistic evidence provides us with sources that were usually accessible to more people than written texts.

Artistic evidence has been used to answer a wide range of historical questions about early civilizations. Some of these are technical: What level of engineering skill in a culture would enable it to construct certain types of buildings? What chemical or other technological processes did a culture use in the production of writing materials, metal work, or other products? Some are economic: What proportion of a culture's wealth went into the production of what types of artistic products? Who paid for and benefited from artistic production? Some questions are aesthetic: How skillful were certain artists? How would one describe an individual artist's or a civilization's style, particularly in comparison to that of others? Some are cultural: Why were certain subjects depicted, and depicted the way they were? What did a civilization view as important enough to include in its permanent visual record?

The questions that we might term aesthetic or cultural are perhaps the trickiest for historians or art historians, particularly if they involve comparisons between civilizations. Assessing the skill of an artist requires not only appreciating the technical aspects of production, but also understanding ideas about the purpose of artistic products as well as the cultural context in which the artist worked. We may be able to say immediately that we "like" or "don't like" an artistic product, but we certainly need information on the culture in which it was created to assess its meaning and use it as historical evidence. It is often difficult to gain much understanding of a culture from a few pieces of artistic evidence, particularly when we view them, not where they were intended to be displayed, but on a gallery wall or in a museum case. Thus using artistic evidence is in some ways a circular process: We learn about a culture from the available written and artistic sources, then use that background to analyze a single piece of art, which may in turn make us change or refine our ideas about the written record or other artistic creations, and eventually may lead to new conclusions about the culture as a whole.

Though most historians and art historians regard some knowledge of a culture as important for an understanding of its artistic products, there are those who discount such a prerequisite. Some people, though usually not art historians, assert that aesthetic judgments are not culturally or historically based, but derive from universal standards, so that "good" art, or at least a masterpiece, is recognizable to all. Others contend that knowing about a culture shapes one's impressions too strongly, making it impossible to view an artistic product objectively. To them what is most important is seeing with a fresh eye, and they stress that to use visual evidence correctly, we must both sharpen our powers of

observation, and also *unlearn* previous ideas about art.

You may agree with either or both of these arguments and may wish to test them with this chapter. To do this, turn immediately to the Evidence and look carefully at each sculpture or painting. They come from three different early cultures: Egypt in the Old and New Kingdom (2600–1200 B.C.E.), Archaic and Classical Greece (600–350 B.C.E.), and Buddhist India (200 B.C.E.–600 C.E.). In all three cultures, one of the most common subjects for artistic presentation was the human form.

Record your general impressions, which will enable you to assess later how much even a slight understanding of a culture may alter your viewing. Do any of these impressions or answers come from what you already know about any one of these cultures, or do they come solely from looking at the art?

As we turn now to background information, we begin with characteristics common to all of the sources. For each of the three cultures, the sculptures and paintings are arranged roughly in chronological order, though they span different amounts of time. All the pieces served some sort of religious function and come from either tombs or religious buildings such as temples. All were created in cultures that believed in *anthropomorphic* gods; in other words, their gods were conceptualized in human form so that human form and divine power were linked. (The Egyptians had other gods that were thought of as animals or as part animal and part human.) In all three cultures, making an image of a god and honoring that image were seen as meritorious, and thus the creative process was linked to spiritual or religious values.

In ancient Egypt, art was an integral aspect of religion, with much of the art that has survived made not for human eyes but for the inside of tombs, part of the Egyptian cult of the dead. The Egyptians had an extremely strong belief in the afterlife, an afterlife that was very much like life in this world and that required both physical objects and funeral rituals to attain. In the Archaic Period and the Old Kingdom (about 3100–2200 B.C.E.), only the pharaoh was regarded as capable of achieving a full afterlife. Nobles built their tombs as close to his as possible, pledging in carved inscriptions to continue their allegiance to the pharaoh after death; if he engaged their services, they, too, might achieve eternal life. By the Middle Kingdom (ca. 2050–1800 B.C.E.), eternal life was viewed as a hope for all, as long as the body was preserved through mummification and the spirit led to Osiris, the god of the dead, through the proper mortuary ceremonies. Funerary objects and statues or paintings of the deceased all helped lead him or her to Osiris by depicting the deceased in rituals that ensured eternal life. Throughout all periods of ancient Egyptian history, the statue of a deceased person in a tomb or temple was regarded as a home for his or her *ka*, the spirit or immortal alter ego, which entered the sculpture during a funeral ritual. The *ka* within the sculpture made the deceased a participant in festivities held in the temple even after death. Though we might view this preoccupation with death and the afterlife as morbid and reflecting a rejection of life, it does not seem to have been so for the ancient Egyptians whose portraits and tomb paintings have been preserved; they enjoyed their life here on earth so much that they simply wanted to continue it after death.

Because most statues were regarded as substitutes for a particular deceased person, and paintings were to show the deceased involved in activities or rituals, it was extremely important that depictions be recognized as the correct individual. Egyptian artists achieved this objective not by individualistic portraiture of a physical likeness, but by painting or inscribing the name on the statue or painting. The portrait itself could then be used to depict stereotyped qualities: plumpness represented wealth and well-being; signs of age, maturity and wisdom; a trim build, confidence and vitality. Egyptian art also sought to link the impermanent individual clearly to the permanent office or occupation, so it was important to include unmistakable symbols of office—a scribe was always portrayed with a scroll, and the pharaoh with the crown of Upper and Lower Egypt and a crooked staff. By the Middle Kingdom there was some attempt to individualize facial features, but the bodies remained stock types and the faces continued to be idealized.

The emphasis on permanence emerges in many aspects of Egyptian art, most noticeably perhaps in the

[83]

lack of change over thousands of years in the basic style of portraying the human body. The deceased was rendered motionless, in standardized standing or sitting poses, so that there was no indication of change. Throughout Egyptian history, the pharaoh was regarded and portrayed as divine, though there were slight variations on this, with the emphasis in wall paintings sometimes on his handling of earthly problems and participation in earthly activities, and at other times on his role as executor of divine will and participation in celestial ceremonies. After every period of turbulence and violence, such as an invasion or a civil war, there was a return to the old artistic styles, a deliberate *archaism*.

Egyptian artists did not attempt to portray scenes or figures as they appeared to the eye, but as they actually were, what we might call a depiction of their essence. Thus individual figures are not foreshortened or drawn from one particular vantage point, for one's vantage point might easily change; instead they are shown in a way that presents many sides or angles at once. The most famous example of this is the Egyptian way of depicting the human body, which you can see most clearly in Sources 2 and 4. The Egyptian way of setting elements in a scene is also one that does not reproduce a visual image, but reflects the content of what is being represented. Thus, artists use what is sometimes termed an *aspective* rather than a *perspective* approach, basing the size of the figures not on their placement in the scene, but on their importance in the social hierarchy.

Many of the earliest Greek depictions of the human form were also from tombs or temples, the male *kouros* and female *kore* figures. These were not portraits or ceremonial substitutes for the deceased the way Egyptian tomb sculptures were, but were rather erected in memory of an individual or by a living person to fulfill a vow to the gods. These large stone sculptures began to be made in Greece beginning in the mid-seventh century B.C.E., and many art historians have linked them stylistically with much earlier Egyptian statuary. Unlike in Egypt, however, the portrayal of the human body in Greece changed rapidly over the next two hundred years, with sculptors basing their work more and more on actual human anatomy. This concern with the way that the body actually looked can also be observed in Greek painting. Unfortunately most large-scale Greek paintings have been lost, but Greek pottery was frequently decorated with painted figures and scenes that allow us to see human forms in a setting.

Along with the kore and kouros figures, Greek statuary from the Archaic period (ca 630–480 B.C.E.) also portrayed gods and mythological heroes who are sometimes part divine and sometimes fully human. Because the gods bore no physical sign of their divinity, it is often difficult to tell exactly who is being depicted unless the subject is accompanied by a standard symbol such as the sea god Poseidon's trident or the hero Herakles' lion skin. Gods and heroes continued to be the most common subject matter for

Greek sculpture in the Classical period (ca 480–330 B.C.E.), with actual historical events shown only rarely, though mythological events appear frequently, especially in reliefs.

Like the Egyptians, the Greeks saw their gods as having all the bodily qualities that humans did, but qualities that were perfected because they did not die and did not require food or sleep to sustain their bodies. The gods feasted, but did not need to eat; they bled when wounded, but did not die. Gods could also change their bodily shape at will, and often disguised themselves either to achieve an end or to shield the radiance of their bodies from human observers. (Humans who looked on a god directly in Greek mythology generally died.) The mythological heroes had died, but were thought to have joined the undying gods in a type of "eternity," an afterlife that consisted of eternal feasting and banqueting rather than the variety of activities characteristic of the Egyptian afterlife. Whether normal humans could aspire to such an afterlife is unclear, though at least those men who died in war were thought to have a chance. For most humans, the afterlife was a sort of shadowy existence in the underworld (Hades), neither good nor bad; correct funeral practices were important to allow one's psyche (usually translated as "soul" or "spirit") to go to Hades, but these were much less elaborate than those of the Egyptians and did not involve preservation of the body.

As mentioned above, Greek pottery often shows mythological scenes, but it also depicts everyday life—women weaving, men banqueting, people going in and out of doors. Some of its subjects are pornographic, showing men with prostitutes or gods and satyrs chasing nymphs. Because of such subject matter, pottery has traditionally been viewed as having no religious or ceremonial significance. This view has recently changed somewhat as scholars have recognized that, for example, the banqueting scenes depict not only the setting in which the pottery was actually used, but also envision a certain type of afterlife for those using it. The doors may not be simply entrances of houses, but also the gateway between this life and the next. The mythological scenes are not simply decorative, but are meant to reinforce cultural norms.

The Greek view of the human body was determined by philosophy as well as religion, particularly after the time of Plato (427–347 B.C.E.). Plato saw the human body as in some ways a microcosm of the universe (an idea that influenced Western thought until the time of the Renaissance), a universe that was itself a living creature. Both the body and the universe are material and perishable, but the soul is immortal, as is the perfect form of the universe and all that exists within it. For Plato these perfect forms, which are sometimes called "ideal types," were not simply mental constructs but had an existence somewhere and were actually more "real" than the transitory, material world around us. (The notion of ideal types, or idealism, has also been a long-lasting one in Western thought. It operates, for instance, in many people's understanding of such concepts as justice. Their concept of a just society comes not so much from observing societies that actually exist in the world as from abstract principles regarding what might be termed "ideal justice.") As a proponent of idealism, Plato scorned the attempts of the artists and sculptors who were his contemporaries to depict the human body based on visual observation. Plato thought the chief purpose of art was to represent eternal forms as understood by the soul, not to imitate fleeting external appearances. He praised Egyptian art for its elevated portrayals, and he regarded mathematical forms as the most beautiful because their beauty was absolute and not based on—or biased by—either intellectual or physical points of view.

In many ways, sculptors in India working within both Buddhist and Hindu traditions fit Plato's ideal better than did his Athenian contemporaries. Sculpture, in Indian religion and philosophy, is not to depict the physical body but to give concrete shape to an invisible spirit within the body. Indian artists sought to give visible form to the living principles within the body, conceptualized as breath (*prana*) and sap (*rasa*). *Prana* pushes against the walls of the body, making the skin appear taut and keeping the body erect, so that the muscles are less important. Indian sculpture does not aim to record the appearance or structure of the body, but instead to express the awareness of life within the body, of the breath

that sustains and moves the body. Sculptors achieve this, not by looking at other bodies as models, but by feeling the breath and pulse of life within their own bodies and by meditating or contemplating. There is a link between the body and the natural world, which also has breath and sap. When a sculpture was completed, it was consecrated by a priest, given the breath of life. Then it was placed in a position within a temple where it could be seen, worshiped, and perhaps eventually copied, for the replication of images was considered auspicious.

Buddhist teachings did not reject earlier Indian ideas about art or the body, but built on them. The religious teachings generally termed Buddhism were first taught in India by Siddhartha Gautama, a nobleman living in the sixth century B.C.E. who came to be known as the Buddha, or the Awakened One. Buddhist teachings are extremely complex, though at their heart is an emphasis on morality, meditation, and achieving wisdom. Part of the wisdom one strives to achieve is the understanding that there is nothing permanent, including the individual soul, and that the ideal state of being (*nirvana*) is a life that transcends individual desires. On achieving nirvana, an individual would become awakened to a transcendental eternal realm of being, that is, a buddha.

Over the centuries, many divisions developed within Buddhism, one of the most significant being a split beginning in the first century B.C.E. over how strictly one needed to follow the Buddhist path in order to achieve nirvana. Mahayana Buddhism taught that many people, not simply a small spiritual elite of monks, could become fully buddha, an idea that gave this branch of Buddhism a wide popular base. As it spread, Mahayana Buddhism absorbed a number of local deities, transforming them to fit with Buddhist ideas by turning them into guardians of the Buddha, or *bodhisattvas*. A bodhisattva is a being who has almost achieved nirvana but decides instead to turn away from this final, blissful, transcendental state to help others on their way to becoming buddha. Although bodhisattvas had human bodies, they were no longer subject to the physical limitations of human life and were often worshiped in their own right. Their merits could be shared by their worshipers, and their intervention, combined with devotion, could allow the worshiper to achieve nirvana. The Buddha himself had been a bodhisattva in his earlier lives, and stories of his actions and exploits during these previous lives became an important part of Buddhist literature.

Though there was no explicit prohibition against portraying the Buddha as Buddha, there are no images of him until several centuries after his death; he was symbolized by an empty throne or a hemispheric mound containing a relic, termed a *stupa*. With the spread of Mahayana Buddhism, people became more devoted to Buddha's person and not simply his teachings, so they wanted physical likenesses. Images of the Buddha showed up first on coins and temple railings and, by the first century C.E., as free-standing sculpture. Sculptors adopted existing ideas about portraying the body to the portrayal of the Buddha's body, striving to produce a sacred image that both transcended and represented perfect human beauty. The links between the body and the natural world were stressed in the shapes of the Buddha's body parts, and a system of proportions was developed based on the height of the head or the breadth of the finger. These calculations for the correct proportions of the Buddha were based not on actual human anatomy, but on the magical properties of certain numbers, and they became the standard for images of the Buddha for centuries.

Our questions for this chapter ask you to analyze individual pieces of artistic evidence and make cultural inferences based on this analysis: How do artists in these three cultures depict the human form? What do these depictions suggest about the values of these cultures?

SOURCES AND METHOD

The single most important method for using visual sources is to look at them. This may seem self-evident, and we may feel our "looking" skills are well-honed because of the visual culture of advertising and television in which we live. Too often, however, we view visual material as merely illustrations of a text (this is often

[87]

how graphics are integrated into textbooks) and don't really look at the images themselves. To answer the first question in this chapter, turn to the Evidence (which you may already have done if you decided to do the pretest suggested in the Problem section). Look carefully at Sources 1 through 4, all of which present pharaohs and queens of Egypt. What do you notice most about these figures; in other words, what details stand out? What words would you use to describe the individuals as they are portrayed? How do their expression and stance sway your description? How would you compare the portrayal of humans with that of animals—for example, the birds in Source 2? How would you compare the portrayal of Queen Nefertari in Source 4 with that of the goddess Isis in the same tomb painting? How would you compare the depiction of the pharaoh Mycerinus in Source 1 with that of the pharaoh Ramesses II in Source 3? How is clothing depicted in these examples of Egyptian art?

Now look at the artistic evidence from Greece, Sources 5 through 9. What main differences do you see in the depiction of the human form in the kore and kouros figures from the early sixth century B.C.E., Sources 5 and 6? How would you compare these to the statues of the Egyptian pharaoh? Would you make any distinction in your comparisons between the body and the head? Judging by the vase painting in Source 7 and the sculpture in Source 8, what changes do you see in the representation of the human form over the next century? What differences do you see

between the depiction of female and male forms in Source 7? Now look at Source 9, which is about one hundred years more recent than Source 8 and is one of the first depictions of the nude female form in Greek art. (Until this period, the only women depicted nude were prostitutes; even Aphrodite, the goddess of love and beauty, was shown clothed.) What words would you use to describe Aphrodite as she is shown here? Looking at Sources 8 and 9, what differences do you see in the way male and female bodies are depicted? How would you compare these depictions of the human body with those in Source 1?

Now look at the examples from India, Sources 10 through 13. What details stand out in these portrayals? How would you describe the body of the female deity (*yakshi*) in Source 10? How would you compare this with the female bodies portrayed in Egyptian and Greek art? Sources 11 and 12 show the Buddha. How does his body differ from the bodies in the other sources? How would you describe his expression and demeanor? How would you compare the treatment of clothing in these two sculptures with the treatment of clothing in Egyptian and Greek sculpture? Source 13 is a bodhisattva, usually identified as Vajrapani because he is holding a thunderbolt. (Bodhisattvas can often be identified only by items they wear or carry, for no names are inscribed on these sculptures. Both Egyptian tomb sculptures and Greek statues were mostly inscribed, but in Greece the inscriptions are often destroyed or missing, so that we identify them as well by their dress or other details.) How would you describe the bodhisattva's body? his stance? his clothing? How would you compare these with those of the Buddha? with those of a Greek male body such as the one in Source 8?

From looking at the Sources and considering questions like those suggested above, you can formulate your answer to the first question for this chapter: How do these three cultures depict the human form? The second question—what do these depictions tell us about the values of these cultures?—involves extrapolating from the sources and combining your observations with your previous knowledge of the cultures. Here you (or any historian) must be more speculative, for we generally can't know exactly how individuals living at the time a statue or painting was made looked at it, or how their view of the artist's intent differed from ours. We must also be especially careful, when using visual sources, to choose ones that are representative or typical rather than unusual. (On this issue you will have to trust our choice of evidence or do some further research in books of reproductions or museums in your area.)

These reservations apply, of course, just as much to historical arguments based on written sources as to those based on visual evidence, and in both cases the best method of historical interpretation is the same: stick as closely as possible to arguments that are based on the sources themselves. In this case, then, your exploration of the values of these cultures needs to be based primarily on the careful observations you have already made.

Think about your observations of the depiction of the body in Egypt. Whose bodies are shown? What does their stance or expression indicate were admirable qualities in such individuals? What does the similaity between the portrayals of the pharaoh over more than a thousand years indicate about Egyptian culture? What do the similarities between the depiction of Isis and Nefertari indicate about Egyptian ideas about the relationship between the human (or at least the royal) and the divine?

Next, think about the Greek art. Why might the depiction of the body become more anatomically accurate earlier than the head? Why might the Greeks have broken with the Egyptian pattern and portrayed men nude, even in scenes (such as the battle scene in Source 7) in which men were not normally naked? What might account for the differences in the portrayal of male and female nudes you noted in Sources 8 and 9? Though we generally think of nakedness as revealing, are there certain facts that nakedness obscures?

Now turn to the Indian art. What does Source 10 indicate about cultural attitudes toward the female body? How does this portrayal of a goddess differ from those of Egyptian or Greek female deities (Isis in Source 4 and Aphrodite in Source 9)? What does the Buddha's expression indicate about the qualities admired in a leader? How does this differ from the qualities suggested in the depictions of the Egyptian pharaohs and Greek heroes? What do the differences you have noted between the Buddha and the bodhisattva indicate about attitudes toward each of these revered individuals?

[89]

Source 1 from Harvard University–MFA Expedition. Courtesy, Museum of Fine Arts, Boston.

1. King Mycerinus and Queen Khamerernebti, from Funerary Temple near his Pyramid at Giza, ca 2600 B.C.E.

2. Nebamum Hunting Birds, with his Wife and Servant, from his Tomb at Thebes, ca 1400 B.C.E.

Source 3 from Hirmer Fotoarchiv.

3. Statues of King Ramesses II and his Wife, Queen Nefertari, at Luxor, ca 1250 B.C.E.

The statue of Nefertari is much smaller than that of Ramesses; her head is just below his knee.

4. Wall Painting from Nefertari's Tomb near Thebes, ca 1250 B.C.E.

The goddess Isis is holding an ankh—the symbol of life—to Nefertari's nostrils.

Source 5 from Archaeological Receipts Fund/National Archaeological Museum, Athens.

5. Anavyssos Kouros, Attica near Athens, ca 525 B.C.E.

6. Peplos Kore, Athens, ca 530 B.C.E.

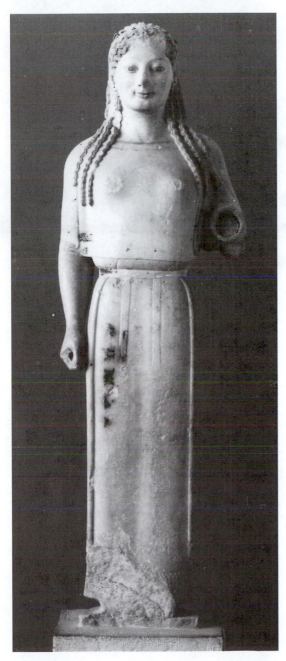

7. Theseus and the Amazons, from an Attic Red-figured Krater,[1] ca 440 B.C.E.

1. **Krater:** a wide, two-handled bowl common in ancient Greece.

8. Polykleitos, Doryphoros or "The Canon," ca 440 **B.C.E. (Roman copy)**

9. Praxiteles, Aphrodite of Knidos, ca 340 B.C.E. (Roman copy)

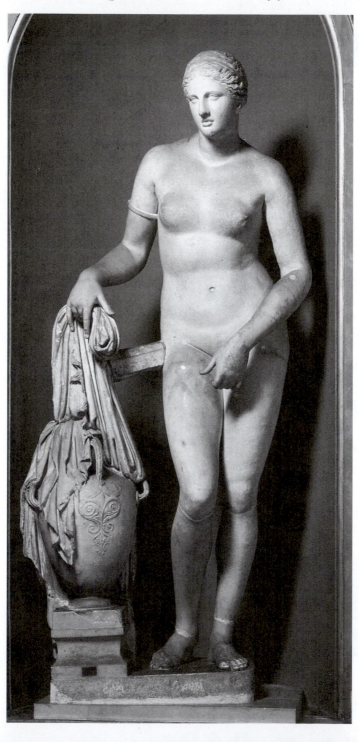

10. Yakshi, from a Pillar at the Great Stupa of Bharhut, ca 100 B.C.E.

Source 11: Courtesy of The Huntington Archive.

11. Standing Buddha, from Gandhara, ca 200 C.E.

12. Preaching Buddha, from Sarnath, ca 475 C.E.

13. Bodhisattva Vajrapani, Nepal, 6th or 7th century C.E.

QUESTIONS TO CONSIDER

As you examine the evidence for this chapter, you may be discovering that your viewing is shaped to a greater or lesser extent both by what you already know about one or more of the cultures and by your previous experience with sculpture and paintings of the human form. Some of the sources may thus seem very familiar, whereas others appear strange and exotic. This has caused some people who work with visual evidence to deny that we can ever view things with the "fresh eye" that other scholars deem indispensable. Does your experience in working with the evidence in this chapter lead you to support either side of this dispute? If you did the pretest, did your observations and impressions change after reading the Problem section?

Though all of the evidence in this chapter depicts the human form, some of the portrayed individuals were regarded as fully human, some as fully divine, and many as both human and divine or as moving between a human and divine state. Do these differences affect the way these individuals are depicted?

What does this tell you about the three cultures?

When making any sort of cultural comparison, it is often easiest to think in terms of similarities and differences. What similarities have you found in the depictions of the human body among the three cultures? Are there any words that you could use to describe the bodies in all or most of the sources accurately? Do any of these words suggest cultural values that may be similar? Do any two of the cultures handle representations of the human body in a similar fashion? What might this tell you about other ways in which these two cultures are similar? What do you see as the most important differences among the sculpture and painting from the three cultures? Are any of these the result of technological differences (such as differences in the material out of which the sculpture is made), or do they indicate cultural differences?

You are now ready to answer the central questions for this chapter: How do these three cultures depict the human form? What do these depictions tell us about the values of these cultures?

EPILOGUE

In all three of the cultures we have investigated here, a certain way of depicting the human form came to be accepted as the norm and was then copied extensively. Over many cen-

turies after this norm developed, variations occurred from time to time, but these digressions were always followed by returns to the original standards (or what were perceived as the original standards).

In Egypt, this copying was largely internal, as the form developed in the

Old Kingdom (Source 1) was repeated for thousands of years. There were occasional deviations from this, such as that under the pharaoh Akhenaton (ruled ca 1372–1354 B.C.E.), who abandoned traditional Egyptian religion in favor of the worship of one god, the sun god Aton. Akhenaton supported an artistic style that was much more naturalistic, and paintings of him show him with narrow shoulders and a potbelly. As soon as he died, however, his new religious system was abandoned, and both art and religion returned to its traditional form. This artistic form was even adopted centuries after the fall of pharaonic Egypt by the Macedonian dynasty of the Ptolemies, who were established as rulers through the conquests of Alexander the Great. The most famous of the Ptolemies, Cleopatra (69–30 B.C.E.), the sister and wife to Ptolemy XII, had herself portrayed looking very similar to Nefertari in Source 4, using this archaic form to stress her link with the ancient pharaohs.

The way in which the human body was portrayed in fourth-century B.C.E. Greece (Sources 8 and 9) was even more influential than that of Egypt. These depictions came to be regarded by later Greeks and Romans as the ultimate standard of perfection, and these pieces were copied and recopied hundreds of times. (This is very fortunate, for the Greek originals have in many cases been lost, and what remains are Roman copies; Sources 8 and 9 are actually Roman copies of the originals.) The Roman historian Pliny[2] (ca 23–79 C.E.), in fact, noted that Polykleitos' sculpture of the athlete (Source 8) was "called the Canon by artists, who drew from it the rudiments of art as from a code," and judged Praxiteles' Aphrodite (Source 9) the finest statue "not only by Praxiteles but in the whole world." When Romans took or copied Greek images, they generally took them out of their religious setting as temple statuary and placed them in gardens, homes, or public squares. The statues thus lost their religious functions as objects of veneration and became secular objects prized primarily for their aesthetic appeal.

Greek style from this period, which has come to be called classical in the West, has been consciously emulated during many periods since, including the Italian Renaissance, the French Revolution, and the early decades of the United States. You need only to visit your state capitol or other local government buildings to assess the ways in which classical Greek standards still influence our portrayal of heroes and leaders.

Like Greek art, Buddhist art in India is generally regarded as having gone through a formative period and then achieved a level of perfection regarded as classical. Source 11 comes from the formative period, from an area of western India called Gandhara (now a part of Afghanistan) in which artists may have been influenced by Greek statues or sculptors. Sources 12 and 13 come from

2. Pliny, *Historia naturalis*, xxxiv, 55, and xxxvi, 20. Quoted in Gisela M. A. Richter, *A Handbook of Greek Art* (New York: Da Capo Press, 1987), pp. 120, 141.

northern India or Nepal in the Gupta period (ca 300–600 C.E.), a time during which the Gandharan merged with styles from other parts of India. The Gupta period was one of Indian cultural expansion into central and southeastern Asia, and Gupta styles were copied over a very broad area. Just as in Egypt, there were periods of deviation followed by a return to the classical style for the Buddha and bodhisattvas. In areas of southeast Asia, such as Cambodia, where the ruler was viewed as a god-king, the statues often looked slightly like the ruling king, though they still were not portraits in the modern sense. Unlike Greek statuary, Buddhist images did not lose their religious function, for they were copied because of their sanctity, not solely their artistic merit. Images modeled on those of Gupta India are still produced today for use in worship, particularly in areas where Buddhism is strong, such as Sri Lanka and parts of southeast Asia.

CHAPTER FIVE

THE IDEAL AND THE REALITY

OF CLASSICAL ATHENS

Athens during the fifth century B.C.E. is often identified as one of the main sources of Western values and standards. Later Europeans and Americans regarded the Athenians as the originators of democracy, drama, representational or realistic art, history, philosophy, and science. At different times over the past 2,500 years they have attempted to imitate this "Golden Age" of classical Athens in everything from buildings to literature. Many U.S. state capitols and government buildings are modeled on the Parthenon or other temples, complete with statuary of former governers in the manner of Greek gods. We still divide drama into tragedies and comedies in the same way the Athenians did, though now we sometimes use a prerecorded laugh track instead of grinning masks to indicate that a given work is a comedy. During some historical periods, such as the Renaissance, thinkers and writers made conscious attempts to return to classical ideals in all areas of life, combing the works of Athenian authors for previously overlooked material in their quest to draw guidance and learn everything possible from this unique flowering of culture.

Even more than as a model for literature and art, classical Athens has continued to serve as a relevant source for answers to basic questions about human existence. Though all cultures have sought to identify the ultimate aim and meaning of human life, the ancient Greeks, especially the Athenians, were the first in the West to provide answers that were not expressed in religious or mythological terms. Their thoughts on these matters grew out of speculations on the nature of the universe made by earlier Greeks, particularly Thales and his followers Anaximander and Heraclitus. These thinkers, living in the seventh and sixth centuries B.C.E., theorized about how the universe had been formed and what it was made of by means of rational explanations drawn from observation rather than from myth or religious tradition. Because they believed the natural universe could be explained in other than supernatural terms, they are often termed the first true scientists or first philosophers.

During the fifth century B.C.E., several Athenian thinkers turned their attention from the world around them to the human beings living in that world. They used this new method of philosophical inquiry to question the workings of the human mind and the societies humans create. They asked such questions as, How do we learn things? What should we try to learn? How do we know what is right or wrong, good or bad? If we can know what is good, how can we create things that are good? What kind of government is best? This type of questioning is perhaps most often associated with Socrates (469–399 B.C.E.) and his pupil Plato (427?–347 B.C.E.), who are generally called the founders of Western philosophy. Thales and his followers are thus known as the pre-Socratics; and a twentieth-century philosopher, Alfred North Whitehead, noted—only half jokingly—that "the European philosophical tradition . . . consists of a series of footnotes to Plato."

Both Socrates and Plato believed that goodness is related to knowledge and that excellence could be learned. For Plato especially, true knowledge was gained not by observation of the world but by contemplation of what an ideal world would be like. In their view, to understand goodness, justice, or beauty, it is necessary to think about what pure and ultimate good-

ness, justice, or beauty means. Plato thus introduced into Western thought a strong strain of idealism and was the first to write works on what an ideal society or set of laws would look like. He also described the education required to train citizens for governing this ideal state and the social and economic structure necessary to keep them at their posts. Though he probably recognized that these standards could never be achieved, he believed that the creation of ideals was an important component of the discipline of philosophy, a sentiment shared by many Western thinkers after him.

Plato's most brilliant pupil, Aristotle (384–322 B.C.E.), originally agreed with his teacher but then began to depart somewhat from idealism. Like the pre-Socratics, Aristotle was fascinated by the world around him, and many of his writings on scientific subjects reveal keen powers of observation. Even his treatises on standards of human behavior, such as those concerning ethics and politics, are based on close observation of Athenian society and not simply on speculation. Aristotle further intended that these works should not only describe ideal human behavior or political systems, but also provide suggestions about how to alter current practice to conform more closely to the ideal. Thus, although Aristotle was still to some degree an idealist, both the source and the recipient of his ideals was the real world.

In classical Athens, human nature was a subject contemplated not only by scientists and philosophers, but also by historians, such as Herodotus and Thucydides. They, too, searched for explanations about the natural order that did not involve the gods. For Herodotus and Thucydides, the Persian and Peloponnesian wars were caused by human failings, not by actions of vengeful gods such as those that Homer, following tradition, depicted in the Iliad as causing the Trojan War. Like Aristotle, they were interested in describing real events and finding explanations for them; like Plato, they were also interested in the possible as well as the actual. History, in their opinion, was the best arena for observing the true worth of various ideals to human society.

To the Athenians, war was the ultimate test of human ideals, morals, and values, but these could also be tested and observed on a much smaller scale in the way people conducted their everyday lives. Although for Plato the basis of an ideal government was the perfectly trained ruler or group of rulers, for Aristotle and other writers it was the perfectly managed household, which they regarded as a microcosm of society. Observing that the household was the smallest economic and political unit in Athenian society, Aristotle began his consideration of the ideal governmental system with thoughts on how households should be run. Other writers on politics and economics followed suit, giving advice after observing households they regarded as particularly well managed.

Whereas Plato clearly indicated that he was describing an ideal, in the case of Aristotle and other Athenians, it is sometimes difficult to determine whether they were attempting to describe reality, what they wished were reality, or a pure ideal. Your task in this chapter will be to examine the relationship between ideal and reality in the writings of several Athenian philosophers, historians, and commentators and in architectural diagrams of Athenian buildings and houses. What ideals do the writers set forth for the individual, the household, and the government? How are these ideals reflected in more realistic descriptions of life in Athens and in the way Athenians built their houses and their city?

SOURCES AND METHOD

All the written sources we will use come from Athenians who lived during the classical period and are thus what we term original or primary sources. They differ greatly from modern primary sources, however, in that their textual accuracy cannot be checked. Before the development of the printing press, the only way to obtain a copy of a work was to write it out by hand yourself or hire someone to do so. Therefore, each manuscript copy might be slightly different. Because the originals of the works of Aristotle or Thucydides have long since disappeared, what we have to work with are translations of composites based on as many of the oldest copies still in existence after 2,500 years that the translators could find.

The problem of accuracy is further complicated with some of the authors we will read because they did not actually write the works attributed to them. Many of Aristotle's works, for instance, are probably copies of his students' notes combined with (perhaps) some of his own. If you think of the way in which you record your own instructors' remarks, you can see why we must be cautious about assuming that these secondhand works contain everything Aristotle taught exactly as he intended it. Socrates, in fact, wrote nothing at all; all his ideas and words come to us through his pupil Plato. Scholars have long debated how much of the written record represents Socrates and how much represents Plato, especially when we consider that Socrates generally spoke at social gatherings or informally while walking around Athens, when Plato was not taking notes. These problems do not mean that we should discount these sources; they simply mean that we should realize that they differ from the printed documents and tape-recorded speeches of later eras.

We will begin our investigation with what is probably the most famous description of classical Athens: a funeral speech delivered by Pericles (Source 1). Pericles, one of the leaders of Athens when the Peloponnesian War opened, gave this speech in 430 B.C.E. in honor of those who had died during the first year of the war. It was recorded by Thucydides and, though there is some disagreement over who actually wrote it, reflects Pericles' opinions. Read the speech carefully. Is Pericles describing an ideal he hopes Athens will achieve or reality as he sees it? How does he depict Athenian democracy and the Athenian attitude toward wealth? How does he compare Athens with Sparta? How does Athens treat its neighbors? What role does Pericles see for Athenian women? Before going on to the next readings, jot down some words that you feel best describe Athens and the Athenians. Would you want to live in the Athens Pericles describes?

Source 2 comes from a later section of Thucydides' Peloponnesian War, and it describes Athenian actions in the sixteenth year of the war. As you read it, think about the virtues that Pericles ascribed to the Athenians. Are these virtues reflected in the debate with the Melians or in the actions against them? How do the Athenians justify their actions? After reading this selection, jot down a few more words that you think describe the Athenians. Would you now erase some entries from your first list?

Source 3 is taken from the first book of Aristotle's *The Politics*. In this selection, he describes the proper functioning of a household and the role of each person in it. As you read it, you will notice that Aristotle is concerned equally with the economic role of household members and their moral status. What qualities does he see as important in the ideal head of household? the ideal wife or child? the ideal slave? How does he justify the differences between household members? How do these qualities compare with those described by Pericles or exhibited by the Athenians in their contact with the Melians?

Add a few more words to your list describing the Athenians.

The fourth selection (Source 4), by an unknown author, presents another view of Athenian democracy and the Athenian empire. This passage was written about five years after the speech made by Pericles and about ten years before the Melian debate. How does this author view democracy and Athens's relations with its neighbors? What words might he add to your list to describe his fellow Athenians? How do you think he would have responded had he been in the audience listening to Pericles' funeral speech?

The fifth selection (Source 5) is a discussion of household management cast in the form of a dialogue, from a treatise by Xenophon called *The Economist*. What does the main speaker, whose name is Ischomachus, see as the main roles of husband and wife? Would he have agreed with Aristotle's conclusions about the qualities necessary in an ideal husband and wife? What suggestions does he make for encouraging ideal behavior in wives and slaves? Does he appear to be describing an actual or an ideal marital relationship? What words would you now add to or subtract from your list?

The sixth selection (Source 6) is a very small part of *The Republic*, in which Plato sets out his views on the ideal government. Plato did not favor democracy; he advocated training a group of leaders, whom he called guardians, to work for the best interests of all. What qualities does Plato feel are most important in the guardians? What economic and family structures does he feel will help them maintain these qualities? How does his description of the ideal female guardian compare with Pericles' and Xenophon's descriptions of the ideal Athenian wife? Do the qualities he finds important in guardians match up with any of those on your list?

Once you have read all the selections carefully, go back to Pericles' speech and read it again. Do you still have the same opinion about whether he is describing an ideal or reality? Which of the words describing Athens that were on your original list are left?

Now look at the two diagrams, which are based on archaeological discoveries. They are thus clear representations of physical reality in classical Greece, but they tell us something about ideals as well, for people construct the space they live in according to their ideas about how society should operate. The first diagram, Source 7, is the floor plan of a house from fifth-century B.C.E. Olynthus. Does the actual house correspond to the one described by Xenophon? How does the layout of the house reinforce the roles prescribed for the ideal husband and wife? The second diagram, Source 8, is a plan of the Athenian *agora*, the open square in the center of Athens that served as both the political and commercial center of the city. The west side of the agora was a line of government buildings, including the *bouleuterion*, where the council met. The agora was bordered by several *stoa*, roofed-over open colonnades in front of lines of shops and offices. Because the climate of Greece is mild

[109]

a good part of the year, much business could take place outside or in one of the stoa. What qualities from your list does the openness of the agora encourage? As you can see from the diagram, the agora was bordered by buildings with religious, governmental, and commercial functions. What does the placement of these buildings indicate about how Athenians valued the different areas of their lives?

THE EVIDENCE

Sources 1 and 2 from Thucydides, History of the Peloponnesian War, *translated by Richard Crawley (New York: Modern Library, 1951), pp. 103–106; p. 109.*

1. Pericles' Funeral Speech,
430 B.C.E.

That part of our history which tells of the military achievements which gave us our several possessions, or of the ready valour with which either we or our fathers stemmed the tide of Hellenic or foreign aggression, is a theme too familiar to my hearers for me to dilate on, and I shall therefore pass it by. But what was the road by which we reached our position, what the form of government under which our greatness grew, what the national habits out of which it sprang; these are questions which I may try to solve before I proceed to my panegyric upon these men: since I think this to be a subject upon which on the present occasion a speaker may properly dwell, and to which the whole assemblage, whether citizens or foreigners, may listen with advantage.

Our constitution does not copy the laws of neighbouring states; we are rather a pattern to others than imitators ourselves. Its administration favours the many instead of the few; this is why it is called a democracy. If we look to the laws, they afford equal justice to all in their private differences; if to social standing, advancement in public life falls to reputation for capacity, class considerations not being allowed to interfere with merit; nor again does poverty bar the way, if a man is able to serve the state, he is not hindered by the obscurity of his condition. The freedom which we enjoy in our government extends also to our ordinary life. There, far from exercising a jealous surveillance over each other, we do not feel called upon to be angry with our neighbour for doing what he likes, or even to indulge in those injurious looks which cannot fail to be offensive, although they inflict no positive penalty. But all this ease in our private relations does not make us lawless as citizens. Against this fear is our chief safeguard, teaching us to obey the magistrates and the laws, particularly such as regard the protection of the injured, whether they are actually on the statute book, or belong to that code which, although unwritten, yet cannot be broken without acknowledged disgrace.

Further, we provide plenty of means for the mind to refresh itself from business. We celebrate games and sacrifices all the year round, and the elegance of our private establishments forms a daily source of pleasure and helps to banish the spleen; while the magnitude of our city draws the produce of the world into our harbour, so that to the Athenian the fruits of other countries are as familiar a luxury as those of his own.

If we turn to our military policy, there also we differ from our antagonists. We throw open our city to the world, and never by alien acts exclude foreigners from any opportunity of learning or observing, although the eyes of an enemy may occasionally profit by our liberality; trusting less in system and policy than to the native spirit of our citizens; while in education, where our rivals from their very cradles by a painful discipline seek after manliness, at Athens we live exactly as we please, and yet are just as ready to encounter every legitimate danger. In proof of this it may be noticed that the Lacedæmonians[1] do not invade our country alone, but bring with them all their confederates; while we Athenians advance unsupported into the territory of a neighbour, and fighting upon a foreign soil usually vanquish with ease men who are defending their homes. Our united force was never yet encountered by any enemy, because we have at once to attend to our marine and to despatch our citizens by land upon a hundred different services; so that, wherever they engage with some such fraction of our strength, a success against a detachment is magnified into a victory over the nation, and a defeat into a reverse suffered at the hands of our entire people. And yet if with habits not of labour but of ease, and courage not of art but of nature, we are still willing to encounter danger, we have the double advantage of escaping the experience of hardships in anticipation and of facing them in the hour of need as fearlessly as those who are never free from them.

Nor are these the only points in which our city is worthy of admiration. We cultivate refinement without extravagance and knowledge without effeminacy; wealth we employ more for use than for show, and place the real disgrace of poverty not in owning to the fact but in declining the struggle against it. Our public men have, besides politics, their private affairs to attend to, and our ordinary citizens, though occupied with the pursuits of industry, are still fair judges of public matters; for, unlike any other nation, regarding him who takes no part in these duties not as unambitious but as useless, we Athenians are able to judge at all events if we cannot originate, and instead of looking on discussion as a stumbling-block in the way of action, we think it an indispensable preliminary to any wise action at all. Again, in our enterprises we present the singular spectacle of daring and deliberation, each carried to its

1. **Lacedæmonions:** Spartans.

highest point, and both united in the same persons; although usually decision is the fruit of ignorance, hesitation of reflexion. But the palm of courage will surely be adjudged most justly to those, who best know the difference between hardship and pleasure and yet are never tempted to shrink from danger. In generosity we are equally singular, acquiring our friends by conferring not by receiving favours. Yet, of course, the doer of the favour is the firmer friend of the two, in order by continued kindness to keep the recipient in his debt; while the debtor feels less keenly from the very consciousness that the return he makes will be a payment, not a free gift. And it is only the Athenians who, fearless of consequences, confer their benefits not from calculations of expediency, but in the confidence of liberality.

In short, I say that as a city we are the school of Hellas; while I doubt if the world can produce a man, who where he has only himself to depend upon, is equal to so many emergencies, and graced by so happy a versatility as the Athenian. And that this is no mere boast thrown out for the occasion, but plain matter of fact, the power of the state acquired by these habits proves. For Athens alone of her contemporaries is found when tested to be greater than her reputation, and alone gives no occasion to her assailants to blush at the antagonist by whom they have been worsted, or to her subjects to question her title by merit to rule. Rather, the admiration of the present and succeeding ages will be ours, since we have not left our power without witness, but have shown it by mighty proofs; and far from needing a Homer for our panegyrist, or other of his craft whose verses might charm for the moment only for the impression which they gave to melt at the touch of fact, we have forced every sea and land to be the highway of our daring, and everywhere, whether for evil or for good, have left imperishable monuments behind us. Such is the Athens for which these men, in the assertion of their resolve not to lose her, nobly fought and died; and well may every one of their survivors be ready to suffer in her cause. . . .

[I]f I must say anything on the subject of female excellence to those of you who will now be in widowhood, it will be all comprised in this brief exhortation. Great will be your glory in not falling short of your natural character; and greatest will be hers who is least talked of among the men whether for good or for bad.

My task is now finished. I have performed it to the best of my ability, and in words, at least, the requirements of the law are now satisfied. If deeds be in question, those who are here interred have received part of their honours already, and for the rest, their children will be brought up till manhood at the public expense: the state thus offers a valuable prize, as the garland of victory in this race of valour, for the reward both of those who have fallen and their survivors. And where the rewards for merit are greatest, there are found the best citizens.

And now that you have brought to a close your lamentations for your relatives, you may depart.

2. The Melian Debate,
415 B.C.E.

The Athenians also made an expedition against the isle of Melos with thirty ships of their own, six Chian, and two Lesbian vessels, sixteen hundred heavy infantry, three hundred archers, and twenty mounted archers from Athens, and about fifteen hundred heavy infantry from the allies and the islanders. The Melians are a colony of Lacedæmon[2] that would not submit to the Athenians like the other islanders, and at first remained neutral and took no part in the struggle, but afterwards upon the Athenians using violence and plundering their territory, assumed an attitude of open hostility. Cleomedes, son of Lycomedes, and Tisias, son of Tisimachus, the generals, encamping in their territory with the above armament, before doing any harm to their land, sent envoys to negotiate. These the Melians did not bring before the people, but bade them state the object of their mission to the magistrates and the few; upon which the Athenian envoys spoke as follows: . . .

ATHENIANS: We will now proceed to show you that we are come here in the interest of our empire, and that we shall say what we are now going to say, for the preservation of your country; as we would fain exercise that empire over you without trouble, and see you preserved for the good of us both.

MELIANS: And how, pray, could it turn out as good for us to serve as for you to rule?

ATHENIANS: Because you would have the advantage of submitting before suffering the worst, and we should gain by not destroying you.

MELIANS: So that you would not consent to our being neutral, friends instead of enemies, but allies of neither side.

ATHENIANS: No; for your hostility cannot so much hurt us as your friendship will be an argument to our subjects of our weakness, and your enmity of our power.

MELIANS: Is that your subjects' idea of equity, to put those who have nothing to do with you in the same category with peoples that are most of them your own colonists, and some conquered rebels?

ATHENIANS: As far as right goes they think one has as much of it as the other, and if any maintain their independence it is because they are strong, and that if we do not molest them it is because we are afraid; so that besides extending our empire we should gain in security by your subjection; the fact that you are islanders and weaker than others rendering it all the more important that you should not succeed in baffling the masters of the sea.

MELIANS: But do you consider that there is no security in the policy which we indicate? For here again if you debar us from talking about justice and invite us to obey your interest, we also must explain ours, and try to persuade you, if

2. **Lacedæmon:** Sparta.

the two happen to coincide. How can you avoid making enemies of all existing neutrals who shall look at our case and conclude from it that one day or another you will attack them? And what is this but to make greater the enemies that you have already, and to force others to become so who would otherwise have never thought of it?

ATHENIANS: Why, the fact is that continentals generally give us but little alarm; the liberty which they enjoy will long prevent their taking precautions against us; it is rather islanders like yourselves, outside our empire, and subjects smarting under the yoke, who would be the most likely to take a rash step and lead themselves and us into obvious danger.

MELIANS: Well then, if you risk so much to retain your empire, and your subjects to get rid of it, it were surely great baseness and cowardice in us who are still free not to try everything that can be tried, before submitting to your yoke.

ATHENIANS: Not if you are well advised, the contest not being an equal one, with honour as the prize and shame as the penalty, but a question of self-preservation and of not resisting those who are far stronger than you are. . . .

Of the gods we believe, and of men we know, that by a necessary law of their nature they rule wherever they can. And it is not as if we were the first to make this law, or to act upon it when made: we found it existing before us, and shall leave it to exist for ever after us; all we do is to make use of it, knowing that you and everybody else, having the same power as we have, would do the same as we do. . . . You will surely not be caught by that idea of disgrace, which in dangers that are disgraceful, and at the same time too plain to be mistaken, proves so fatal to mankind; since in too many cases the very men that have their eyes perfectly open to what they are rushing into, let the thing called disgrace, by the mere influence of a seductive name, lead them on to a point at which they become so enslaved by the phrase as in fact to fall wilfully into hopeless disaster, and incur disgrace more disgraceful as the companion of error, than when it comes as the result of misfortune. This, if you are well advised, you will guard against; and you will not think it dishonourable to submit to the greatest city in Hellas, when it makes you the moderate offer of becoming its tributary ally, without ceasing to enjoy the country that belongs to you; nor when you have the choice given you between war and security, will you be so blinded as to choose the worse. And it is certain that those who do not yield to their equals, who keep terms with their superiors, and are moderate towards their inferiors, on the whole succeed best. Think over the matter, therefore, after our withdrawal, and reflect once and again that it is for your country that you are consulting, that you have not more than one, and that upon this one deliberation depends its prosperity or ruin.

The Athenians now withdrew from the conference; and the Melians, left to themselves, came to a decision corresponding with what they had maintained in the discussion, and answered, 'Our resolution, Athenians, is the same as it was at first. We will not in a moment deprive of freedom a city that has been inhabited these seven hundred years; but we put our trust in the fortune by which the gods have preserved it until now, and in the help of men, that is, of the Lacedæmonians; and so we will try and save ourselves. Meanwhile we invite you to allow us to be friends to you and foes to neither party, and to retire from our country after making such a treaty as shall seem fit to us both. . . .

The Athenian envoys now returned to the army; and the Melians showing no signs of yielding, the generals at once betook themselves to hostilities, and drew a line of circumvallation[3] round the Melians, dividing the work among the different states. Subsequently the Athenians returned with most of their army, leaving behind them a certain number of their own citizens and of the allies to keep guard by land and sea. The force thus left stayed on and besieged the place. . . .

Meanwhile the Melians attacked by night and took the part of the Athenian lines over against the market, and killed some of the men, and brought in corn and all else that they could find useful to them, and so returned and kept quiet, while the Athenians took measures to keep better guard in future.

Summer was now over. The next winter . . . the Melians again took another part of the Athenian lines which were but feebly garrisoned. Reinforcements afterwards arriving from Athens in consequence, under the command of Philocrates, son of Demeas, the siege was now pressed vigorously; and some treachery taking place inside, the Melians surrendered at discretion to the Athenians, who put to death all the grown men whom they took, and sold the women and children for slaves, and subsequently sent out five hundred colonists and inhabited the place themselves.

Source 3 from Aristotle, The Politics, *translated by T. A. Sinclair and revised by Trevor J. Saunders (Baltimore: Penguin Classics, Revised Edition, 1981), pp. 26–27, 31, 34, 50–53. Translation copyright © the estate of T. A. Sinclair, 1962; revised translation copyright © Trevor J. Saunders, 1981. Reprinted with permission of Penguin Books Ltd. (UK).*

3. From Aristotle, *The Politics*

We shall, I think, in this as in other subjects, get the best view of the matter if we look at the natural growth of things from the beginning. . . .

It was out of the association formed by men with these two, women and slaves, that the first household was formed; and the poet Hesiod was right when he wrote, "Get first a house and a wife and an ox to draw the plough." (The ox is the poor man's slave.) This association of persons, established according to the law of nature and continuing day after day, is the household. . . .

3. **circumvallation:** ramparts and walls.

Now property is part of a household and the acquisition of property part of the economics of a household; for neither life itself nor the good life is possible without a certain minimum standard of wealth. Again, for any given craft the existence of the proper tools will be essential for the performance of its task. Tools may be animate as well as inanimate; a ship's captain uses a lifeless rudder, but a living man for watch; for the worker in a craft is, from the point of view of the craft, one of its tools. So any piece of property can be regarded as a tool enabling a man to live; and his property is an assemblage of such tools, including his slaves; and a slave, being a living creature like any other servant, is a tool worth many tools. . . .

The "slave by nature" then is he that can and therefore does belong to another, and he that participates in the reasoning faculty so far as to understand but not so as to possess it. For the other animals serve their owner not by exercise of reason but passively. The use, too, of slaves hardly differs at all from that of domestic animals; from both we derive that which is essential for our bodily needs. . . . It is clear then that in household management the people are of greater importance than the material property, and their quality of more account than that of the goods that make up their wealth, and also that free men are of more account than slaves. About slaves the first question to be asked is whether in addition to their value as tools and servants there is some other quality or virtue, superior to these, that belongs to slaves. Can they possess self-respect, courage, justice, and virtues of that kind, or have they in fact nothing but the serviceable quality of their persons?

The question may be answered in either of two ways, but both present a difficulty. If we say that slaves have these virtues, how then will they differ from free men? If we say that they have not, the position is anomalous, since they are human beings and capable of reason. Roughly the same question can be put in relation to wife and child: Have not these also virtues? Ought not a woman to be self-respecting, brave, and just? Is not a child sometimes naughty, sometimes good? . . .

This mention of virtue leads us straightaway to a consideration of the soul; for it is here that the natural ruler and the natural subject, whose virtue we regard as different, are to be found. In the soul the difference between ruler and ruled is that between the rational and the nonrational. It is therefore clear that in other connexions also there will be natural differences. And so generally in cases of ruler and ruled; the differences will be natural but they need not be the same. For rule of free over slave, male over female, man over boy, are all natural, but they are also different, because, while parts of the soul are present in each case, the distribution is different. Thus the deliberative faculty in the soul is not present at all in a slave; in a female it is inoperative, in a child undeveloped. We must therefore take it that the same conditions prevail also in regard to the ethical virtues, namely that all must participate in them but not all to the same extent, but only as may be required by each for his proper function. The ruler then must have ethical virtue in its entirety; for his task is simply that of chief maker and reason is chief maker. And the other members must have what amount is appropriate to each. So it is evident that each of the classes spoken of must have ethical virtue. It is also clear that there is some variation in the ethical virtues; self-respect is not the same in a man as in a woman, nor justice, nor courage either, as Socrates thought; the one is courage of a ruler, the other courage of a servant, and likewise with the other virtues.

If we look at the matter in greater detail it will become clearer. For those who talk in generalities and say that virtue is "a good condition of the soul," or that it is "right conduct" or the like, delude themselves. Better than those who look for general definitions are those who, like Gorgias, enumerate the different virtues. So the poet Sophocles singles out "silence" as "bringing credit to a woman," but that is not so for a man. This method of assessing virtue according to function is one that we should always follow. Take the child: he is not yet fully developed and his function is to grow up, so we cannot speak of his virtue as belonging absolutely to him, but only in relation to the progress of his development and to whoever is in charge of him. So too with slave and master; we laid it down that a slave's function is to perform menial tasks; so the amount of virtue required will not be very great, only enough to ensure that he does not neglect his work through loose living or mere fecklessness.

Source 4 from B. K. Workman, editor and translator, They Saw It Happen in Classical Times *(New York: Barnes & Noble, 1964), pp. 32–34. Reprinted by permission of Littlefield, Adams & Company and Basil Blackwell, Publishers.*

4. An Unknown Author's View of Athenian Democracy

Insolent conduct of slaves and resident aliens is everywhere rife in Athens. You cannot strike a slave there, and he will not get out of your way in the street. There is good reason for this being the local custom. If the law allowed a free-born citizen to strike a slave, an alien, or a freedman, then you would often strike an Athenian citizen in the mistaken impression that he was a slave. For the common people dress as poorly as slaves or aliens and their general appearance is no better. . . .

The common people take no supervisory interest in athletic or aesthetic shows, feeling that it is not right for them, since they know that they have not the ability to become expert at them. When it is necessary to provide men to put on stageshows or games or to finance and build triremes,[4] they know that

4. **trireme:** standard Greek warship, about 120 feet long and rowed by 150 to 175 men; a ram on the bow was the trireme's main weapon.

impresarios come from the rich, the actors and chorus from the people. In the same way, organizers and ship-masters are the rich, while the common people take a subordinate part in the games and act as oarsmen for the triremes. But they do at least think it right to receive pay for singing or running or dancing or rowing in the fleet, to level up the incomes of rich and poor. The same holds good for the law courts as well; they are more interested in what profit they can make than in the true ends of justice. . . .

Of the mainland cities in the Athenian Empire, the large ones are governed by fear, the small ones by want. For all states must import and export, and this they cannot do unless they remain subject to the mistress of the seas.

Source 5 from Julia O'Faolain and Lauro Martines, editors, Not in God's Image: Women in History from the Greeks to the Victorians *(New York: Harper & Row, 1973), pp. 20–22. Adapted from several translations. Copyright © 1973 by Julia O'Faolain and Lauro Martines. Reprinted with permission of the authors.*

5. From Xenophon, *The Economist*

"Here's another thing I'd like to ask you," said I. "Did you train your wife yourself or did she already know how to run a house when you got her from her father and mother?"

"What could she have known, Socrates," said he, "when I took her from her family? She wasn't yet fifteen. Until then she had been under careful supervision and meant to see, hear, and ask as little as possible. Don't you think it was already a lot that she should have known how to make a cloak of the wool she was given and how to dole out spinning to the servants? She had been taught to moderate her appetites, which, to my mind, is basic for both men's and women's education."

"So, apart from that," I asked, "it was you, Ischomachus, who had to train and teach her her household duties?"

"Yes," said Ischomachus, "but not before sacrificing to the gods. . . . And she solemnly swore before heaven that she would behave as I wanted, and it was clear that she would neglect none of my lessons."

"Tell me what you taught her first. . . ."

"Well, Socrates, as soon as I had tamed her and she was relaxed enough to talk, I asked her the following question: 'Tell me, my dear,' said I, 'do you understand why I married you and why your parents gave you to me? You know as well as I do that neither of us would have had trouble finding someone else to share our beds. But, after thinking about it carefully, it was you I chose and me your parents chose as the best partners we could find for our home and our children. Now, if God sends us children, we shall think about how best to raise them, for we share an interest in securing the best allies and support for our old age. For the moment we only share our home." . . .'

"My wife answered, 'But how can I help? What am I capable of doing? It is on you that everything depends. My duty, my mother said, is to be well behaved.'"

"'Oh, by Zeus,' said I, 'my father said the same to me. But the best behavior in a man and woman is that which will keep up their property and increase it as far as may be done by honest and legal means.'"

"'And do you see some way,' asked my wife, 'in which I can help in this?'"

"'. . . It seems to me that God adapted women's nature to indoor and man's to outdoor work. . . . As Nature has entrusted woman with guarding the household supplies, and a timid nature is no disadvantage in such a job, it has endowed woman with more fear than man. . . . It is more proper for a woman to stay in the house than out of doors and less so for a man to be indoors instead of out. If anyone goes against the nature given him by God and leaves his appointed post . . . he will be punished. . . . You must stay indoors and send out the servants whose work is outside and supervise those who work indoors, receive what is brought in, give out what is to be spent, plan ahead what should be stored and ensure that provisions for a year are not used up in a month. When the wool is brought in, you must see to it that clothes are made from it for whoever needs them and see to it that the corn is still edible. . . . Many of your duties will give you pleasure: for instance, if you teach spinning and weaving to a slave who did not know how to do this when you got her, you double her usefulness to yourself, or if you make a good housekeeper of one who didn't know how to do anything'. . . . Then I took her around the family living rooms, which are pleasantly decorated, cool in summer and warm in winter. I pointed out how the whole house faces south so as to enjoy the winter sun. . . . I showed her the women's quarters which are separated from the men's by a bolted door to prevent anything being improperly removed and also to ensure that the slaves should not have children without our permission. For good slaves are usually even more devoted once they have a family; but good-for-nothings, once they begin to cohabit, have extra chances to get up to mischief."

Source 6 from B. Jowett, translator, The Dialogues of Plato, *revised edition, vol. 3 (Oxford: Oxford University Press, 1895, revised 1924), pp. 58, 100–101, 103, 106, 140–142, 147–148, 151, 159.*

6. From Plato, *The Republic*

Is not the love of learning the love of wisdom, which is philosophy?
　They are the same, he replied.

And may we not say confidently of man also, that he who is likely to be gentle to his friends and acquaintances, must by nature be a lover of wisdom and knowledge?

That we may safely affirm.

Then he who is to be a really good and noble guardian of the State will require to unite in himself philosophy and spirit and swiftness and strength?

Undoubtedly.

Then we have found the desired natures; and now that we have found them, how are they to be reared and educated? Is not this an enquiry which may be expected to throw light on the greater enquiry which is our final end—How do justice and injustice grow up in States?

Adeimantus thought that the enquiry would be of great service to us. . . .

Come then, and let us pass a leisure hour in storytelling, and our story shall be the education of our heroes.

By all means.

And what shall be their education? Can we find a better than the traditional sort?—and this has two divisions, gymnastic for the body, and music[5] for the soul.

True. . . .

Very good, I said; then what is the next question? Must we not ask who are to be rulers and who subjects?

Certainly.

There can be no doubt that the elder must rule the younger.

Clearly.

And that the best of these must rule.

That is also clear.

Now, are not the best husbandmen those who are most devoted to husbandry?

Yes.

And as we are to have the best of guardians for our city, must they not be those who have most the character of guardians?

Yes. . . .

Then there must be a selection. Let us note among the guardians those who in their whole life show the greatest eagerness to do what is for the good of their country, and the greatest repugnance to do what is against her interests.

Those are the right men.

And they will have to be watched at every age, in order that we may see whether they preserve their resolution, and never, under the influence either of force or enchantment, forget or cast off their sense of duty to the State. . . . And he who at every age, as boy and youth and in mature life, has come out of the trial victorious and pure, shall be appointed a ruler and guardian of the

---

5. By "music," the Athenians meant all that was sacred to the muses, the patron goddesses of the arts and sciences.

State; he shall be honoured in life and death, and shall receive sepulture[6] and other memorials of honour, the greatest that we have to give. But him who fails, we must reject. I am inclined to think that this is the sort of way in which our rulers and guardians should be chosen and appointed. I speak generally, and not with any pretension to exactness.

And, speaking generally, I agree with you, he said. . . .

Then let us consider what will be their way of life, if they are to realize our idea of them. In the first place, none of them should have any property of his own beyond what is absolutely necessary; neither should they have a private house or store closed against any one who has a mind to enter; their provisions should be only such as are required by trained warriors, who are men of temperance and courage; they should agree to receive from the citizens a fixed rate of pay, enough to meet the expenses of the year and no more; and they will go to mess and live together like soldiers in a camp. Gold and silver we will tell them that they have from God; the diviner metal is within them, and they have therefore no need of the dross which is current among men, and ought not to pollute the divine by any such earthly admixture; for that commoner metal has been the source of many unholy deeds, but their own is undefiled. And they alone of all the citizens may not touch or handle silver or gold, or be under the same roof with them, or wear them, or drink from them. And this will be their salvation, and they will be the saviours of the State. But should they ever acquire homes or lands or moneys of their own, they will become housekeepers and husbandmen instead of guardians, enemies and tyrants instead of allies of the other citizens; hating and being hated, plotting and being plotted against, they will pass their whole life in much greater terror of internal than of external enemies, and the hour of ruin, both to themselves and to the rest of the State, will be at hand. For all which reasons may we not say that thus shall our State be ordered, and that these shall be the regulations appointed by us for our guardians concerning their houses and all other matters?

Yes, said Glaucon. . . .

The part of the men has been played out, and now properly enough comes the turn of the women. Of them I will proceed to speak, and the more readily since I am invited by you.

For men born and educated like our citizens, the only way, in my opinion, of arriving at a right conclusion about the possession and use of women and children is to follow the path on which we originally started, when we said that the men were to be the guardians and watchdogs of the herd.

True.

Let us further suppose the birth and education of our women to be subject to similar or nearly similar regulations; then we shall see whether the result accords with our design.

---

6. **sepulture:** a special burial ceremony.

What do you mean?

What I mean may be put into the form of a question, I said: Are dogs divided into hes and shes, or do they both share equally in hunting and in keeping watch and in the other duties of dogs? or do we entrust to the males the entire and exclusive care of the flocks, while we leave the females at home, under the idea that the bearing and suckling their puppies is labour enough for them?

No, he said, they share alike; the only difference between them is that the males are stronger and the females weaker.

But can you use different animals for the same purpose, unless they are bred and fed in the same way?

You cannot.

Then, if women are to have the same duties as men, they must have the same nurture and education?

Yes. . . .

My friend, I said, there is no special faculty of administration in a state which a woman has because she is a woman, or which a man has by virtue of his sex, but the gifts of nature are alike diffused in both; all the pursuits of men are the pursuits of women also, but in all of them a woman is inferior to a man.

Very true.

Then are we to impose all our enactments on men and none of them on women?

That will never do.

One woman has a gift of healing, another not; one is a musician, and another has no music in her nature?

Very true.

And one woman has a turn for gymnastic and military exercises, and another is unwarlike and hates gymnastics?

Certainly.

And one woman is a philosopher, and another is an enemy of philosophy; one has spirit, and another is without spirit?

That is also true.

Then one woman will have the temper of a guardian, and another not. Was not the selection of the male guardians determined by differences of this sort?

Yes.

Men and women alike possess the qualities which make a guardian; they differ only in their comparative strength or weakness.

Obviously.

And those women who have such qualities are to be selected as the companions and colleagues of men who have similar qualities and whom they resemble in capacity and in character?

Very true. . . .

The law, I said, which is the sequel of this and of all that has preceded, is to the following effect—"that the wives of our guardians are to be common, and their children are to be common, and no parent is to know his own child, nor any child his parent."

Yes, he said, that is a much greater wave than the other; and the possibility as well as the utility of such a law are far more questionable. . . .

Both the community of property and the community of families, as I am saying, tend to make them more truly guardians; they will not tear the city in pieces by differing about "mine" and "not mine"; each man dragging any acquisition which he has made into a separate house of his own, where he has a separate wife and children and private pleasures and pains; but all will be affected as far as may be by the same pleasures and pains because they are all of one opinion about what is near and dear to them, and therefore they all tend towards a common end.

Certainly, he replied.

Source 7 adapted from Orestis B. Doumanis and Paul Oliver, editors, Shelter in Greece *(Athens: Architecture in Greece Press, 1974), p. 25.*

7. Floor Plan of a House from Olynthus, 5th century B.C.E.

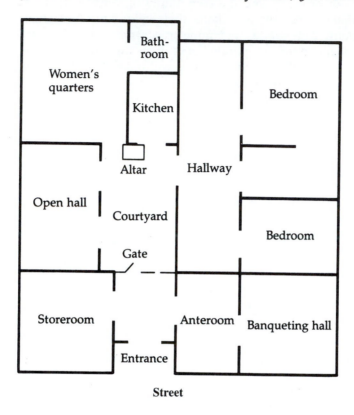

Source 8 adapted from A. W. Lawrence, Greek Architecture *(Yale University Press, 1957), p. 257. Copyright © 1955 by Yale University Press. Reprinted by permission of Yale University Press.*

8. The Athenian Agora, 4th century B.C.E.

QUESTIONS TO CONSIDER

Before you start to think about the questions in this section, you may want to turn to your text to read (or reread) the section on Athens during the classical period. This can give you more background on the authors and on the political events that might have affected what they wrote.

Though some of the written selections in this chapter clearly describe ideals and others reality, still others blend realism and idealism, creating an idealized view of actual persons or situations. Which selections would you put in this last category? Why would these authors describe reality in an idealized manner? (To answer this question, you need to think about both the purpose of each selection and whether the author truly thought that what he was describing actually existed—in other words, whether this was a conscious or unconscious alteration of reality.)

Once you have labeled the written sources as ideals, reality, and idealizations of reality, go back to your list of the personal qualities of Athenians. Which qualities would you put in each of these three categories? Now that you know you are describing only an ideal or real characteristic, would you add any further qualities? The next step is to divide your list into categories of persons, for it is clear that most of the authors make great distinctions between male and female, adult and child, slave and free. Do all the authors agree on the qualities important in an ideal man,

woman, or slave? Which authors have opposing ideas? Why might this be so? Sometimes distinctions between categories are not clearly set out by the author; when Pericles, for instance, uses the words *person* and *people* in his funeral oration, one might think he was talking about all Athenians. Looking at your list divided into categories, of whom is Pericles speaking when he says "person" and "people"? Do any of the authors make distinctions between individuals of the same category based on such factors as wealth or education; for example, do they describe wealthy men differently from poor men, or set out different ideals for women who are interested in learning than for those who are not? If Athenians lived up to the ideals prescribed for them, what types of people would you expect to meet in the agora? What types of people would you not expect to meet?

Turning from the individual to social units, what qualities should the ideal Athenian household possess? How might real households work to emulate these ideals? Judging from information in the selections and in your text about Athenian marriage patterns, family life, and social life in general, did real Athenian households approach the ideal at all? How did their beliefs about the way households should be run affect the way Athenians designed their houses? How did the layout of a house work to make reality correspond with those ideals?

The qualities of governments as presented in the selections may also be classified as real, ideal, or idealized. Were any of the words you used to describe the Athenian government after first reading Pericles included in your final list? Does his idealized view of Athens come closer to the realistic view provided in the Melian debate or to the purely ideal view of Plato? After reading all the selections, would you put the quality "democracy" into the real or the ideal column for Athens? How would Athenians define democracy? How does the layout of the agora reflect this definition? Do all the authors agree that democracy is a desirable form of government? Judging from information in your text about politics in Athens in the fifth century, why would authors disagree on this matter? If you put democracy in the ideal column, what changes in existing conditions would have been necessary for it to become a reality?

The selections you have read offer varying opinions on a great many subjects, including the benefits of wealth and private property, the relationship between dominant and dependent states and between dominant and dependent individuals, the reasons for the differences between men and women, the role of naval power in foreign policy, and the causes of imperialism. All these issues have both ideal and real components, and you may want to think about them before you draw your final conclusions about classical Athens. How well did Athens live up to the ideals it set for itself? How did the different ideals held up for different categories of persons affect their participation in Athenian life?

EPILOGUE

We can find the ideals of the Athenians expressed not only in their philosophy, history, and architecture, as you have discovered here, but also in their drama, poetry, and sculpture. Indeed, most of the original sources we have from Athens are not realistic descriptions but either thoughts about ideals or idealizations of actual persons and episodes. That they are idealizations may be very clear to us as modern skeptical readers, but for a long time the statements in these sources were taken as literal truth. To give you an example, here is a quotation from Edith Hamilton, one of the foremost historians of Greece, published in 1930:

> For a hundred years Athens was a city where the great spiritual forces that war in men's minds flowed together along in peace; law and freedom, truth and religion, beauty and goodness, the objective and the subjective—there was a truce to their eternal warfare, and the result was the balance and clarity, the harmony and completeness, that the word Greek has come to stand for.[7]

Given what you have just read, would you agree with her? Do you

7. Edith Hamilton, *The Greek Way* (New York: Norton, 1930), p. 206.

think everyone living in classical Athens would have agreed with her?

No matter how you have judged the relationship between ideal and reality in classical Athens, the ideals for the individual and state created there have significantly shaped the development of Western philosophy and social institutions. Roman philosophers closely studied Plato's *Republic*, and medieval philosophers were strongly influenced by Aristotle's *Politics*. Writers from the Renaissance to the present have invented ideal societies, "utopias" guided by wise leaders like Plato's guardians. Occasionally small groups of people have actually tried to set up working replicas of these ideal societies, frequently forbidding private property and the nuclear family as Plato did. Educational theorists have devised "perfect" school systems that, if not entirely successful when put into practice, have had their effect on real-life pedagogy. The Athenian ideal of government by the people is reflected in the constitutions of modern democratic states, with the category "people" now including groups unthinkable to Pericles.

In terms of Athenian history, democracy was an extremely short-lived phenomenon. Widespread revolt broke out in the Athenian empire, and Sparta ultimately defeated Athens, bringing the Peloponnesian War to a close after twenty-seven years. This did not end warfare in Greece, however, as the city-states continued to battle among themselves. Finally, in 338 B.C.E., Greece was conquered by Philip of Macedon, and Athens became simply one small part of a much larger empire. From that point on, Athenian ideals of individual behavior would be emulated in Western culture, but democratic government would not again be attempted as an experiment in the real world for another 2,000 years.

CHAPTER SIX

THE EQUINE REVOLUTION

(3700 B.C.E.–100 C.E.)

According to Greek mythology, Athena, goddess of wisdom, and Poseidon, god of the seas, held a contest to determine the right name to give a new and beautiful Attican city in Greece. Whichever of the two who could give the city the gift that would be most useful to its citizens would win. For her part, Athena produced an olive tree, which had many uses. Poseidon then raised his trident[1] and struck the ground. From that spot emerged the first horse, who leaped up and galloped about. The other gods who were judges of the contest gasped in awe.[2]

The duel between Athena and Poseidon is not the only episode in which the horse figured prominently in ancient religion or mythology. Throughout central Asia, Egypt, India, the Middle East, Europe, and North America, humans frequently held the horse in such high regard as to approach veneration. In many cultures, rulers and warriors were buried with their horses beside them, and in several places the sacrificing of horses was considered to be among the most pleasing gifts to the gods. Alexander the Great ceremoniously buried his favorite steed, Bucephalus, on the banks of the Hydaspes River, and the city founded there was named Bucephala.

The prominence of the horse in ancient religion and mythology is evidence of how important the horse was to humans. Before the widespread domestication and expanded use of the horse—the so-called *equine revolution*[3]—travel, agriculture, warfare, and society were extremely different. Although dogs, cattle, and reindeer had been domesticated earlier, many

---

1. **trident**: a three-pronged spear.

2. Because Poseidon made the mistake of emphasizing only the horse's advantages in warfare, Athena was declared the winner and, characteristically, named the new city for herself: Athens. As a consolation prize, Poseidon was named god of horses. But Athena's olive branch became the symbol of peace.

3. **equine**: pertaining to the horse.

[129]

ancient peoples believed that the taming of the horse was their most significant accomplishment.

By the time that humans met horses, the horse had gone through a considerable evolution, much of which was to humans' advantage. The ancestor of the modern horse can be traced, through archaeological findings, to both North America and Europe roughly 50 million years ago. The "dawn horse" (Eohippus) was only around fifteen to twenty inches tall at the shoulder (withers) and probably weighed no more than 100 pounds. Its front feet had four toes each, padded on the underside not unlike the feet of present dogs, and the back feet had three padded toes. The Eohippus primarily was a leaf eater, and its principal defense against its enemies was its impressive speed.

Over thousands of generations, the horse evolved into a creature quite different from its original ancestor. Most important perhaps, a change in the animal's teeth alignment turned it into a grass eater, a fact that probably added considerable height and weight. Foot pads gradually disappeared, and the toenails of the hooves became a thick and solid nail. The legs gradually grew longer and the muzzle became elongated. In North America, on the eastern slopes of the Rocky Mountains, the horse found sufficient grass for food.

In Europe, the Eohippus for some reason became extinct. But in North America, these larger and stronger horses began to migrate north and east, across the land bridge that at the time existed between present-day Alaska and Russia.[4] Indeed, it is probable that at the same time horses were migrating eastward across this land bridge, the ancestors of present-day Native Americans were migrating westward across this same route.

Sometime between 10,000 and 8,000 years ago, the remaining horses in North America became extinct. Their disappearance is something of a mystery. Many reputable scholars believe that the incoming humans butchered these animals en masse for food.[5] Other equally respected historians claim that a disease wiped out the horse population and, along with it, the mastodons, elephants, rhinoceroses, camels, and saber-toothed tigers that once existed in North America. Whatever the reason, the Western Hemisphere did not see another horse until Spanish conquerors (conquistadors) and settlers reintroduced the horse to the Americas in the sixteenth century.[6]

By the time that the migrating horse spread across Asia, southern Russia, and Europe, three distinct breeds had emerged. In Europe, the forest pony (Equus abeli) probably most resembled the horses that had migrated from North America. Short,

4. Today the Bering Strait is only 180 feet deep. Thus, a lowering of ocean levels 250 to 300 feet deep (which was the case in the middle of the Pleistocene Age) would have exposed a considerable land bridge between Asia and North America.

5. See, for example, John Keegan, *A History of Warfare* (New York: Vintage Books, 1993), p. 156.

6. Native Americans of Central America called Cortes's horses "deer." See Miguel Leon-Portilla, ed., *The Broken Spears: The Aztec Account of the Conquest of Mexico*, trans. Lysander Kemp (Boston: Beacon Press, 1962), p. 30.

squat, with a blunt muzzle, they were small (about nine to eleven hands high)[7] and quick. In eastern Europe and the Ukraine, the tarpan (*Equus gmelini*) was somewhat larger and probably swifter. And in Asia, especially on the steppes of central Asia, emerged Przewalski's horse, strong and large (approximately thirteen hands high).[8]

It was on the steppe that the horse began to reach its near-present development. The steppe is a vast, treeless grassland that runs 3,000 miles from the river valleys of China to the Carpathian Mountains of the Ukraine and eastern Romania. Unsuited to agriculture (unless expensively irrigated), the steppe provides exceptionally fine grazing, which permitted the horse almost to achieve its present size and weight. Because an adult horse needs twenty to thirty pounds of vegetation each day, the horse needed to roam over fairly large territories, which the steppe provided.

Early humans encountered wild horses beyond the steppe. At first they probably thought of horses exclusively as food. At the base of a rock shelter at Solutré, France, the bones of around 40,000 horses have been found, dating back to about 25,000 years ago. Because horses had such strong bonding instincts, hu-

mans found that they could drive a few horses into canyons to be trapped there and the rest would follow. Then the butchering could begin.

It is not clear when (or where) humans first reasoned that they could domesticate horses for food rather than chasing wild bands over the steppe. Previous to the horse, the reindeer had been domesticated and bred in central Asia, and it probably was not long before peoples on the steppe were domesticating and breeding horses, probably for food. In sites along the lower Dneiper and Don Rivers in what is now the Ukraine, the number of bones from what were young and healthy horses seems far too high to reflect only animals killed in the wild. Those sites have been dated (using carbon dating of the horse bones) at around 3640 B.C.E. By 1000 B.C.E., the domestication of the horse had spread to Europe, Asia, and northern Africa, although wild horses existed until well into our own time.[9]

As with much of the history of the equine revolution, it is not clear precisely when humans began to ride their horses. At the same archaeological sites noted above (dated at approximately 3640 B.C.E.), pieces of carved antlers and bones are thought to be the remains of bridle cheek pieces, which held cord or leather bits that were fitted into the horse's mouth to hold the two (left and right) reins. Similar cheek pieces and even some metal loops have been found in somewhat later sites from central

7. A hand is equal to four inches. Therefore, a horse that is ten hands high would be forty inches tall at the shoulder.

8. Przewalski's horse (alternative spelling Przevalskii) was named for Nikolai Przewalski (1839–1888), who "discovered" the horse in the wild in 1879. As a comparison, the present Arabian horse is approximately fourteen to fifteen hands high and the massive Clydesdale is sixteen to seventeen hands high.

9. Wild Przewalski horses were last sighted in Mongolia in the 1960s, and are thought now to exist only in zoos.

Asia to eastern Europe, evidence that horseback riding spread quickly beyond its original homeland. Yet horseback riding was not done south of the steppe (in the lower Mesopotamia, the Indus Valley, or the Mediterranean region) until considerably later. The Scythians of Asia and southeastern Europe brought the horse to Greece sometime between the eighth and seventh centuries B.C.E.

In the 1960s, a magnificent archaeological find was discovered by Russian explorers in the high Ulagan Valley in the Altai Mountains west of Mongolia. Dated at around the fifth century B.C.E., the site was marvelously preserved by a series of climatic accidents that formed ice masses in graves that almost completely halted decomposition. Sixty-nine almost perfect horse cadavers were found, including hair, hide, flesh, and even stomach contents. The horses were very close to the modern horse (*Equus caballus*) in size and weight, and clear evidence indicated that they had been carefully bred for size and strength. The animals were light tan with black manes and tails. Some of the horses were geldings (castrated stallions), certain evidence that the horses' owners were breeding their animals. Saddles, saddlebags, and bridles were found as well, although no traces of breakable objects (like pottery) were discovered—evidence that the animals' owners were nomads. Thus the horse became valuable to humans not only as a food source, but also as an important means of transportation, one that would be critical to human movement until the development of the railroad in the nine-

teenth century and the automobile in the twentieth.

The use of the horse as a load puller came somewhat later, having to wait for technological innovations for the horse to be adapted to this work. Sumerians of the Fertile Crescent had developed both the two-wheeled cart and the four-wheeled wagon as early as 2800 or 2700 B.C.E., but these vehicles were designed to be hauled by oxen, not horses (which the Sumerians called "asses from the mountains" and considered of little practical value). With solid disk wheels and heavy carriages, these vehicles weighed up to a half-ton each. Moreover, the animals that pulled them were yoked, a device suitable for oxen but one that would almost surely choke a horse. To us these carts and wagons would be pitifully slow—traveling at only about 1.5 miles per hour (ten to twelve miles per day under the best of circumstances)—and would be almost immobile in hilly or wet terrain. Similar vehicles have been unearthed in the Middle East, the Indus Valley, and the regions now known as Armenia and Georgia (between the Black and Caspian seas). And pottery models of similar oxen-drawn wagons have been found in graves as remote as Denmark. Most of these wagons were used by sedentary peoples, for nomads would have found them far too slow and inefficient.

The key technological challenge, therefore, was to make these vehicles lighter and to devise a type of harness that would not choke a horse. The earliest evidence of spoked wheels comes from cylinder seals discovered in an Assyrian commercial outpost in what is now north central Turkey and dated at around the early nineteenth century B.C.E. The carts had been lightened considerably and another important technological innovation had been developed: wheel hubs allowed the wheels to revolve independently around the axle so as to allow sharper turning where inner and outer wheels spin at different speeds. A special neck yoke for horses, which put the pulling pressure on the horse's chest instead of its throat, soon followed.

Hittites or some other early people from the Caucasus Mountains or the Ukrainian steppe also developed the chariot (ca 2000 B.C.E.), designed for the rapid transportation of humans rather than for freight. Between 1700 and 1600 B.C.E., the chariot spread throughout the Near East, North Africa, Europe, Iran, India, and even China. Originally ownership was confined to the very wealthy. Ancient records from both China and the Middle East indicate that chariots were eyed as one of the most prized gifts that rulers could bestow on their followers, and chariots became a great status symbol in those societies. Indeed, there is evidence that members of the elite had their chariots as well as their horses buried with them. In societies in which the great majority of people walked or rode donkeys or asses, the chariot was a sign of privilege and power. Of course, it was not lost on these people that, with their potential for great speed, chariots might have military value as well. Again, the Hittites probably led the way.

Thus from the steppe of central Asia and eastern Europe, the hunting, domesticating, breeding, riding, and harnessing of the horse as a draft animal together formed an equine revolution, a revolution that was arguably as important to human development as any other before or since.

Your task in this chapter will require a considerable amount of inference and imagination. From the evidence presented, you are to determine the impact of the equine revolution on humans. At one level, think of how the horse affected travel, agriculture, warfare, and general standards of living. And at a somewhat more sophisticated level, imagine how the horse would have affected social organization (including gender relations), thought, and perspectives.

SOURCES AND METHOD

Your task in this chapter is to infer from the evidence the impact that the equine revolution had on humans—on travel, agriculture, warfare, standards of living (including diet, clothing, and other factors), social organization, gender relations, and even thought. Much of the evidence comes from archaeological discoveries and must be examined and analyzed (archaeologists would say "read") with considerable imagination.

As you examine the evidence, it would be extremely helpful to make a chart like the top one on page 134 so as to organize your notes.

Once you have completed your chart, then use the evidence, the chart, and your imagination to add a fourth column to your chart (see charts below). Be sure you leave enough space on your chart for each source, so that you can write down your thoughts fully.

Sources 1 and 2 are cave and rock paintings, respectively—Source 1 from France and Source 2 from Egypt. The animals in Source 2 may well be asses and not horses.

Source Number	Description	Deductions
1	Cave painting from Lascaux, France, 15,000—10,000 B.C.E.	By painting them on cave wall, artist attached great importance to horse, probably for food.
2		

Source Number	Description	Deductions	Impact of the horse on humans
1	Cave painting from Lascaux France, 15,000–10,000 B.C.E.	By painting them on cave wall, artist attached great importance to horse, probably for food.	Impact on diet; would decrease starvation, since horses could be eaten year-round (when fruits and berries were only seasonal). Good protein. Perhaps sped up use of fire to cook raw horsemeat.
2			

Source 3 is a Scythian frieze. A frieze is a decorative horizontal band, usually along the upper part of a wall but also found on urns and vases (in this case, a jar with a narrow neck). "Read" the bottom row of the frieze first, left to right, then move to the top row and repeat the process. What is being depicted here?

The map in Source 4 gives you a good idea of how horse breeding spread from the steppe to the east, west, and south. Source 5 is an Iranian-style portrait of a king and hunter. How would the horse have helped hunters?

Herodotus (Source 6), a Greek historian of the fifth century B.C.E., has been called the father of history because of his extraordinary work. This selection from his masterpiece *The Persian Wars* gives an interesting description of a group of mid-fifth-century B.C.E. nomadic warriors known to Herodotus as the Massagetae. How does Herodotus, a "civilized" Greek, view these horse people? In his view, how has the horse affected the lives of the Massagetae?

Sources 7 through 11 show the various ways humans used mounted horses. Sources 7 and 11 are reliefs (projections of figures from flat backgrounds), Source 8 is a felt appliqué, and Sources 9 and 10 are statuettes. What do these artistic representations tell you about the impact of the horse on human development?

Source 12 is a toy model of a Sumerian cart and a drawing of a Sumerian cart wheel; Source 13 is a sketch of a wagon dating from the second millennium B.C.E. that was found by Russian archaeologists in present-day Armenia. These wagons could not have been drawn by horses (see above), whereas the wagons and chariots in Sources 14 through 16 and 18 clearly could have been. What were the differences between these two types of vehicles? How did wagons and chariots affect their human users?

Source 17 is a photograph of a grave from China's Shang dynasty, dated about 1700 B.C.E. What does the photograph tell you?

Source 19, a photograph of early Greek figurines, shows a representation of an early plow. Why would early cultivators have preferred oxen over horses to pull plows? What would be needed before horses could pull plows? Would there be any advantages in using horses instead of oxen?

THE EVIDENCE

Source 1: Art Resource, NY.

1. Cave Painting, Lascaux, France, 15,000–10,000 B.C.E.

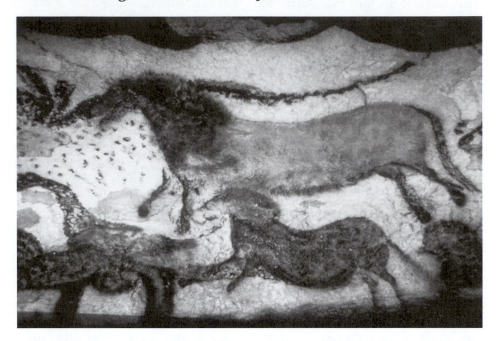

Source 2 from Anthony Dent, The Horse Through Fifty Centuries of Civilization *(New York: Holt, Rinehart & Winston, 1974), p. 11.*

2. Rock Painting, North Africa

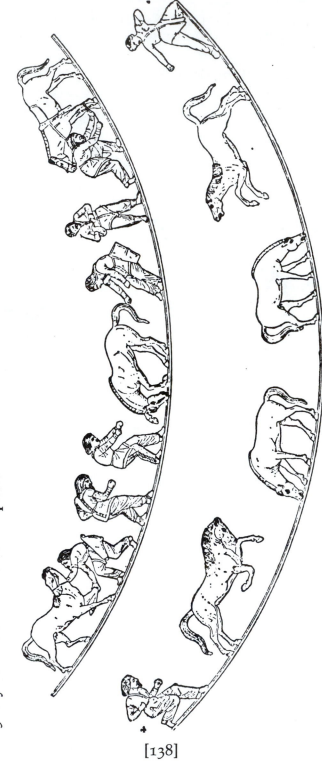

Source 3 from E. H. Minns, Scythians and Greeks (Cambridge: Cambridge University Press, 1913). Reproduced with permission of Cambridge University Press.

3. Scythian Frieze on Silver Amphora

Source 4 from Miklos Jankovich, They Rode Into Europe: The Fruitful Exchange in the Arts of Horsemanship Between East and West, *trans. Anthony Dent (London: George G. Harrap, 1971), p. 26.*

4. The Migrations of Horse-Breeding People in Asia and Europe

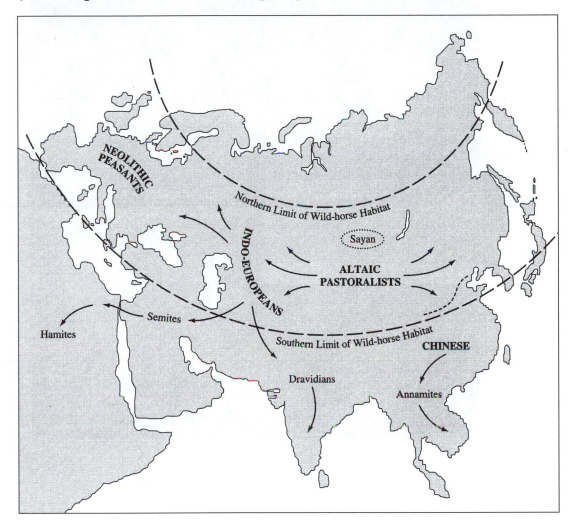

5. Iranian-Style Royal Portrait from Sasanian-Type Silver Plate

Source 6 from Herodotus, The Persian Wars, *trans. George Rawlinson (New York: Modern Library, 1942), Book I, Chs. 201, 215–216.*

6. From Herodotus, *The Persian Wars,* 5th century B.C.E.

201. When Cyrus had achieved the conquest of the Babylonians, he conceived the desire of bringing the Massagetae under his dominion. Now the Massagetae are said to be a great and warlike nation, dwelling eastward, towards the rising of the sun, beyond the river Araxes, and opposite the Issedonians. By many they are regarded as a Scythian race. . . .

215. In their dress and mode of living the Massagetae resemble the Scythians. They fight both on horseback and on foot, neither method is strange to them: they use bows and lances, but their favourite weapon is the battle-axe. Their arms are all either of gold or brass. For their spearpoints, and arrowheads, and for their battle-axes, they make use of brass; for head-gear, belts, and girdles, of gold. So too with the caparison[10] of their horses, they give them breastplates of brass, but employ gold about the reins, the bit, and the cheek-plates. They use neither iron nor silver, having none in their country; but they have brass and gold in abundance.

216. The following are some of their customs: Each man has but one wife, yet all the wives are held in common; for this is a custom of the Massagetae and not of the Scythians, as the Greeks wrongly say. When a man desires a woman he hangs his quiver in front of her wagon and has intercourse with her unhindered. Human life does not come to its natural close with this people; but when a man grows very old, all his kinsfolk collect together and offer him up in sacrifice; offering at the same time some cattle also. After the sacrifice they boil the flesh and feast on it; and those who thus end their days are reckoned the happiest. If a man dies of disease they do not eat him, but bury him in the ground, bewailing his ill fortune that he did not come to be sacrificed. They sow no grain, but live on their herds, and on fish, of which there is great plenty in the Araxes. Milk is what they chiefly drink. The only god they worship is the sun, and to him they offer the horse in sacrifice; under the notion of giving to the swiftest of the gods the swiftest of all mortal creatures.

---

10. **caparison:** a cover put over a horse's saddle or harness, usually for ornamentation.

7. Assyrian Horsemen, Relief from the Palace of Nineveh, ca 639 B.C.E.

8. Felt Hanging Found at Pazyryk, Siberia, 5th century B.C.E.

9. Parthian Mounted Archer, Etruscan Vase

Source 10: Seth Joel/Laurie Platt Winfrey, Inc.

10. Chinese Pottery Figures, 3rd century B.C.E.

Source 11 from Miklos Jankovich, They Rode Into Europe: The Fruitful Exchange in the Arts of Horsemanship Between East and West, *trans. Anthony Dent (London: George G. Harrap, 1971), opposite p. 48. Photograph: Landesmuseum Mainz.*

11. Relief Tombstone of a Trooper of the Roman Auxiliary Cavalry Regiment Recruited in Noricum

Source 12 from M. A. Litauer and J. H. Crouwel, Wheeled Vehicles and Ridden Animals in the Ancient Near East *(Leiden, The Netherlands: E. J. Brill Publishers, 1979), Fig. 1. Wagon: After a photograph from the Ashmolean Museum, Oxford; Wheel: After de Mecquenem, 1943, Fig. 89:1–2 and Pl. X:2. Reproduced with permission.*

12. Toy Model of a Sumerian Wagon and Drawing of a Wheel from a Sumerian Cart, early 3rd millennium B.C.E.

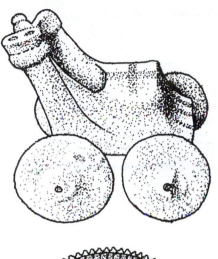

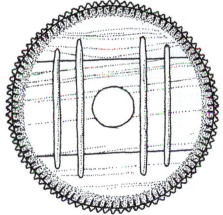

13. Drawing of Caucasian Wagon and Cart, early 2nd millennium B.C.E.

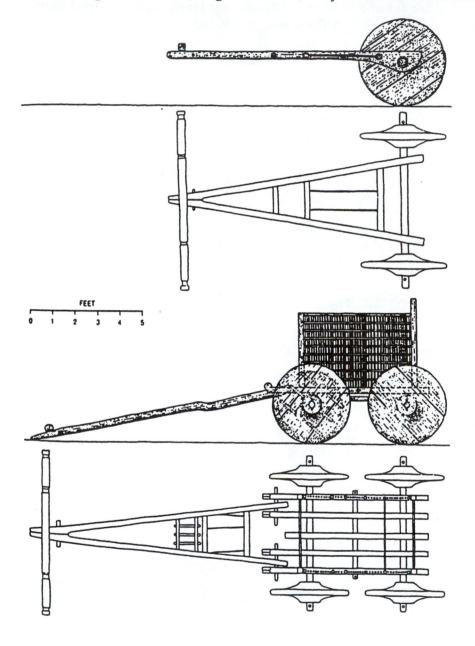

Source 14 from Miklos Jankovich, They Rode Into Europe: The Fruitful Exchange in the Arts of Horsemanship Between East and West, *trans. Anthony Dent (London: George G. Harrap, 1971), opposite p. 48. Photograph: Hungarian National Museum, Budapest. Inv. Nr. 56.1900.*

14. Roman Wagon, from Roman Tombstone in Pannonia (in Modern Hungary)

Source 15 from M. A. Litauer and J. H. Crouwel, Wheeled Vehicles and Ridden Animals in the Ancient Near East *(Leiden, The Netherlands: E. J. Brill, 1979), Fig. 29. Photograph: The Metropolitan Museum of Art, Gift of Mr. & Mrs. J. J. Klejman, 1966 Accession 66.245.17b.*

15. Anatolian Chariot, from Assyrian Seal, early 2nd millennium B.C.E.

16. Egyptian Chariot, mid-2nd millennium B.C.E.

This Greek drawing is based on an Egyptian relief.

Source 17 from Anthony Dent, The Horse Through Fifty Centuries of Civilization (New York: Holt, Rinehart & Winston, 1974), p. 20. Rijksmuseum voor Volkenkunde, Leiden.

17. Photograph of Gravesite from China's Shang Dynasty, ca 1700 B.C.E.

Source 18 from Scala/Art Resource, NY.

18. Roman Triumphal Chariot

Source 19 from Anthony Dent, The Horse Through Fifty Centuries of Civilization *(New York: Holt, Rinehart & Winston, 1974), p. 62. Photographs: Erich Lessing/Art Resource, NY.*

19. Early Greek Clay Figurines Depicting a Plow Team and a Chariot

On the left, oxen are yoked to a plow; on the right, horses pull a chariot.

QUESTIONS TO CONSIDER

Continue to work on your chart as the questions in this section prompt new ideas. At the same time, be willing to ask questions yourself; for example, in terms of using the horse for food, what advantages would there have been to capturing horses, putting them in corrals, and breeding them?

Source 1 is a painting made by Cro-Magnon people of the Magdalenian era, and many of these have been found by archaeologists and explorers, from France to North Africa (Source 2). Why do you think people painted images of the horse as often as they did? Most scholars theorize that the paintings were part of magic rituals conducted before hunts. If so, what might these hunters have been thinking?

Source 3, from a Scythian frieze, appears to show how Scythians domesticated horses. After catching the horse, it looks as if the man is trying to get the horse to kneel or bow before him (which actually was part of the Scythian domestication ritual). How would you explain this? At the top left, the forefeet of the saddled horse appear to have been bound, or hobbled, by the man. Why would he do this?

Source 4 represents the migration of people who bred horses. Note how far many of them traveled, and how they passed on their knowledge to other people, who in turn also moved. How would horse breeding have affected the horse? the people who bred them? Remember that the western Asian horse was only between ten and eleven hands high, whereas today's Arabian horse is roughly fourteen to fifteen hands high.

Source 5 is a representation of a mounted hunter. How would the horse affect the process of hunting (note that in Source 2, from ancient Egypt, the hunters are on foot)? How would that change affect the diet, dress, family life, and so on of nomadic hunters?

Source 6 is the historian Herodotus's account of the failed efforts of the Persians under Cyrus the Great to subdue the Massagetae, an Iranian-speaking group of Scyths or a kindred people who lived on the steppe east of the Caspian Sea. Although Herodotus obviously understood the value of mounted warriors, he also appreciated the fact that the horse played other important roles in the lives of the Massagetae. For example, Herodotus notes that the Massagetae "sow no grain." On what does he say they lived? The milk that he claims served as their principal drink undoubtedly came from mares, too. And horses also were important in the religious life of the Massagetae (why were horses sacrificed to the sun god?).

Sources 7, 9, and 11 demonstrate clearly the power of the mounted warrior. How did the introduction of cavalry change military tactics? How could nonmounted peoples defend themselves? How might weaponry and armor have changed, both for the mounted warriors as well as for foot soldiers battling against cavalry?

Source 8 is a fascinating wall hanging that comes from a grave in the Altai Mountains. In the picture, the Great Goddess is shown holding a tree of life in her hand. What symbolism do you see?

Source 10, a pottery figure of an officer who served China's first emperor, Qin Shi Huangdi, tells us a great deal about the horse's effect on Chinese life. What is he wearing? This is not the traditional garb of the Chinese, who preferred loose-fitting robes, and so where did this type of clothing originate?

Sources 12, 13, and 14 show the evolution of the wagon that could be drawn by a horse, or by a team of horses. What were the drawbacks of the Sumerian wagon (Source 12)? How did the Caucasian cart and wagon improve on the Sumerian (Source 13)? What were the problems with the Caucasian vehicles? How did the wagon in Source 14 finally reach the desired goal? What effects on human lifestyles might the evolution of the horse-drawn wagon have had? Think about commerce, migration, the ability to move more breakable objects (pottery), the ability to carry adequate food, and other implications.

Undoubtedly the chariot spurred a revolution in warfare. The Assyrians

[155]

would use massed vehicles in a frontal assault on an enemy while mounted archers attacked the enemy's flanks. The carnage, as you might imagine, could be ghastly. But the chariot had other important consequences as well. Note the chariot in Source 18, obviously not a military vehicle but a ceremonial one. And think about why a man would have wanted to have been buried with his chariot and horses, slain for the occasion (Source 17). Think about the chariot not in terms of its functions but rather in terms of its status.

Source 19 is a photograph of Greek figurines depicting an oxen-drawn plow and a horse-drawn chariot. Why couldn't the horse have been used to pull the plow (recall what you learned earlier about problems with the first wagons)? What alterations would have to be made before the plow was compatible with horse power? One answer was to breed and raise larger horses (the Clydesdale, for example, weighs between 1,600 and 2,200 pounds and has enormous pulling strength). Were there other (easier) solutions?

The evidence has given you some very good clues about the impact of the horse on human diet, dress, transportation, and warfare. From those clues, you should also be able to infer ways in which the horse also affected religion, social organization and classes, gender roles, and even child-raising (for example, how would boys be raised differently from girls, and who would perform the child-raising functions for each?). And you may be able to imagine other important effects as well.

EPILOGUE

The evolving relationship between horses and humans is far more than just a story of human ingenuity. At another level, it is the story of the interdependence of the earth's life forms and the interrelationships between human beings and other species in their environment. In one sense, the equine revolution is the history of two of those species— humans and horses—evolving together, each needing the other for its own particular evolution. Just as the original horse (Eohippus) is vastly different from the modern horse (*Equus caballus*), so also are humans today radically different from their Cro-Magnon ancestors who hunted horses and devoured them by the tens of thousands. The ways in which each has changed can be attributed in part to their relationships with one another. As human beings pave over pastures with asphalt and clear-cut forests for farmland, perhaps we should remember that earlier peoples owed their development—and perhaps even their own existence—to other species that today we threaten to eradicate.

Similarly, people today often regard their nomadic cousins as barbarians who made no contribution to human development. They forget that the nomads of the steppe of central Asia and the Ukraine were innovative and intelligent peoples, humans who tamed the horse, invented saddles, bridles, stirrups, and wheeled vehicles that gave people new possibilities and new visions. Often ignored, nomadic or seminomadic pastoralists are important groups in the larger drama of historical change.

To be sure, some of the innovations involving horses were used for war and terror. Referring to the invading Chaldeans, the Israelite prophet Habakkuk wrote, "Their horses are swifter than leopards, more fierce than the evening wolves" (Habakkuk 1:8). And the Roman chronicler Ammianus Marcellinus, on observing the Hun horsemen in 392 C.E., noted that "because of their extraordinary rapidity of movement . . . you would not hesitate to call them the most terrible of all warriors."[11] For their part, the Aztecs of Central America in 1519 C.E. were terrified of Cortes's horses (they called them deer).[12]

But, as you have learned from the evidence, the impact of the horse on human beings was far greater than just as a military weapon. The equine revolution altered the ways in which people waged war, yes, but also the ways in which they ate, dressed, traveled, related to one another, raised children, and confronted strangers. Indeed, the equine revolution brought about a human revolution as well.

11. J. Otto Maenchen-Helfen, *The World of the Huns* (Berkeley: University of California Press, 1973), p. 202.

12. See Miguel Leon-Portilla, ed., *The Broken Spears: The Aztec Account of the Conquest of Mexico*, trans. Lysander Kemp (Boston: Beacon Press, 1962), p. 30.

CHAPTER SEVEN

THE ACHIEVEMENTS OF AUGUSTUS

THE PROBLEM

For many centuries, the seat of power in Rome was the senate, a body of men drawn from the most powerful and prominent Roman families that made all major political and military decisions. Under the leadership of the senate, Rome had gradually taken control of the entire Italian peninsula. It then conquered southern France and much of Spain, and, after defeating Carthage in the Punic Wars, occupied northern Africa. These territorial conquests altered the nature of power in Rome, however, because the armies that conquered and held the new territories pledged loyalty to their military leaders and not to the senate. During the first century before Christ, several of these semi-independent armies challenged the senate's power, and civil war erupted in many parts of the Roman territory. The city itself was plundered several times by rival legions, and trade and communications were frequently disrupted. In 60 B.C.E.,

three army generals—Pompey, Crassus, and Julius Caesar—decided to form a political alliance, the triumvirate, leaving the senate intact but without much actual power.

All three of these generals were ambitious men who were unwilling to share power with anyone for very long. The senate was especially worried about Julius Caesar, who was gathering an increasingly larger army in Gaul (present-day France), and decided to put its trust in Pompey, whose base of power lay in Greece. (Crassus had meanwhile died in battle.) It ordered Caesar to disband his army and not to return to Rome, setting the Rubicon River near Ravenna in northern Italy as the line he must not cross. In 49 B.C.E., Caesar crossed the Rubicon (an expression we still use for an irrevocable decision), directly challenging the power of the senate and of Pompey. His armies quickly defeated those of the senate in Italy, and within a few months he held the entire Italian peninsula. From there Caesar turned his attention to Pompey's army, which his forces also defeated in 48 B.C.E., leaving him in control of all the Roman territory. Though he did not disband the senate, he did begin to shape the government to his liking, appointing officials and army officers and directly overseeing the administration of the provinces. He increased the size of the senate from 600 to 900 members by padding it with his followers, many of whom came from the provinces.

Caesar's meteoric and extralegal rise to power created great resentment among many Roman senators. Intensely proud of Roman traditions and of their own families' long-standing political power, they felt that Caesar was degrading the senate by adding unsophisticated rural representatives. A group of senators, led by Brutus and Cassius, decided to assassinate Caesar, which they did on the steps of the Roman senate on March 15, 44 B.C.E. The conspirators had not thought much beyond this act, however, and Caesar's death led not to peace but to a renewal of civil war. Some of the army was loyal to the assassins; some to Mark Antony, an associate of Caesar's; and some to Caesar's nephew and adopted son, Octavian. At first Mark Antony and Octavian cooperated to defeat the assassins, but then they turned against each other. The war dragged on for over a decade, with Octavian's forces gradually gaining more territory. Octavian won the support of many Romans by convincing them that Antony was plotting with Cleopatra, queen of Egypt, and in 31 B.C.E. his forces decisively defeated those of Antony at the naval battle of Actium. Antony and his ally Cleopatra committed suicide, leaving Octavian sole ruler of the Mediterranean world.

The problem now facing Octavian was the same one Julius Caesar had confronted twelve years earlier: how to transform a state won by military force into a stable political system. Caesar's answer—personal, autocratic rule—had led to his assassination at the hands of disgruntled senators. This lesson was not lost on Octavian, who realized that directly opposing the strong republican tradition in Rome could be very dangerous.

This tradition had arisen from both political reality—the senate had held actual power for many generations—and Roman political theory. The Romans held that their form of government had been given to them by the gods, who had conferred authority on Romulus, the mythical founder of Rome. That authority was later passed on to the senate, whose original function was to consult the gods about actions Rome should take. The senate in turn passed on authority to the rest of the government bureaucracy and to male heads of household, for in Rome households were considered, as in Athens, the smallest unit of government. Only male heads of household could sit in the senate, for only such individuals were regarded as worthy enough to consult the gods on matters of great importance to the state. This meant that Roman society was extremely patriarchal, with fathers having (at least in theory) absolute control over their wives, children, and servants.

This divinely ordained authority could always be distributed downward as the political bureaucracy grew, but to do away with existing institutions was extremely dangerous. Any radical transformation of the structure of government, especially any change in the authority of the senate, would have been regarded as impious.

Octavian had himself grown up in this tradition and at least to some degree shared these ideas about authority and the divine roots of the Roman political system. He realized that he could be more effective—and probably would live longer—if he worked through, rather than against, existing political institutions. Moreover, serious problems existed that had to be faced immediately, and after years of civil war, the govern-ment bureaucracy was no longer firmly in place to deal with them. Octavian needed to appoint officials and governors and reestablish law and order throughout Roman territory without offending the senate by acting like an autocrat or dictator.

In the eyes of many of his contemporaries, Octavian accomplished this admittedly difficult task very well. The senate conferred on him the name he is usually known by, Augustus, meaning "blessed" or "magnificent." Later historians regarded Augustus, rather than Julius Caesar, as the creator of the Roman Empire. Your task in this chapter will be to evaluate these judgments. How did Augustus transform the Roman republic into an empire? Why was he successful where Julius Caesar had not been?

SOURCES AND METHOD

As you think about these questions, you can see that they involve two somewhat different components: the process by which Augustus made changes and the results of these changes, or what we might term the means and the ends. Both are important to consider in assessing the achievements of any political leader, and both have been used by the contemporaries of Augustus, later Roman writers, and modern historians in evaluating the first Roman emperor's reign.

One of the best sources for observing the process of political change is laws, especially basic laws such as constitutions that set out governmental structure. Rome was a society in which law was extremely important and was explicitly written down, unlike many early societies, in which laws were handed down orally from generation to generation. As the Romans conquered Europe and the Mediterranean, they brought their legal system with them; consequently, Roman law forms the basis of most modern Western legal systems, with England and thus the United States the most notable exceptions.

We encounter some serious difficulties in using laws as our source material for the reign of Augustus, however. Given Roman ideas about authority and the strength of Roman tradition, would you expect him to have made major legal changes? Augustus, after all, described his aims and his actions as restoring republican government; if we use only the constitution of Rome as a source, we might be tempted to believe him. No new office was created for the emperor. Instead, he carefully preserved all traditional offices while gradually taking over many of them himself. Augustus was both a consul and a tribune, although the former office was usually reserved for a patrician and the latter for a plebeian. Later the senate appointed him imperator, or commander-in-chief of the army, and gave him direct control of many of the outlying provinces. These provinces furnished grain supplies essential to the people of Rome as well as soldiers loyal to Augustus rather than to the senate. The senate also gave him the honorary title of princeps (or "first citizen"), the title he preferred, which gradually lost its republican origins and gained the overtones of "monarch" evident in its modern English derivative, "prince." Augustus recognized the importance of religion to most Romans, and in 12 B.C.E. he had himself named pontifex maximus, or "supreme priest." He encouraged the building of temples dedicated to "Rome and Augustus," laying the foundations for the growth of a ruler cult closely linked with patriotic loyalty to Rome.

None of these innovations required any alteration in the basic constitution of Rome. What did change, however, was the tone of many laws, particularly those from the outlying provinces, where Augustus could be more open about the transformation he was working without bringing on the wrath of the senate. Our first two selections, then, are decrees and laws from Roman territories, where we can perhaps see some hint of the gradual development of the republic into an empire.

Source 1 is a decree by Augustus himself, an inscription dated 4 B.C.E. from the Greek city of Cyrene. Like all laws, it was passed in response to a perceived problem. What problem does the decree confront? What procedure does it provide to solve this problem? What complications does it anticipate, and how does it try to solve them? You will notice that the decree itself is set within a long framework giving the reasons it was issued. This is true for many laws, including the American Constitution, which begins, "We the people of the United States, in order to form a more perfect union, establish justice, insure domestic tranquillity." Why does Augustus say he is passing this law? This framework can also give you clues to the relationship between Augustus and the senate. How is this relationship described, and what does Augustus's attitude appear to be?

The second law is an inscription dated 11 C.E. from an altar in the city of Narbonne in southern France (Source 2). This law was passed by the local government, not the central Roman authorities. What does it order the population to do? Although the law itself does not state why it was passed, what might some reasons have been? What does the law indicate about attitudes toward Augustus and toward Roman authorities?

Another valuable source for examining the achievements of Augustus consists of the comments of his contemporaries and later Roman historians. Because Romans had such a strong sense of their own traditions, they were fascinated by history and were ever eager to point out how the hand of the gods operated in a way that allowed Rome to conquer most of the Western world. In the century before Augustus took over, it looked to many Romans as if the gods had forgotten Rome, leaving its citizens to kill each other in revolutions and civil wars. Augustus's military successes and political acumen seemed to show that he had the gods on his side, so writers delighted in extolling his accomplishments. Augustus's astuteness also extended to the world of literature and the arts, and he hired writers, sculptors, architects, and painters to glorify Rome, causing his own reputation no harm in the process. Many of the poems and histories are blatant hero worship, others communicate a more balanced view, and, because Augustus was not totally successful at winning everyone over to his side, some authors are openly critical.

Sources 3 through 6 are assessments by various Romans of Augustus's rule. As you read them, first try to gauge each author's basic attitude toward Augustus. What does he find to praise or blame? Does his judgment appear overly positive or negative? Does he sound objective? In answering these questions, you will need to pay attention not only to the content of the selection but also to the specific words each author chooses.

What kinds of adjectives does he use to describe Augustus's person and political actions? Once you have assessed the basic attitude of each author, identify what he regards as important in Augustus's reign. To what factors does he attribute Augustus's success? How does he describe the process by which the Roman republic was turned into an empire? What reasons does he give for Augustus's success and Julius Caesar's failure?

A bit of background on each of these selections will help you put them in better perspective. Source 3 was written by Horace, a poet living at the court of Augustus. This is an excerpt from his *Odes*, a literary rather than a primarily historical work. Source 4, an excerpt from Suetonius's biography of Augustus, was composed during the first half of the second century. Suetonius, private secretary to the emperor Hadrian, was keenly interested in the private as well as the public lives of the Roman emperors. Source 5 is taken from the long history of Rome by the politician and historian Dio Cassius (ca 150–235). Source 6 is drawn from the *Annals* of Tacitus, an orator and historian from a well-to-do Roman family. Sources 4 through 6 were written between one and two centuries after the events they present and are thus "history" as we know it, describing events after they happened.

Source 7 is a third type of evidence, namely, Augustus's own description of his rule. Usually called the *Res Gestae Divi Augusti*, it is an inscription he composed shortly before the end of his life. In this piece, following a long Roman tradition of inscriptions commemorating distinguished citizens, he describes the honors conferred on him as well as his accomplishments. Like all autobiographical statements, it is intended not simply as an objective description of a ruler's deeds but specifically as a vehicle for all that Augustus most wanted people to remember about this reign. Even though it is subjective, the *Res Gestae* is unique and invaluable as a primary source because it gives us Augustus's own version of the transformations he wrought in Roman society. As you read it, compare Augustus's descriptions of his deeds with those of the historians you have just read. What does Augustus regard as his most important accomplishments?

Many of the best sources for Augustus, of course, as for all of ancient history, are not written but archaeological. In fact, two of the sources we have looked at so far, the decree issued by Augustus and the inscription from Narbonne (Sources 1 and 2), are actually archaeological as well as written sources because they are inscriptions carved in stone. Thus, unlike other texts from the ancient world, including such basic ones as Plato's *Republic*, we have the original text and not a later copy.

Inscriptions are just one of many types of archaeological evidence. As the Romans conquered land after land, they introduced not only their legal code but their monetary system as well. Roman coins have been found throughout all of Europe and the Near East, far beyond the borders of the Roman Empire. Numismatics, the study of coins, can thus provide us with clues available from no other source, for coins have the great advantage of being both durable and valuable. Though their value sometimes works to render them less durable—people melt them down to make other coins or to use the metal in other ways—it also makes them one of the few material goods that people hide in great quantities. Their owners intend to dig them up later, of course, but die or forget where they have buried them, leaving great caches of coins for later archaeologists and historians.

Roman coins differ markedly from modern coins in some respects. Though the primary function of both is to serve as a means of exchange, Roman coins were also transmitters of political propaganda. One side usually displayed a portrait of the emperor, chosen very carefully by the emperor himself to emphasize certain qualities. The reverse side often depicted a recent victory, anniversary, or other important event, or the personification of an abstract quality of virtue such as health or liberty. Modern coins also feature portraits, pictures, and slogans, but they tend to stay the same for decades, and so we pay very little attention to what is on them. Roman emperors, on the other hand, issued new coins frequently, expecting people to look at them. Most of the people who lived in the Roman Empire were illiterate, with no chance to read about the illustrious deeds of the emperor, but they did come into contact with coins nearly every day. From these coins they learned what the emperor looked like, what he had recently done, or what qualities to associate with him, for even illiterate people could identify the symbols for such abstract virtues as liberty or victory. Over 100 different portraits of Augustus have been found on coins, providing us with additional clues about the achievements he most wanted to emphasize.

Once you have read the written documents, look at the two illustrations of coins, Sources 8 and 9. On the first, issued in 2 B.C.E., the lettering reads CAESAR AUGUSTUS DIVI F PATER PATRIAE, or "Augustus Caesar, son of a God, Father of the Fatherland." (Julius Caesar had been deified by the senate after his assassination, which is why Augustus called himself "son of a God.") Augustus is crowned with what appears to be a wreath of wheat stalks; this crown was the exclusive right of the priests of one of Rome's oldest religious groups that honored agricultural gods. The second coin, issued between 20 and 16 B.C.E., shows Augustus alongside the winged figure of the goddess Victory in a chariot atop a triumphal arch that stands itself on top of a viaduct; the inscription reads QUOD VIAE MUN SUNT, "because the roads have been reinforced." Think about the message Augustus was trying to convey with each of these coins. Even if you could not read the words, what impression of the emperor would you have from coins like these?

Issuing coins was one way for an emperor to celebrate and communicate his achievements; building was another. As you have read in Augustus's autobiography, he had many structures—stadiums, marketplaces, and temples—built for various purposes. He, and later Roman emperors, also built structures that were purely symbolic, the most impressive of which were celebratory arches, built to commemorate an achievement or a military victory. The second coin shows Augustus standing on top of such an arch; Source 10 is a photograph of the arch of Augustus that still stands at Rimini. This arch was built at one end of the Flaminian Way, which Augustus reconstructed, as you have read in his autobiography; a similar arch was built at the other end in Rome. As you did when looking at the coins, think about the message such an arch conveys. It was put up with the agreement of the senate; does it give you a sense of republicanism or empire?

Roads are another prime archaeological source, closely related to the aqueducts we examined in the chapter on the need for water in ancient societies. The Romans initially built roads to help their army move more quickly; once built, however, the road system facilitated trade and commerce as well. Roads are thus symbols of power as well as a means to maintain and extend it. Archaeologists have long studied the expansion of the Roman road system, and their findings can most easily be seen diagrammed on maps. Though maps do not have the immediacy of actual archaeological remains, they are based on such remains and enable us to detect patterns and make comparisons over time.

Sources 11 and 12 are maps of the major Roman roads existing before the reign of Augustus, those built or reconstructed during his reign, and the Roman road system at its farthest extent. Compare the first map with the information you have obtained from Augustus himself about his expansion of the frontiers of Rome (Source 7, paragraph 26). Notice that he mentions only the western part of the Roman Empire; do the roads built during his reign reflect this western orientation? What do the later road-building patterns shown in Source 12 tell us about the goals and successes of later Roman emperors?

THE EVIDENCE

Sources 1 through 3 from Naphtali Lewis and Meyer Reinhold, editors and translators, Roman Civilization, *vol. 2,* The Empire *(New York: Columbia University Press, 1955), pp. 39–42; p. 62; p. 20. © 1955 by Columbia University Press. Reprinted with the permission of the publisher.*

1. Decree Issued by Emperor Augustus, 4 B.C.E.

The Emperor Caesar Augustus, *pontifex maximus*, holding the tribunician power for the nineteenth year, declares:

A decree of the senate was passed in the consulship of Gaius Calvisius and Lucius Passienus, with me as one of those present at the writing. Since it affects the welfare of the allies of the Roman people, I have decided to send it into the provinces, appended to this my prefatory edict, so that it may be known to all who are under our care. From this it will be evident to all the inhabitants of the provinces how much both I and the senate are concerned that none of our subjects should suffer any improper treatment or any extortion.

DECREE OF THE SENATE

Whereas the consuls Gaius Calvisius Sabinus and Lucius Passienus Rufus spoke "Concerning matters affecting the security of the allies of the Roman people which the Emperor Caesar Augustus, our *princeps*, following the recommendation of the council which he had drawn by lot from among the senate, desired to be brought before the senate by us," the senate passed the following decree:

Whereas our ancestors established legal process for extortion so that the allies might more easily be able to take action for any wrongs done them and recover moneys extorted from them, and whereas this type of process is sometimes very expensive and troublesome for those in whose interest the law was enacted, because poor people or persons weak with illness or age are dragged from far-distant provinces as witnesses, the senate decrees as follows:

If after the passage of this decree of the senate any of the allies, desiring to recover extorted moneys, public or private, appear and so depose before one of the magistrates who is authorized to convene the senate, the magistrate—except where the extorter faces a capital charge—shall bring them before the senate as soon as possible and shall assign them any advocate they themselves request to speak in their behalf before the senate; but no one who has in accordance with the laws been excused from this duty shall be required to serve as advocate against his will. . . .

The judges chosen shall hear and inquire into only those cases in which a man is accused of having appropriated money from a community or from private parties; and, rendering their decision within thirty days, they shall order him to restore such sum of money, public or private, as the accusers prove was taken from them. Those whose duty it is to inquire into and pronounce judgment in these cases shall, until they complete the inquiry and pronounce their judgment, be exempted from all public duties except public worship. . . .

The senate likewise decrees that the judges who are selected in accordance with this decree of the senate shall pronounce in open court each his several finding, and what the majority pronounces shall be the verdict.

2. Inscription from the City of Narbonne, 11 C.E.

In the consulship of Titus Statilius Taurus and Lucius Cassius Longinus, September 22. Vow taken to the divine spirit of Augustus by the populace of the Narbonensians in perpetuity: "May it be good, favorable, and auspicious to the Emperor Caesar Augustus, son of a god, father of his country, *pontifex maximus*, holding the tribunician power for the thirty-fourth year; to his wife, children, and house; to the Roman senate and people; and to the colonists[1] and residents of the Colonia Julia Paterna of Narbo Martius,[2] who have bound themselves to worship his divine spirit in perpetuity!"

The populace of the Narbonensians has erected in the forum at Narbo an altar at which every year on September 23—the day on which the good fortune

1. The word *colonist* has a very specific meaning in Roman history. Colonists were Romans, often retired soldiers, who were granted land in the outlying provinces in order to build up Roman strength there. They were legally somewhat distinct from native residents, which is why this law uses the phrase "colonists and residents" to make it clear that both groups were required to follow its provisions.

2. The long phrase "Colonia Julia Pasterna of Narbo Martius" is the official and complete Roman name for the town of Narbo, which we now call Narbonne.

of the age bore him to be ruler of the world—three Roman *equites*[3] from the populace and three freedmen shall sacrifice one animal each and shall at their own expense on that day provide the colonists and residents with incense and wine for supplication to his divine spirit. And on September 24 they shall likewise provide incense and wine for the colonists and residents. Also on January 1 they shall provide incense and wine for the colonists and residents. Also on January 7, the day on which he first entered upon the command of the world, they shall make supplication with incense and wine, and shall sacrifice one animal each, and shall provide incense and wine for the colonists and residents on that day. And on May 31, because on that day in the consulship of Titus Statilius Taurus and Manius Aemilius Lepidus he reconciled the populace to the decurions,[4] they shall sacrifice one animal each and shall provide the colonists and residents with incense and wine for supplication to his divine spirit. And of these three Roman *equites* and three freedmen one. . . . [The rest of this inscription is lost.]

3. From Horace, *Odes*

Thine age, O Caesar, has brought back fertile crops to the fields and has restored to our own Jupiter the military standards stripped from the proud columns of the Parthians;[5] has closed Janus' temple[6] freed of wars; has put reins on license overstepping righteous bounds; has wiped away our sins and revived the ancient virtues through which the Latin name and the might of Italy waxed great, and the fame and majesty of our empire were spread from the sun's bed in the west to the east. As long as Caesar is the guardian of the state, neither civil dissension nor violence shall banish peace, nor wrath that forges swords and brings discord and misery to cities. Not those who drink the deep Danube shall violate the orders of Caesar, nor the Getae, nor the Seres,[7] nor the perfidious Parthians, nor those born by the Don River. And we, both on profane and sacred days, amidst the gifts of merry Bacchus, together with our wives and children, will first duly pray to the gods; then, after the tradition of our ancestors, in songs to the accompaniment of Lydian flutes we will hymn leaders whose duty is done.

3. **equites:** cavalry of the Roman army.

4. **decurion:** member of a town council.

5. The Parthians were an empire located in the region occupied by present-day Iraq. They had defeated Roman armies led by Mark Antony and had taken the Roman military standards, that is, the flags and banners of the army they defeated. Augustus recovered these standards, an important symbolic act, even though he did not conquer the Parthians.

6. This was a small temple in Rome that was ordered closed whenever peace reigned throughout the whole Roman Empire. During the reign of Augustus it was closed three times.

7. The Getae and the Seres were people who lived in the regions occupied by present-day Romania and Ukraine.

Source 4 from Suetonius, The Lives of the Twelve Caesars, *edited and translated by Joseph Gavorse (New York: Modern Library, 1931), p. 89.*

4. From Suetonius, *Life of Augustus*

The whole body of citizens with a sudden unanimous impulse proffered him the title of "father of his country"—first the plebs, by a deputation sent to Antium, and then, because he declined it, again at Rome as he entered the theater, which they attended in throngs, all wearing laurel wreaths; the senate afterwards in the senate house, not by a decree or by acclamation, but through Valerius Messala. He, speaking for the whole body, said: "Good fortune and divine favor attend thee and thy house, Caesar Augustus; for thus we feel that we are praying for lasting prosperity for our country and happiness for our city. The senate in accord with the Roman people hails thee 'Father of thy Country.' " Then Augustus with tears in his eyes replied as follows (and I have given his exact words, as I did those of Messala): "Having attained my highest hopes, members of the senate, what more have I to ask of the immortal gods than that I may retain this same unanimous approval of yours to the very end of my life?"

Sources 5 through 7 from Naphtali Lewis and Meyer Reinhold, editors and translators, Roman Civilization, *vol. 2,* The Empire *(New York: Columbia University Press, 1955), pp. 4–8; p. 4; pp. 9–10, 12, 14–16, 17, 19. © 1955 by Columbia University Press. Reprinted with the permission of the publisher.*

5. From Dio Cassius, *Roman History*

In this way the power of both people and senate passed entirely into the hands of Augustus, and from this time there was, strictly speaking, a monarchy; for monarchy would be the truest name for it, even if two or three men later held the power jointly. Now, the Romans so detested the title "monarch" that they called their emperors neither dictators nor kings nor anything of this sort. Yet, since the final authority for the government devolves upon them, they needs must be kings. The offices established by the laws, it is true, are maintained even now, except that of censor; but the entire direction and administration is absolutely in accordance with the wishes of the one in power at the time. And yet, in order to preserve the appearance of having this authority not through their power but by virtue of the laws, the emperors have taken to themselves all the offices (including the titles) which under the Republic possessed great power with the consent of the people—with the exception of the dictatorship. Thus, they very often become consuls, and they are always styled proconsuls whenever they are outside the *pomerium*.[8] The title *imperator* is held by them for life, not only by those who have won victories in battle but also by all the rest, to indicate their absolute power, instead of the title "king" or "dictator." These latter titles they have never assumed since they fell out of use in the constitution, but the actuality of those offices is secured to them by the appellation *imperator*. By virtue of the titles named, they secure the right to make levies, collect funds, declare war, make peace, and rule foreigners and citizens alike everywhere and always—even to the extent of being able to put to death both *equites* and senators inside the *pomerium*—and all the other powers once granted to the consuls and other officials possessing independent authority; and by virtue of holding the censorship they investigate our lives and morals as well as take the census, enrolling some in the equestrian and senatorial orders and removing others from these orders according to their will. By virtue of being consecrated in all the priesthoods and, in addition, from their right to bestow most of them upon others, as well as from the fact that, even if two or three persons rule jointly, one of them is *pontifex maximus*, they hold in their own hands supreme authority over all matters both profane and sacred. The tribunician power, as it is called, which once the most influential men used to hold, gives them the right to nullify the effects of the measures taken by any other official, in case they do not approve, and makes their persons inviolable; and if they appear to be wronged in even the slightest degree, not merely by deed but even by word, they may destroy the guilty party as one accursed, without a trial.

Thus by virtue of these Republican titles they have clothed themselves with all the powers of the government, so that they actually possess all the prerogatives of kings without the usual title. For the appellation "Caesar" or "Augustus" confers upon them no actual power but merely shows in the one case that they are the successors of their family line, and in the other the splendor of their rank. The name "Father" perhaps gives them a certain authority over us all—the authority which fathers once had over their children; yet it did not signify this at first, but betokened honor and served as an admonition both to them to love their subjects as they would their children; and to their subjects to revere them as they would their fathers. . . .

The senate as a body, it is true, continued to sit in judgment as before, and in certain cases transacted business with embassies and envoys from both peoples and kings; and the people and the plebs, moreover, continued to come together for the elections; but nothing was actually done that did not please Caesar. At any rate, in the case of those who were to hold office, he himself selected and nominated some; and though he left the election of others in the hands of the people and the plebs, in accordance with the ancient practice, yet he took care that no persons should hold office who were unfit or elected as the result of factious combinations or bribery.

---

8. **pomerium:** the city limits of Rome.

Such were the arrangements made, generally speaking, at that time; for in reality Caesar himself was destined to have absolute power in all matters for life, because he was not only in control of money matters (nominally, to be sure, he had separated the public funds from his own, but as a matter of fact he spent the former also as he saw fit) but also in control of the army. At all events, when his ten-year period came to an end, there was voted him another five years, then five more, after that ten, and again another ten, and then ten for the fifth time, so that by the succession of ten-year periods he continued to be sole ruler for life. And it is for this reason that the subsequent monarchs, though no longer appointed for a specified period but for their whole life once for all, nevertheless always held a celebration every ten years, as if then renewing their sovereignty once more; and this is done even at the present day.

Now, Caesar had received many privileges previously, when the question of declining the sovereignty and that of apportioning the provinces were under discussion. For the right to fasten laurels to the front of the imperial residence and to hang the civic crown above the doors was then voted him to symbolize the fact that he was always victorious over enemies and savior of the citizens. The imperial palace is called Palatium, not because it was ever decreed that this should be its name but because Caesar dwelt on the Palatine and had his military headquarters there. . . . Hence, even if the emperor resides somewhere else, his dwelling retains the name of Palatium.

And when he had actually completed the reorganization, the name Augustus was at length bestowed upon him by the senate and by the people. . . . He took the title of Augustus, signifying that he was more than human; for all most precious and sacred objects are termed augusta. For which reason they called him also in Greek sebastos . . . meaning an august person.

6. From Tacitus, *Annals*

After the death of Brutus and Cassius, there was no longer any army loyal to the Republic. . . . Then, laying aside the title of triumvir and parading as a consul, and professing himself satisfied with the tribunician power for the protection of the plebs, Augustus enticed the soldiers with gifts, the people with grain, and all men with the allurement of peace, and gradually grew in power, concentrating in his own hands the functions of the senate, the magistrates, and the laws. No one opposed him, for the most courageous had fallen in battle or in the proscription. As for the remaining nobles, the readier they were for slavery, the higher were they raised in wealth and offices, so that, aggrandized by the revolution, they preferred the safety of the present to the perils of the past. Nor did the provinces view with disfavor this state of affairs, for they distrusted the government of the senate and the people on account of the struggles of the powerful and the rapacity of the officials, while the protection afforded them by the laws was inoperative, as the provinces were repeatedly thrown into confusion by violence, intrigue, and finally bribery. . . .

At home all was peaceful; the officials bore the same titles as before. The younger generation was born after the victory of Actium, and even many of the older generation had been born during the civil wars. How few were left who had seen the Republic!

Thus the constitution had been transformed, and there was nothing at all left of the good old way of life. Stripped of equality, all looked to the directives of a *princeps* with no apprehension for the present, while Augustus in the vigorous years of his life maintained his power, that of his family, and peace.

7. From Augustus, *Res Gestae Divi Augusti*

1. At the age of nineteen, on my own initiative and at my own expense, I raised an army by means of which I liberated the Republic, which was oppressed by the tyranny of a faction. For which reason the senate, with honorific decrees, made me a member of its order in the consulship of Gaius Pansa and Aulus Hirtius, giving me at the same time consular rank in voting, and granted me the *imperium*. It ordered me as propraetor, together with the consuls, to see to it that the state suffered no harm. Moreover, in the same year, when both consuls had fallen in the war, the people elected me consul and a triumvir for the settlement of the commonwealth.

2. Those who assassinated my father I drove into exile, avenging their crime by due process of law; and afterwards when they waged war against the state, I conquered them twice on the battlefield.

3. I waged many wars throughout the whole world by land and by sea, both civil and foreign, and when victorious I spared all citizens who sought pardon. Foreign peoples who could safely be pardoned I preferred to spare rather than to extirpate. . . . Though the Roman senate and people unitedly agreed that I should be elected soul guardian of the laws and morals with supreme authority, I refused to accept any office offered me which was contrary to the traditions of our ancestors. . . .

9. The senate decreed that vows for my health should be offered up every fifth year by the consuls and priests. In fulfillment of those vows, games were often celebrated during my lifetime, sometimes by the four most distinguished colleges of priests, sometimes by the consuls. Moreover, the whole citizen body, with one accord, both individually and as members of municipalities, prayed continuously for my health at all the shrines.

10. My name was inserted, by decree of the senate, in the hymn of the Salian priests. And it was enacted by law that I should be sacrosanct in perpetuity and that I should possess the tribunician power as long as I live. I declined to become *pontifex maximus* in place of a colleague while he was still alive, when the people offered me that priesthood, which my father had held. A few years

later, in the consulship of Publius Sulpicius and Gaius Valgius, I accepted this priesthood, when death removed the man who had taken possession of it at a time of civil disturbance; and from all Italy a multitude flocked to my election such as had never previously been recorded at Rome. . . .

17. Four times I came to the assistance of the treasury with my own money, transferring to those in charge of the treasury 150,000,000 sesterces. And in the consulship of Marcus Lepidus and Lucius Arruntius I transferred out of my own patrimony 170,000,000 sesterces to the soldiers' bonus fund, which was established on my advice for the purpose of providing bonuses for soldiers who had completed twenty or more years of service.

18. From the year in which Gnaeus Lentulus and Publius Lentulus were consuls, whenever the provincial taxes fell short, in the case sometimes of 100,000 persons and sometimes of many more, I made up their tribute in grain and in money from my own grain stores and my own patrimony. . . .

20. I repaired the Capitol and the theater of Pompey with enormous expenditures on both works, without having my name inscribed on them. I repaired the conduits of the aqueducts which were falling into ruin in many places because of age, and I doubled the capacity of the aqueduct called Marcia by admitting a new spring into its conduit. I completed the Julian Forum and the basilica which was between the temple of Castor and the temple of Saturn, works begun and far advanced by my father, and when the same basilica was destroyed by fire, I enlarged its site and began rebuilding the structure, which is to be inscribed with the names of my sons; and in case it should not be completed while I am still alive, I left instructions that the work be completed by my heirs. In my sixth consulship I repaired eighty-two temples of the gods in the city, in accordance with a resolution of the senate, neglecting none which at that time required repair. In my seventh consulship I reconstructed the Flaminian Way from the city as far as Ariminum,[9] and also all the bridges except the Mulvian and the Minucian. . . .

22. I gave a gladiatorial show three times in my own name, and five times in the names of my sons or grandsons; at these shows about 10,000 fought. Twice I presented to the people in my own name an exhibition of athletes invited from all parts of the world, and a third time in the name of my grandson. I presented games in my own name four times, and in addition twenty-three times in the place of other magistrates. On behalf of the college of fifteen, as master of that college, with Marcus Agrippa as my colleague, I celebrated the Secular Games[10] in the consulship of Gaius Furnius and Gaius Silanus. In my

9. Present-day Rimini, Italy.

10. The Secular Games were an enormous series of athletic games, festivals, and banquets that Augustus ordered held in 17 B.C.E. Though called "secular," they were held in honor of the gods and were directed by the College of Fifteen, a board that oversaw sacrifices to the gods. All adult Roman citizens were expected to view the games out of religious duty.

thirteenth consulship I was the first to celebrate the Games of Mars, which subsequently the consuls, in accordance with a decree of the senate and a law, have regularly celebrated in the succeeding years. Twenty-six times I provided for the people, in my own name or in the names of my sons or grandsons, hunting spectacles of African wild beasts in the circus or in the Forum or in the amphitheaters; in these exhibitions about 3,500 animals were killed.

23. I presented to the people an exhibition of a naval battle across the Tiber where the grove of the Caesars now is, having had the site excavated 1,800 feet in length and 1,200 feet in width. In this exhibition thirty beaked ships, triremes or biremes, and in addition a great number of smaller vessels engaged in combat. On board these fleets, exclusive of rowers, there were about 3,000 combatants. . . .

26. I extended the frontiers of all the provinces of the Roman people on whose boundaries were peoples subject to our empire. I restored peace to the Gallic and Spanish provinces and likewise to Germany, that is, to the entire region bounded by the Ocean from Gades to the mouth of the Elbe River. I caused peace to be restored in the Alps, from the region nearest to the Adriatic Sea as far as the Tuscan Sea, without undeservedly making war against any people. My fleet sailed the Ocean from the mouth of the Rhine eastward as far as the territory of the Cimbrians,[11] to which no Roman previously had penetrated either by land or by sea. . . .

34. In my sixth and seventh consulships, after I had put an end to the civil wars, having attained supreme power by universal consent, I transferred the state from my own power to the control of the Roman senate and people. For this service of mine I received the title of Augustus by decree of the senate, and the doorposts of my house were publicly decked with laurels, the civic crown was affixed over my doorway, and a golden shield was set up in the Julian senate house, which, as the inscription on this shield testifies, the Roman senate and people gave me in recognition of my valor, clemency, justice, and devotion. After that time I excelled all in authority, but I possessed no more power than the others who were my colleagues in each magistracy.

35. When I held my thirteenth consulship, the senate, the equestrian order, and the entire Roman people gave me the title of "father of the country" and decreed that this title should be inscribed in the vestibule of my house, in the Julian senate house, and in the Augustan Forum on the pedestal of the chariot which was set up in my honor by decree of the senate. At the time I wrote this document I was in my seventy-sixth year.

11. Near present-day Hamburg, Germany.

Sources 8 and 9 from The American Numismatic Society, New York.

8. Roman Coin Issued 2 B.C.E.

9. Roman Coin Issued 20–16 B.C.E.

Source 10 from Alinari/Art Resource. Photo by Stab D. Anderson, 1931.

10. Arch of Augustus at Rimini

Source 11 adapted from sketches by Merry E. Wiesner.

11. Main Roman Roads, 31 BCE–14 CE

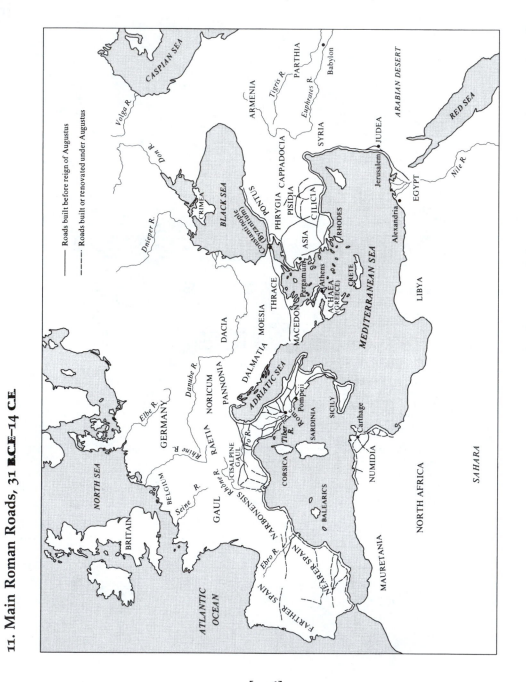

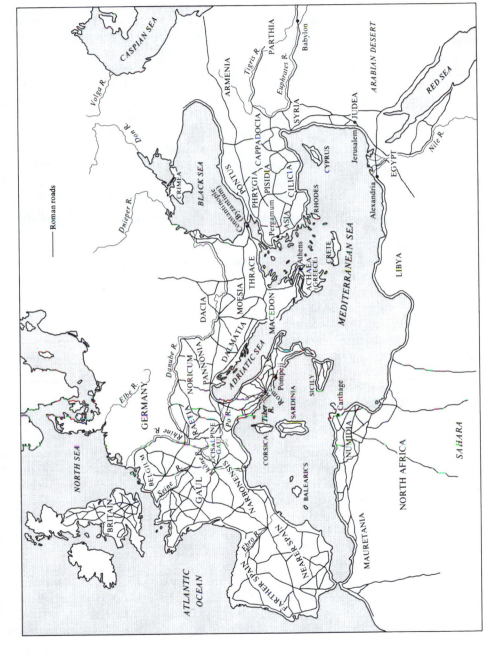

Source 12 from Victor W. Von Hagen, *The Roads That Led to Rome*
(Cleveland and New York: World Publishing Co., © 1967 by George
Weidenfeld and Nicolson, London), pp. 18–19.

12. Main Roman Roads at Their Greatest Extent, 180 C.E.

QUESTIONS TO CONSIDER

Now that you have examined various pieces of evidence, you need to put them together to arrive at a conclusion that you can support. Do not worry about not having all the evidence you need; no historian can ever discover "all" the facts about an event or person. He or she makes conclusions on the basis of the evidence available, alters those conclusions when new material is discovered, and uses those conclusions as a framework for further research. In this respect, historians operate just like physicists learning how the universe works. Do not worry if some of your sources disagree; ten people who witness an auto accident often come up with ten quite contradictory accounts of the event. Why might accounts of Augustus's rule be even more contradictory?

The sources have made you aware of the operation of Roman government on two levels: that of the formal constitution, which remained a republic, and that of the actual locus of power, which was increasingly the emperor. The changes that Augustus instituted thus took place at the second level, and in many areas we can ignore the formal constitution of Rome in describing the process of change. Comparing all the sources, how would you describe the means by which Augustus transformed the republic into a different type of government? Which steps were most important? Which observers seemed to have the clearer view of this process, Augustus himself and those living during his lifetime, or later

historians? In considering this last question, you need to think about the advantages and disadvantages of eyewitness reports versus later, secondary accounts.

The second question concerns results, not process: Why was Augustus successful? To answer this, we must consider not only the changes themselves, but people's perceptions of them. A ruler's place in history depends not only on real accomplishments but also on how these accomplishments are perceived and judged by later generations. Rulers perceived as good or successful are often given credit for everything good that happened during their reigns, even if they had nothing to do with it. Conversely, rulers regarded as unsuccessful, weak, or bad get blamed for many things that were not their fault. A reputation is generally based on actual achievements, but occasionally it is also determined by a ruler's successful manipulation of public opinion, and sometimes by that manipulation alone.

Augustus clearly recognized the importance of public opinion, which in Rome was tied to upholding tradition. How does he make use of Roman traditions in the laws and coins he issues? How do other observers judge his connection with tradition? Many of Rome's traditions were incorporated into public rituals and ceremonies. What sorts of ceremonies did Romans participate in or view? How did Augustus use these ceremonies to demonstrate his power or his personal connections with Roman tradition? Along with rituals, titles are also important demonstrations of power. What does Augustus call himself and what do others call him, both in the written documents and on the coins? Why is there so much discussion of his accepting or not accepting various titles?

Now that you have considered the opinions of a range of commentators, assessed some actual legal changes and road-building patterns, examined some coins, and heard from Augustus himself, you are ready to answer the questions: How did Augustus transform the Roman republic into an empire? Why was he successful? Once you have made your assessment, think about how you would use it to structure future research. What other evidence would be useful in supporting your conclusions? Where might you go to find that evidence?

EPILOGUE

Though Augustus said that his aim was a restoration of the republic, in reality he transformed Roman government into an empire ruled by one individual. His reign is generally termed the *Principate*, a word taken from Augustus's favorite title *princeps*, but the rulers of Rome after him did not hesitate to use the title *emperor*. Like him, they also retained the titles *pontifex maximus*, supreme priest, and *imperator*, commander-in-chief. It is interesting to see how many of our words denoting aspects of royal rule come from Augustus: not only *prince*, *emperor*, and *czar* (the Russian variant of "Caesar") but also *palace*, from Palatine, the hill where Augustus had his house.

The emperors who came after Augustus built on his achievements, both literally and figuratively. They extended the borders of the Roman Empire even farther, so that at its largest it would stretch from Scotland to the Sudan and from Spain to Syria. The Roman road system was expanded to more than 50,000 miles, longer than the current interstate highway system in the United States; some of those roads are still usable today. Roman coins continued to be stamped with the emperor's picture and have been found as far away as southern India. Later emperors continued Augustus's building projects in Rome and throughout the empire. Vespasian built the Colosseum, which could seat 50,000 people; Trajan, the Forum with a number of different buildings and an enormous 125-foot column with his statue on top; Hadrian, the Pantheon and a wall dividing England and Scotland. The emperor Nero may have even ordered part of Rome burned to make room for his urban renewal projects.

Augustus's successors also continued his centralization of power. His stepson Tiberius stripped the assemblies of their right to elect magistrates, and later emperors took this power away from the senate as well. Bureaucrats appointed by the emperor oversaw the grain trade, the army, and the collection of taxes, with the senate gradually dwindling into a rubber stamp for the emperor's decisions. New territories were ruled directly by the emperor through governors and generals; in these jurisdictions, the senate did not have even the pretense of power.

The cult of ruler worship initiated somewhat tentatively in the provinces under Augustus grew enormously after his death, when, like Julius Caesar, he was declared a god. Though Romans officially deified only the memory of deceased emperors, some emperors were not willing to wait that long. Caligula declared himself a god at the age of twenty-five, spent much of his time in the temple of Castor and Pollux, and talked to the statue of Jupiter as an equal. Though Caligula was probably insane and later was stabbed to death, ruler worship in general was serious business for most Romans, closely linked as it was to tradition and patriotism. Groups like the Christians who did not offer sacrifices to the emperor or at least to the emperor's "genius" were felt to be unpatriotic, disloyal, and probably traitorous.

Thus in many ways Augustus laid the foundation for the success and durability of his empire. Historians have always been fascinated with the demise of the Roman Empire, but considering the fact that it lasted more than 400 years after Augustus in western Europe—and, in a significantly altered form, almost 1,500 years in eastern Europe—a more appropriate question might be why it lasted so long. Though the weaknesses that led to the empire's eventual collapse were also outgrowths of the reign of Augustus, the latter still represents a remarkable success story.

We must be careful of attributing too much to one man, however. As we have seen, Augustus had an extremely effective network of supporters and advisers, including Rome's most important men of letters. Their rendering of the glories of Roman civilization and the brilliance of Augustus has shaped much of what has been written about Rome since; you may only need to check the adjectives used in your text to describe Augustus to confirm this. Myths or exaggerations told about a ruler die hard, especially those that have been repeated for nearly 2,000 years.

CHAPTER EIGHT

THE DEVELOPMENT OF ORTHODOXY

IN EARLY CHRISTIANITY

The world in which Christianity began was one in which people practiced many different religions. The Romans generally tolerated the religions of the people they conquered as long as they did not appear to be politically or socially revolutionary, and as long as the people would also participate in ceremonies that honored and appeased the Roman gods. Like most of the peoples of the ancient world, the Romans were *polytheists* who honored many gods and easily added new gods or goddesses to their belief systems. In fact, Romans often adopted the gods of conquered peoples, believing that additional gods would simply make the Roman state stronger. In their religious life, most people who lived in the Roman Empire were *syncretistic*, that is, they not only easily added new deities, but also combined parts of various religious and philosophical systems together in an individualized way.

One group living within the Roman Empire had very different religious ideas, however. These were the Jews, who were strictly *monotheistic*, believing that they were to worship only one single god, whom they termed *Yahweh*. They would thus not participate in events that honored other gods or those in which living or deceased Roman emperors were described as divine. Though one would think this would have led to trouble with Roman authorities, usually it did not, for the Romans recognized that Jewish monotheism had a long tradition behind it. The Romans' respect for their own traditions led them to make an exception in the case of the Jews; the Jews were also not actively seeking converts, so the Romans did not have to worry that Judaism would spread.

Though all Jews were monotheistic, during the lifetime of Jesus of Nazareth (ca 5 B.C.E.–29 C.E.), on whose ideas Christianity was based, there were a number of groups within Judaism that stressed different parts of the Jewish tradition or had slightly

[181]

different ideas. Thus when Jesus' early followers—all of them Jews—began to talk about his ideas, they appeared to Roman authorities as simply another Jewish sect. In fact, many of Jesus' early followers, who regarded him as the Messiah (the one foretold in Jewish prophecy who would bring about a period of happiness for Jews), thought of their movement as one primarily to reform Judaism.

By the last half of the first century, this way of thinking began to change, as those who followed Jesus' ideas began to set themselves apart from other Jews by participating in a special commemorative meal and by aggressively preaching. Many of them began to preach to non-Jews (termed *Gentiles*), leading to disagreements about whether those who accepted Jesus' ideas first had to become Jews to become full members of the movement. This issue was resolved at a meeting in Jerusalem in favor of the more universalist position, for it was decided that Gentile followers should have equal status without having to be circumcised or follow Jewish laws and customs. This decision enabled the movement to spread much more widely, with men and women traveling as missionaries throughout the Roman Empire. Instead of being a group within Judaism, Jesus' followers were now a distinct religion, taking the name that the Romans had first given them, *Christians,* a word derived from Christ, a Greek translation of the Hebrew word *Messiah* and a title given to Jesus by his followers.

Though Christians separated themselves from Jews, they took many of their religious ideas from Judaism, most importantly its monotheism, moral standards, and refusal to honor other gods. Christians also refused to participate in public religious ceremonies or honor the emperor as divine, but because their ideas were new and not part of a long-standing tradition, Romans did not feel that they warranted the same respect that Jews did. Beginning with the reign of the emperor Nero (54– 68), Roman authorities began to persecute Christians, decreeing the death penalty for any who would not recant. These persecutions were stepped up during periods of unrest in the Empire, when Christians were blamed for provoking the displeasure of the traditional gods by refusing to honor them, so that the gods allowed turmoil and crisis. Many Christian beliefs and practices also appeared to be suspect or dangerous to Roman eyes: They talked about their king, who sounded like a rival to the emperor, and held ceremonies in which they claimed to eat the body and blood of this king, which to Romans appeared to be cannibalism; husbands and wives called each other brother and sister, suggesting incest; Christians spoke of an imminent end of the world, which would of course mean the end of the Roman Empire, and so appeared to be preaching political revolution. Christians' refusal to participate in the state cult implied disloyalty to Rome. They held secret meetings, which only the initiates could attend; this suggested they had something to hide and contrasted sharply with the public religious ceremonies common in Roman polytheism.

Despite Roman suspicion, however, the campaigns against Christians were never very thorough. Most of the emperors and the governors of Roman provinces followed the advice of the emperor Trajan (98–117) that Christians were not to be sought out, but only arrested if a responsible citizen accused them, and only executed if they did not recant. He recommended that authorities avoid general investigations or listening to rumors, and called for the arrest of anyone who accused someone of being a Christian without clear proof. Trajan and many of the emperors who followed him thus did not take Christianity very seriously, and let local governors decide how to handle Christians in their territories. The persecutions that did take place often led to dramatic public martyrdoms, giving Christianity great publicity and convincing many people throughout the Roman Empire that this new religion offered something distinctive.

The heroism of the early martyrs combined with the sporadic nature of the persecutions gave Christianity breathing space to expand. The number of Christians, particularly in urban areas, grew slowly but steadily, and began to include highly educated people who were familiar with a wide variety of religious and philosophical ideas. This was a time in the Roman Empire when many people appear to have been dissatisfied with traditional religion, and a number of groups that offered salvation to converts gained in popularity. Because it combined a promise of life after death with a spirit of community and gave believers a sense of purpose in life, Christianity grew faster than most other religions. This growth created problems for Christianity, however, for there was great diversity among early Christian communities, with each interpreting the accounts of Jesus' life related to them by missionaries and the main points of his message slightly differently. Because they had been brought up in a tradition of religious syncretism, many people adopted only some of the ideas of Christianity or combined Christian ideas with those from other sources. The sayings of Jesus and the accounts of his preaching were often enigmatic, so that people were able to use them in support of widely differing ideas.

This diversity was troubling to many of the leaders of early Christianity, who thought it extremely important that there be unity among all those who called themselves Christians. They thus began to declare certain ideas as *orthodox*, that is, acceptable or correct, and others as *heretical*, that is, unacceptable or incorrect, breaking with the Greco-Roman tradition of religious syncretism and toleration. They realized this could not be done simply on their own authority, but that some type of standards needed to be devised by which to judge ideas and practices. The establishment of orthodox ideas and authoritative standards did not happen in a vacuum, however, but was shaped by the preconceptions of early Church leaders and the social and political situation of the Roman Empire in which they lived. Your task in this chapter will be to use the

[183]

writings of both those authors judged orthodox and those judged heretical to assess the way in which early Christianity developed. How was the initial diversity of Christianity changed into a split between orthodoxy and heresy? What ideas and institutions came to be the most important determinants of orthodoxy?

SOURCES AND METHOD

Studying the history of any religious movement poses special problems for historians, for sources are very rarely objective. Even in the tolerant Roman Empire, some religious ideas were judged dangerous or deviant, so the writings of these groups were destroyed or not preserved, and the only record we have of them is from hostile observers. This is even more the case with Christianity, for most of our records come from those whose ideas were later judged orthodox. It is thus important for us to remember when using such sources that orthodoxy and heresy are relative terms. Only those who don't accept a belief label it as a heresy; those who accept it regard it as correct, of course, so that in their minds the others are the heretics. What we now call heresies within Christianity are beliefs that were rejected as orthodoxy was established.

Along with problems created by subjective sources, we may also have more difficulties in achieving unbiased assessments of the history of religion than other historical topics because we have an intellectual, spiritual, or emotional commitment to certain religious ideas. This does not mean, however, that we should avoid religious topics, particularly when studying Western history in which Judaism, Christianity, and Islam have been key factors, but that we should be cognizant of our own prejudices. Our job as historians is to understand people's religious ideas within their historical context and to see how religious faith manifested itself in historically observable phenomena; it is not to judge whether certain religious ideas are right or wrong. The people we are studying (and perhaps we ourselves) may believe certain developments to be the result of divine will or action, but as historians, we must use the same standards about how or why something happened that we would use in evaluating any event in the past and concentrate on the human actors. Perhaps the most important part of our methodology in exploring religious topics is thus to approach them with both objectivity and respect.

Not only are many of our sources subjective, but very few of them were written simply to describe things that have happened. Rather, they were written to bolster the faith of other followers, to correct perceived errors, or to win converts. You can see this clearly in studying the earliest decades of Christianity. The only contemporary written sources that describe the events in the life of Jesus and in the lives of his first followers were recorded by those who regarded themselves as Christians. These writings were later termed *gospels* (*evangelium* in Latin), a word that means "good news," and were written primarily to spread the "good news" of Jesus' message and not simply to record the biographical details of his life. We can extract historical information from them and compare them with one another, but we have no way of checking them against non-Christian sources except for their references to political events such as the reigns of emperors.

Because gospels are some of the earliest Christian writings that have survived, they are a good place to start our exploration of the development of orthodoxy. During the early centuries of Christianity, many different gospels circulated, but gradually four—those of Matthew, Mark, Luke, and John—came to be considered orthodox and the rest heretical, or at least not as central as Matthew, Mark, Luke, and John. By comparing these orthodox Gospels with those that were excluded, we can see some of the ideas that became central to orthodoxy very early.

The first two sources are from the Gospels of Luke and Matthew, and form the basis for the orthodox interpretation of the resurrection of Jesus and his handing on of authority. In Source 1, who first discovers the empty tomb? What are they told has happened to the body of Jesus? What was the reaction of Jesus' other followers to their report? What point is Jesus trying to make about his own resurrection in verses 36–43? According to Luke, is the resurrection physical or spiritual? Source 2 is the very

end of the Gospel of Matthew, and describes Jesus' final words to his followers. According to this account, to whom does Jesus give authority? What is the source and extent of the authority he is delegating? To whom does Jesus say his message should be communicated?

Sources 3 and 4 offer quite a different view of Jesus' resurrection and handing on of authority, though these were also written by people calling themselves Christians in the first two centuries after the death of Jesus. They come from a movement termed *gnosticism*, with which you may be less familiar than with Christian orthodoxy. Gnosticism was not an organized group, but a diffuse body of beliefs drawn from Greek philosophy, Judaism, Persian religions, and then Christianity. While gnostics disagreed with each other about many things and their beliefs are often very complex, they generally agreed that they had special knowledge, revealed to them by a messenger sent from the creative power or supreme being of the universe; the term *gnostic*, in fact, comes from the Greek word *gnosis*, which means "to know." This special knowledge would enable them to understand the world, and particularly the presence of evil in it, and teach them how to act in order to gain deliverance from the world and achieve salvation. Gnostics believed that the supreme being was totally spiritual and that the material world was either accidentally created or was evil; they were thus uninterested in the things of this world such as politics or human society and were

[185]

very pessimistic about them. They did feel that a small group of humans would be able to return to the purely spiritual world on death—those who had been given the secret knowledge, which would enable the "pure" spirit to escape the "impure" body.

People who were interested in these ideas found much in Christian teachings that appealed to them, and many gnostics became Christian. They created their own body of literature slightly later than the gospels you have read so far, the bulk of which was lost or destroyed. Until quite recently scholars had only fragments of certain gnostic texts and discussions of gnostic ideas in the writings of orthodox thinkers, so that it was difficult to get an unbiased picture. This changed when in 1945 near the town of Nag Hammadi, an Egyptian peasant accidentally found a jar filled with gnostic books, copies made probably in 350–400 of texts first written down as much as three centuries earlier. These were gradually transcribed and translated, and turned out to be fifty-two texts, some of them also labeled "gospels." Sources 3 and 4 are from two of these Nag Hammadi texts, 3 from the gospel of Mary Magdalene and 4 from a text titled "The Wisdom of Jesus Christ."

Source 3 begins with the same event described in the Gospel of Matthew, but then goes on to relate a series of events not included in the orthodox Gospels. How do the instructions Jesus gives his followers differ from those included in Matthew? Who emerges as the strongest of Jesus' followers? What gives her

special authority? What is the reaction of Jesus' other followers to this? Source 4 describes an appearance of Jesus to his followers after his crucifixion. How does its description of his appearance differ from that in the Gospel of Luke? How does the group to whom Jesus appears differ from that described in Matthew? Whom does Jesus say will receive true knowledge? How does this group differ from those whom Matthew describes as the audience of his message?

As you can see from your readings so far, there was great diversity among early Christians in regard to such basic things as the nature of Jesus' Resurrection, the intended audience for his message, and the nature of the group responsible for spreading this message. During the second century, however, many Church leaders felt that this diversity was dangerous, and began to declare certain ideas and interpretations orthodox. The remaining sources in this chapter all stem from second-century orthodox writers, and will help you discover both what ideas were rejected as heresy and the standards devised by Church leaders to make this rejection. We will focus on gnostic ideas, as these were regarded as the most divergent from what became orthodoxy, though the gnostics were not the only heretics in early Christianity. Indeed, many church leaders, including some bishops and the philosopher Origen (185?–254?) held ideas that were, either during their lifetimes or after they died, judged to be heretical. Because of the Nag Hammadi find,

[186]

however, we have more direct access to gnostic ideas than those of most other heretical thinkers.

Source 5 comes from a work generally known as *Against Heresies,* written in the late second century by Irenaeus of Lyons (ca 130–ca 202), a Greek theologian who became bishop of Lyons in France and who was one of the first to systematize Christian doctrine. In *Against Heresies,* Irenaeus seeks to refute gnostic ideas. In this extract, he describes three different types of gnosticism, each of which had different ideas about who Jesus was and the relation between Jesus and the creator of the universe. As you read these three descriptions, it might be useful to write down the variant gnostic answers to the following questions: What was the nature of Jesus—spirit? Human? What actually happened at the crucifixion? What was Jesus' chief purpose while on earth? What is the nature of human salvation—spiritual? Bodily? Because of this, what is the proper attitude of humans toward their bodies— indifference? Rejection?

Though they spent much of their time describing and refuting gnostic ideas, Irenaeus and other leaders recognized that it was also important to devise a positive formulation of the ideas that would be considered orthodox. They took this from the words that many Christian groups were already using when they baptized new initiates, and put together what was termed the "symbol of the faith," or what we would call a creed. This second-century creed became the basis for what later came to be called the Apostles' Creed, first given that

name in a letter of St. Ambrose, the bishop of Milan, in about 390, and assuming its present form in about 650 (Source 6). As you read this source, note which clauses directly refute the various gnostic answers to the questions posed above. What is becoming the orthodox answer to these questions?

The sources thus far have mainly touched on the substance of orthodoxy—the second of the central questions for this chapter—but those remaining will address the first question, regarding the process of the establishment of orthodoxy, more directly. We have already seen, perhaps without noticing, one step in this process—the devising of a uniform statement of belief, with clauses that are unacceptable to most gnostics. Sources 7 and 8 describe another element of this process. Source 7 is another section of Irenaeus's *Against Heresies,* in which he describes the ideas of Marcion, a second-century religious leader influenced by the gnostics. What ideas does Marcion hold that disagree with the statement of faith in the Apostles' Creed? How does Marcion alter the works of other authors so that they support him? Marcion's alteration of Luke and Paul's works led other Church leaders to the realization that some decision needed to be made about which writings from the earliest followers of Jesus were to be accepted as authoritative, and what standards were to be used to make this decision. Source 8 is a fragment from a Greek text probably dating from the late second century, in which the unknown author sets out what he feels are the books and letters (termed *epistles*) that should have special status. This is the earliest known *canon*, or list of the books that later came to be included in the Christian New Testament, and is called the *Muratorian Canon* after the Italian historian who discovered the text. As you read this, note the reasons the author gives for including certain books and excluding others, or for why the authors of these books wrote what they did. How is Luke's authority to write a gospel established, considering that he was not one of the original disciples? What inspires John to write a gospel? In writing Acts, why does Luke exclude certain events? Why does the author feel that the personal letters he regards as written by Paul (to Philemon, Titus, and Timothy) should be included?

As you have probably discovered, the way in which this author judged which books should be included was the same way that orthodox leaders gave authority to their statement of faith—by linking it with the apostles, that is, with Jesus' early followers. As you remember from the first four readings, however, there were wide variations as to whom should be regarded as Jesus' closest followers; Mark speaks of eleven men, "The Wisdom of Jesus Christ" of twelve men and seven women. Mark represents what came to be the orthodox interpretation, which included as true apostles eleven of Jesus' original disciples plus a few other men—most notably Paul, as Source 7 makes clear. By this standard, the works of the gnostics were judged not to be orthodox not only because of their content,

but also because they were generally not as old as the books included in the Christian New Testament. In addition, they did not always make a claim of connection with one of the apostles.

The problem for orthodox leaders was now to affirm their own connection with this original group of men. Sources 9 through 11 give you the writings of three early orthodox leaders on this issue. Source 9 is from a letter of Clement of Rome, the bishop of Rome who was martyred about 97 C.E., to Christians at Corinth in Greece, written at the end of the first century. Source 10 is another section from Irenaeus of Lyons's *Against Heresies*, and Source 11 is a section from *Prescription Against the Heretics,* written by Tertullian (ca 160– ca 230), a theologian from North Africa. As you read these, note the ways in which the idea of apostolic succession, like the creed and canon, was also shaped by gnosticism. How would you compare Clement's discussion of the initial mood of the apostles with that described in the *Gospel of Mary*? How does the way in which Clement alters the Old Testament text of Isaiah help support his argument? How does Irenaeus use apostolic succession to refute the gnostic idea that there was a secret tradition revealed only to a few? Do the authors give evidence of events that contradict their notion of a unity among "true" churches? Whom exactly do they regard as the contemporary holders of apostolic authority?

Before you answer the central questions for this chapter, you may wish to reread all the sources to assess the ways in which the two questions are interrelated. How might the process by which orthodoxy was established have affected the content of orthodox ideas? And, conversely, how might the content of those ideas have shaped the institutions that established orthodoxy?

THE EVIDENCE

1. The Gospel of Luke, Chapter 24

But on the first day of the week, at early dawn, they went to the tomb, taking the spices which they had prepared. [2]And they found the stone rolled away from the tomb, [3]but when they went in they did not find the body. [4]While they were perplexed about this, behold, two men stood by them in dazzling apparel; [5]and as they were frightened and bowed their faces to the ground, the men said to them, "Why do you seek the living among the dead? [6]Remember how he told you, while he was still in Galilee, [7]that the Son of man must be delivered into the hands of sinful men, and be crucified, and on the third day rise." [8]And they remembered his words, [9]and returning from the tomb they told all this to the eleven and to all the rest. [10]Now it was Mary Mag'-dalene and Jo-an-'na and Mary the mother of James and the other women with them who told this to the apostles; [11]but these words seemed to them an idle tale and they did not believe them. . . .

[*Jesus then appeared to two men in a village near Jerusalem, who returned to Jerusalem to tell the disciples what they had seen.*]

[36]As they were saying this, Jesus himself stood among them. [37]But they were startled and frightened, and supposed that they saw a spirit. [38]And he said to them, "Why are you troubled, and why do questionings rise in your hearts? [39]See my hands and my feet, that it is I myself; handle me, and see; for a spirit has not flesh and bones as you see that I have."[1] [41]And while they still disbelieved for joy, and wondered, he said to them, "Have you anything here to eat?" [42]They gave him a piece of broiled fish, [43]and he took it and ate before them.

---

1. Other ancient authorities add verse 40, *And when he had said this, he showed them his hands and feet.*

2. The Gospel of Matthew, Chapter 28

[16]Now the eleven disciples went to Galilee, to the mountain to which Jesus had directed them. [17]And when they saw him they worshiped him; but some doubted. [18]And Jesus came and said to them, "All authority in heaven and on earth has been given to me. [19]Go therefore and make disciples of all nations, baptizing them in the name of the Father and of the Son and of the Holy Spirit, [20]teaching them to observe all that I have commanded you; and lo, I am with you always, to the close of the age."

Sources 3 and 4 from James M. Robinson, editor, The Nag Hammadi Library in English, *3d completely revised edition (San Francisco: Harper and Row, 1988), pp. 525–527; pp. 222–224. Copyright © 1978, 1988 by E. J. Brill, Leiden, The Netherlands. Reprinted by permission of HarperCollins Publishers Inc.*

3. The Gospel of Mary Magdalene

When the blessed one[2] had said this, he greeted them all, saying, "Peace be with you. Receive my peace to yourselves. Beware that no one lead you astray, saying, 'Lo here!' or 'Lo there!' For the Son of Man is within you. Follow after him! Those who seek him will find him. Go then and preach the gospel of the kingdom. Do not lay down any rules beyond what I appointed for you, and do not give a law like the lawgiver lest you be constrained by it." When he had said this, he departed.

But they were grieved. They wept greatly, saying, "How shall we go to the gentiles and preach the gospel of the kingdom of the Son of Man? If they did not spare him, how will they spare us?" Then Mary stood up, greeted them all, and said to her brethren, "Do not weep and do not grieve nor be irresolute, for his grace will be entirely with you and will protect you. But rather let us praise his greatness, for he has prepared us and made us into men." When Mary said this, she turned their hearts to the Good, and they began to discuss the words of the [Savior].

Peter said to Mary, "Sister, we know that the Savior loved you more than the rest of women. Tell us the words of the Savior which you remember—which you know (but) we do not, nor have we heard them." Mary answered and said, "What is hidden from you I will proclaim to you." And she began to speak to them these words: "I," she said, "I saw the Lord in a vision and I said to him, 'Lord, I saw you today in a vision.' He answered and said to me, 'Blessed are you, that you did not waver at the sight of me. For where the mind

2. **the blessed one:** Jesus.

is, there is the treasure.' I said to him, 'Lord, now does he who sees the vision see it (through) the soul (or) through the spirit?' The Savior answered and said, 'He does not see through the soul nor through the spirit, but the mind which [is] between the two—that is [what] sees the vision and it is [. . .].'

[*The next several pages are lost, and then Mary goes on to describe the ascent of the soul.*]

"[. . .] it. And desire that, 'I did not see you descending, but now I see you ascending. Why do you lie, since you belong to me?' The soul answered and said, 'I saw you. You did not see me nor recognize me. I served you as a garment, and you did not know me.' When it had said this, it went away rejoicing greatly.

"Again it came to the third power, which is called ignorance. [It (the power)] questioned the soul saying, 'Where are you going? In wickedness are you bound. But you are bound; do not judge!' And the soul said, 'why do you judge me although I have not judged? I was bound though I have not bound. I was not recognized. But I have recognized that the All is being dissolved, both the earthly (things) and the heavenly.'

When the soul had overcome the third power, it went upwards and saw the fourth power, (which) took seven forms. The first form is darkness, the second desire, the third ignorance, the fourth is the excitement of death, the fifth is the kingdom of the flesh, the sixth is the foolish wisdom of flesh, the seventh is the wrathful wisdom. These are the seven [powers] of wrath. They ask the soul, 'Whence do you come, slayer of men, or where are you going, conqueror of space?' The soul answered and said, 'What binds me has been slain, and what surrounds me has been overcome, and my desire has been ended, and ignorance has died. In a [world] I was released from a world, [and] in a type from a heavenly type, and (from) the fetter of oblivion which is transient. From this time on will I attain to the rest of the time, of the season, of the aeon, in silence.' "

When Mary had said this, she fell silent, since it was to this point that the Savior had spoken with her. But Andrew answered and said to the brethren, "Say what you (wish to) say about what she has said. I at least do not believe that the Savior said this. For certainly these teachings are strange ideas." Peter answered and spoke concerning these same things. He questioned them about the Savior: "Did he really speak with a woman without our knowledge (and) not openly? Are we to turn about and all listen to her? Did he prefer her to us?"

Then Mary wept and said to Peter, "My brother Peter, what do you think? Do you think that I thought this up myself in my heart, or that I am lying about the Savior?" Levi answered and said to Peter, "Peter, you have always been hot-tempered. Now I see you contending against the woman like the adversaries. But if the Savior made her worthy, who are you indeed to reject her? Surely the Savior knows her very well. That is why he loved her more than us. Rather let us be ashamed and put on the perfect man and acquire him for ourselves as he commanded us, and preach the gospel, not laying down any other rule or other law beyond what the Savior said." When [. . .] and they began to go forth [to] proclaim and to preach.

4. "The Wisdom of Jesus Christ"

The Sophia[3] of Jesus Christ.

After he rose from the dead, his twelve disciples and seven women continued to be his followers and went to Galilee onto the mountain called "Divination and Joy." When they gathered together and were perplexed about the underlying reality of the universe and the plan and the holy providence and the power of the authorities and about everything that the Savior is doing with them in the secret of the holy plan, the Savior appeared, not in his previous form, but in the invisible spirit. And his likeness resembles a great angel of light. But his resemblance I must not describe. No mortal flesh could endure it, but only pure (and) perfect flesh, like that which he taught us about on the mountain called "Of Olives" in Galilee. And he said: "Peace be to you! My peace I give to you!" And they all marveled and were afraid.

The Savior laughed and said to them: "What are you thinking about? (Why) are you perplexed? What are you searching for?" Philip said: "For the underlying reality of the universe and the plan."

The Savior said to them: "I want you to know that all men born on earth from the foundation of the world until now, being dust, while they have inquired about God, who he is and what he is like, have not found him. Now the wisest among them have speculated from the ordering of the world and (its) movement. But their speculation has not reached the truth. For it is said that the ordering is directed in three ways by all the philosophers, (and) hence they do not agree. For some of them say about the world that it is directed by itself. Others, that it is providence (that directs it). Others, that it is fate. But it is none of these. Again, of the three voices I have just mentioned, none is close to the truth, and (they are) from man. But I, who came from Infinite Light, I am here—for I know him (Light)—that I might speak to you about the precise nature of the truth. For whatever is from itself is a polluted life; it is self-made. Providence has no wisdom in it. And fate does not discern.

But to you it is given to know; and whoever is worthy of knowledge will receive (it), whoever has not been begotten by the sowing of unclean rubbing but by First Who Was Sent, for he is an immortal in the midst of mortal men."

3. **Sophia:** Greek word for "wisdom."

Source 5 from Henry Bettenson, editor and translator, Documents of the Christian Church, 2d edition (London: Oxford University Press, 1963), pp. 35–37. Reprinted by permission of Oxford University Press.

5. Descriptions of the Ideas of Several Gnostic Thinkers, from Irenaeus of Lyons's *Against Heresies*

Saturninus[4] was of Antioch.[5] . . . Like Menander, [4]he taught that there is one Father, utterly unknown, who made Angels, Archangels, Virtues, Powers; and that the world, and all things therein, was made by certain angels, seven in number. . . .

The Saviour he declared to be unborn, incorporeal and without form, asserting that he was seen as a man in appearance only. The God of the Jews, he affirms, was one of the Angels; and because all the Princes wished to destroy his Father, Christ came to destroy the God of the Jews, and to save them that believed on him, and these are they who have a spark of his life. He was the first to say that two kinds of men were fashioned by the Angels, one bad, the other good. And because the demons aid the worst, The Saviour came to destroy the bad men and the Demons and to save the good. But to marry and procreate they say is of Satan. . . .

Basilides, [4]that he may seem to have found out something higher and more plausible, vastly extends the range of his teaching, declaring that Mind was first born of the Unborn Father, then Reason from Mind, from Reason, Prudence, from Prudence, Wisdom and Power, and from Wisdom and Power the Virtues, Princes and Angels, whom he also calls "the First." By them the First Heaven was made; afterwards others were made, derived from these, and they made another Heaven like to the former, and in like manner others . . . [in all, 365 Heavens].

4. Those Angels who hold sway over the later Heaven, which is seen by us, ordered all things that are in the world, and divided among them the earth and the nations upon the earth. And their chief is he who is held to be the God of the Jews. He wished to subdue the other nations beneath his own people, the Jews, and therefore all the other Princes resisted him and took measures against him. . . . Then the Unborn and Unnamed Father . . . sent his First-begotten Mind (and there is he they call Christ), for the freeing of them that believe in him from those who made the world. And he appeared to the nations of them as a man on the earth, and performed deeds of virtue. Wherefore he suffered not, but a certain Simon, a Cyrenian, was impressed to bear his cross for him; and Simon was crucified in ignorance and error, having

4. **Saturninus, Menander, Basilides, and Cerinthus:** gnostic thinkers.
5. **Antioch:** a city in Syria.

[193]

been transfigured by him, that men should suppose him to be Jesus, while Jesus himself took on the appearance of Simon and stood by and mocked them. . . . If any therefore acknowledge the crucified, he is still a slave and subject to the power of them that made our bodies; but he that denies him is freed from them, and recognises the ordering of the Unborn Father.

A certain Cerinthus [4]also in Asia taught that the world was not made by the first God, but by a certain Virtue far separated and removed from the Principality which is above all things, a Virtue which knows not the God over all. He added that Jesus was not born of a virgin but was the son of Joseph and Mary, like other men, but superior to all others in justice, prudence and wisdom. And that after his baptism Christ descended upon him in the form of a dove, from that Principality which is above all things; and that then he revealed the Unknown Father and performed deeds of virtue, but that in the end Christ flew back, leaving Jesus, and Jesus suffered and rose again, but Christ remained impassible, being by nature spiritual.

6. The Apostles' Creed: Adapted from a Letter of St. Ambrose of Milan, 390

I believe in God, the Father Almighty, maker of heaven and earth, and in Jesus Christ his only Son our Lord, conceived by the Holy Spirit and born of the Virgin Mary. He suffered under Pontius Pilate, was crucified, died and was buried. He descended into hell. On the third day he rose again from the dead. He ascended into heaven and sits at the right hand of God the Father Almighty. From whence he shall come again to judge the quick and the dead. I believe in the Holy Spirit, the Holy catholic[6] church, the communion of saints, the forgiveness of sins, the resurrrection of the body, and the life everlasting.

Sources 7 through 11 from Henry Bettenson, editor and translator, Documents of the Christian Church, *2d edition (London: Oxford University Press, 1963), p. 37; pp. 28–29; p. 63; pp. 68–70; p. 71. Reprinted by permission of Oxford University Press.*

7. Description of the Ideas of Marcion, from Irenaeus of Lyons's *Against Heresies*

Marcion of Pontus took his [Cerdon's[7]] place and amplified his teaching, impudently blaspheming him who is declared to be God by the Law and the

6. "Catholic" in this instance means worldwide.
7. **Cerdon:** a gnostic thinker.

Prophets; calling him a worker of evils, delighting in wars, inconstant in judgement and self-contradictory. While he alleges that Jesus came from the Father who is above the God that made the world; that he came to Judaea in the time of Pontius Pilate the governor, who was the procurator of Tiberius Caesar, and was manifest in the form of a man to all that were in Judaea, destroying the prophets and the Law and all the works of that God who made the world, whom he calls also the Ruler of the Universe. Moreover he mutilated the Gospel according to Luke, removing all the narratives of the Lord's birth, and also removing much of the teaching of the discourses of the Lord wherein he is most manifestly described as acknowledging the maker of this universe to be his father. Thus he persuaded his disciples that he himself was more trustworthy than the apostles, who handed down the Gospel; though he gave to them not a Gospel but a fragment of a Gospel. He mutilated the Epistles of the Apostle Paul in the same manner, removing whatever is manifestly spoken by the Apostle concerning the God who made the world, where he says that he is the father of our Lord Jesus Christ, and setting aside all the Apostle's teaching drawn from the Prophetic writings which predict the advent of the Lord.

2. And then he says that salvation will be of our souls only, of those souls which have learned his teaching; the body, because forsooth it is taken from the earth, cannot partake in salvation.

8. The Muratorian Canon

... The third book of the Gospel is that according to Luke. Luke, the physician, when, after the Ascension of Christ, Paul had taken him to himself as one studious of right [*or, probably,* as travelling companion] wrote in his own name what he had been told [*or in order*], although he had not himself seen the Lord in the flesh. He set down the events as far as he could ascertain them, and began his story with the birth of John.

The fourth gospel is that of John, one of the disciples. ... When his fellow-disciples and bishops exhorted him he said, 'Fast with me for three days from to-day, and then let us relate to each other whatever may be revealed to each of us.' On the same night it was revealed to Andrew, one of the Apostles, that John should narrate all things in his own name as they remembered them. ...

Moreover the Acts of all the Apostles are included in one book. Luke addressed them to the most excellent Theophilus, because the several events took place when he was present; and he makes this plain by the omission of the passion of Peter and of the journey of Paul when he left Rome for Spain.

For the Epistles of Paul ... he wrote to not more than seven churches, in this order: the first to the Corinthians, the second to the Ephesians, the third to the Philippians, the fourth to the Colossians, the fifth to the Galatians, the sixth to the Thessalonians, the seventh to the Romans. ... He wrote besides these one to Philemon, one to Titus, and two to Timothy. These were written in personal affection; but they have been hallowed by being held in honour by the Catholic Church for the regulation of church discipline. There are extant also a letter to the Laodiceans and another to the Alexandrians, forged under Paul's name to further the heresy of Marcion. And there are many others which cannot be received into the Catholic Church. For it is not fitting for gall to be mixed with honey.

The Epistle of Jude indeed, and two bearing the name of John, are accepted in the Catholic Church; also Wisdom, written by the friends of Solomon in his honour. We receive also the Apocalypse of John and that of Peter, which some of us refuse to have read in the Church. But the *Shepherd* was written very recently in our time by Hermas, in the city of Rome, when his brother, Bishop Pius, was sitting in the Chair of the Church of Rome. Therefore it ought also to be read; but it cannot be publicly read in the Church to the people, either among the Prophets, since their number is complete [?], or among the Apostles, to the end of time. . . .

9. Clement of Rome, Letter to the Christians at Corinth

. . . The Apostles for our sakes received the gospel from the Lord Jesus Christ; Jesus Christ was sent from God. Christ then is from God, and the Apostles from Christ. Both therefore came in due order from the will of God. Having therefore received his instructions and being fully assured through the Resurrection of our Lord Jesus Christ, they went forth with confidence in the word of God and with full assurance of the Holy Spirit, preaching the gospel that the Kingdom of God was about to come. And so, as they preached in the country and in the towns, they appointed their firstfruits (having proved them by the Spirit) to be bishops and deacons [overseers and ministers] of them that should believe. And this was no novelty, for of old it had been written concerning bishops and deacons; for the Scripture says in one place, 'I will set up their bishops in righteousness, and their deacons in faith' (Is. lx. 17).[8]

Our Apostles knew also, through our Lord Jesus Christ, that there would be strife over the dignity of the bishop's office. For this reason therefore, having received complete foreknowledge, they appointed the aforesaid, and after a time made provision that on their death other approved men should succeed to their ministry. . . .

---

8. Clement is here changing the original wording of Isaiah 60: 17, which reads *overseers* and *taskmasters* instead of *bishops* and *deacons*.

10. Discussion of Succession from Irenaeus's *Against Heresies*

. . . Those that wish to discern the truth may observe the apostolic tradition made manifest in every church throughout the world. We can enumerate those who were appointed bishops in the churches by the Apostles, and their successors [*or* successions] down to our own day, who never taught, and never knew, absurdities such as these men produce. For if the Apostles had known hidden mysteries which they taught the perfect in private and in secret, they would rather have committed them to those to whom they entrusted the churches. For they wished those men to be perfect and unblameable whom they left as their successors and to whom they handed over their own office of authority. But as it would be very tedious, in a book of this sort, to enumerate the successions in all the churches, we confound all those who in any way, whether for self-pleasing, or vainglory, or blindness, or evilmindedness, hold unauthorized meetings. This we do by pointing to the apostolic tradition and the faith that is preached to men, which has come down to us through the successions of bishops; the tradition and creed of the greatest, the most ancient church, the church known to all men, which was founded and set up at Rome by the two most glorious Apostles, Peter and Paul. For with this church, because of its position of leadership and authority, must needs agree every church, that is, the faithful everywhere; for in her the apostolic tradition has always been preserved by the faithful from all parts.

2. The blessed Apostles, after founding and building up the church, handed over to Linus the office of bishop. Paul mentions this Linus in his epistles to Timothy (2 Tim. iv. 21). He was succeeded by Anacletus, after whom, in the third place after the Apostles, Clement was appointed to the bishopric. He not only saw the blessed Apostles but also conferred with them, and had their preaching ringing in his ears and their tradition before his eyes. In this he was not alone; for many still survived who had been taught by the Apostles. Now while Clement was bishop there arose no small dissension among the brethren in Corinth, and the church in Rome sent a most weighty letter to the Corinthians urging them to reconciliation, renewing their faith and telling them again of the tradition which he had lately received from the Apostles. . . .

3. Euarestus succeeded this Clement, Alexander followed Euarestus; then Sixtus was appointed, the sixth after the Apostles. After him came Telesphorus, who had a glorious martyrdom. Then Hyginus, Pius, Anicetus and Soter; and now, in the twelfth place from the Apostles, Eleutherus occupies the see. In the same order and succession the apostolic tradition in the Church and the preaching of the truth has come down to our time. . . .

4. And then Polycarp, besides being instructed by the Apostles and acquainted with many who had seen the Lord, was also appointed by the Apostles from Asia as bishop of the church in Smyrna.[9] Even I saw him in my early youth; for he remained with us a long time, and at a great age suffered a martyrdom full of glory and renown and departed this life, having taught always the things which he had learnt from the Apostles, which the Church hands down, which alone are true. There testify to these things all the churches throughout Asia, and the successors of Polycarp down to this day, testimonies to the truth far more trustworthy and reliable than Valentinus[10] and Marcion and the other misguided persons.

Polycarp, when staying in Rome in the time of Anicetus, converted many of the before-mentioned heretics to the Church of God, declaring that he had received this one and only truth from the Apostles, the truth which has been handed down by the Church. There are also some who heard him relate that John, the disciple of the Lord, went to the baths at Ephesus; and seeing Cerinthus inside he rushed out without taking a bath, saying, 'Let us flee, before the baths fall in, for Cerinthus the enemy of the truth is inside.' . . .

iv. 1. Since therefore there are so many proofs, there is now no need to seek among others the truth which we can easily obtain from the Church. For the Apostles have lodged all that there is of the truth with her, as with a rich bank, holding back nothing. And so anyone that wishes can draw from her the draught of life. This is the gateway of life; all the rest are thieves and robbers. . . .

Therefore we ought to obey only those presbyters who are in the Church, who have their succession from the Apostles, as we have shown; who with their succession in the episcopate have received the sure gift of the truth according to the pleasure of the Father. The rest, who stand aloof from the primitive succession, and assemble in any place whatever, we must regard with suspicion, either as heretics and evil-minded; or as schismatics, puffed up and complacent; or again as hypocrites, acting thus for the sake of gain and vainglory. All these have fallen from the truth.

11. Discussion of Succession from Tertullian, *Prescription Against the Heretics*

But if any of these [heresies] are bold enough to insert themselves into the Apostolic age, in order to seem to have been handed down from the Apostles because they existed under the Apostles, we can say: Let them then produce the origins of their churches; let them unroll the list of their bishops, an

9. **Smyrna:** a city in Asia Minor (present-day Turkey).
10. **Valentinus and Cerinthus:** gnostic thinkers.

unbroken succession from the beginning so that that first bishop had as his precursor and the source of his authority one of the Apostles or one of the apostolic men who, though not an Apostle, continued with the Apostles. This is how the apostolic churches report their origins; thus the church of the Smyrnaeans relates that Polycarp was appointed by John, the church of Rome that Clement was ordained by Peter. . . .

QUESTIONS TO CONSIDER

As scholars have discovered more about the diversity of early Christian beliefs and practices, they have been increasingly interested in explaining not only *how,* but also *why* certain ideas became identified as orthodox and others were rejected, and why orthodoxy ultimately triumphed. Answers to these questions take us far beyond the sources included here, but you can use the sources, combined with information from your textbook about Roman society in the first centuries after Jesus, to begin to address them. Considering these questions will also allow you to deepen your understanding of the process of this change as you answer the questions for this chapter.

Thinking about gnostic ideas in general, why might the gnostic view that Jesus' true mission was to an elite group able to understand secret knowledge have reduced its popularity among early converts to Christianity? How did the gnostic notion that the inner experience or vision of Christ was what mattered, an experience that anyone could have, challenge Roman ideas of proper structures of authority? How did the gnostic idea that the true message of Jesus had primarily been communi-

cated orally both allow for and limit the spread of gnostic ideas?

Taking some of the actions in the establishment of orthodoxy, why might orthodox views of the crucifixion, which emphasized its bodily nature, be especially appealing at a time when Christians were persecuted by Roman authorities? How did orthodoxy's setting up of objective criteria for membership (that is, taking in anyone who would accept orthodox doctrines and agree to be governed by bishops) increase its appeal as compared to gnosticism's demand for special spiritual insight? Once bishops were established as figures of authority, why would it be increasingly difficult to promote gnostic ideas? How did setting up the criterion of "apostolic" as the central determinant of orthodoxy limit the importance of visions such as that described by Mary Magdalene in Source 3? How would the idea of apostolic authority have worked against groups such as the gnostics who did not think it important to link themselves with the apostles?

Once you begin to understand what ideas became central to orthodox Christianity, you can see that certain events surrounding the life of Jesus were somewhat problematic because they seemed to point to an alternative interpretation. One of these

[199]

events is that related in Source 1, the fact that the empty tomb was discovered by women, not by the disciples, and that women first heard the message that Jesus had risen. How did this conflict with notions of authority being developed in orthodoxy? One solution for problems such as this was to alter the account somewhat, and, in fact, some ancient texts of Luke add an additional verse after verse 11 in Source 1, which reads: "But Peter rose and ran to the tomb; stooping and looking in, he saw the linen cloths by themselves; and he went home wondering at what had happened." How might this addition change one's interpretation of the event?

As we search for human reasons for the developments traced in this chapter, it is important not to forget that the people we are studying regarded these events as signs of divine providence, of God working in history. Early Christians and many non-Christian Romans expected God (or the gods) to act through human agents and so did not regard human explanations as disproof of the divine or miraculous. If the question of how and why orthodoxy triumphed had been put to someone like Irenaeus, how might he have answered? Comparing his hypothetical answer to yours, how have ideas of causation in history changed since ancient times?

EPILOGUE

Christianity was not changed completely to a religion with clear lines between heresy and orthodoxy by 200 C.E., but the establishment of orthodox ideas and authoritative standards has continued to the present day. The original pattern set by the confrontation with gnosticism has been largely followed, however. Christianity generally defined what would be considered orthodoxy only when confronted by a group taking a firm alternative position; the development of Christian theology has thus been reactive rather than spontaneous, and Christianity has tolerated *heterodoxy*, or a range of opinions, on many issues for a long time.

Because of its many denominations, modern Christianity appears at first

glance to be a return to diversity and heterodoxy, yet the ideas and institutions you have traced in this chapter are still present in many Christian denominations. Contemporary theological disputes, particularly within Roman Catholicism but also within Eastern Orthodoxy and many Protestant denominations, are still being decided upon by reference to apostolic authority and the texts of the New Testament. Bishops in many Christian denominations still have a great amount of power, and people still recite the Apostles' Creed. Though it would be hard to find an idea that all Christian denominations today regard as heresy, those of the gnostics would probably come the closest.

The ideas and interpretations put forth by gnostics did not completely die out in the second century, however. Not only did gnostic Christianity survive for several more centuries, but gnostic ideas reemerged in the Middle Ages and in many Christian thinkers down to the present day. The gnostic texts rediscovered at Nag Hammadi have also become increasingly popular with people searching for spiritual answers today. Both those who wish to remain within a Christian tradition but are uncomfortable with the institutionalization and stress on authority that came to mark orthodoxy, and those who are again developing syncretistic personal religions from a variety of traditions have turned to gnosticism for inspiration.

CHAPTER NINE

PHILOSOPHY AND FAITH: THE

PROBLEM OF ANCIENT SUICIDE

THE PROBLEM

Life itself is our most precious possession, and every civilization has viewed suicide, representing as it does the rejection of all human society, as an act of supreme importance, charged with religious, philosophical, and even legal significance. Indeed, the French philosopher Albert Camus (1913–1960) wrote, "There is only one truly philosophical problem, and that is suicide. Judging whether life is or is not worth living amounts to answering the fundamental question of philosophy."[1] Camus was only one of the most recent in a long line of thinkers, extending back at least to the civilization of ancient Egypt, who have written on the fundamental issues raised by the act of self-destruction. This extensive discourse on suicide can afford us a revealing glimpse of the intellectual

1. Albert Camus, *The Myth of Sisyphus and Other Essays*, translated by Justin O'Brien (New York: Vintage Books, 1991), p. 3.

life of past civilizations by allowing us to compare the evolution of their thinkers' ideas on this important act.

In the twentieth century, for example, most of us understand suicide in terms defined by the modern social, psychological, and medical sciences. Émile Durkheim (1858–1917), the pioneering French sociologist, identified several kinds of suicide, but concentrated particularly on the role of modern society in eroding the integrative and regulative aspects of traditional society, resulting, he claimed, in an increase in suicide. We now know that Durkheim's statistical evidence for the increase in suicide in modern times was defective, but his conclusion that suicide is a particular side effect of modern society has endured, even though deprived of its statistical support. Sigmund Freud (1856–1940), the father of modern psychoanalysis, and others of his discipline focused modern attention on the psychological problems that often produce suicide. And since the work of the German physician

Émil Kraepelin (1865–1926), medical professionals have sought to treat the organic causes of depressive disorders that can end in self-destruction.

The earliest Western societies, on the other hand, lacking our modern scientific knowledge, viewed the act of self-destruction in very different, often spiritual, terms. Such societies certainly condemned suicide because it robbed their ranks of productive members. But primitive peoples also believed that the spirits of those who took their own lives would not rest in the world of the dead, but would return to haunt the realm of the living.

In the present chapter we will examine the thought of the ancient world on suicide. The practice was common for much of the period, and ancients seem to have taken their lives for a number of reasons. One had to do with personal honor. Examples abound of ancients extolled in the literature of their time for their nobility in ending their lives to preserve their honor. Perhaps the most famous of these suicides was that of Cato the Younger (95–46 B.C.E.), a leader of the senatorial opposition to Julius Caesar's attempt to control Rome. With his forces defeated in the field, and facing Caesar's imminent attack on Utica, the stronghold under his command, Cato ensured the escape of his followers and took his own life rather than surrender to the man he regarded as a tyrant. Other ancients took their own lives to avoid the pains of old age, perhaps because they saw mental and physical decline as diminishing their honor. Thus, the Greek philosopher Zeno (ca 334–ca 262 B.C.E.) took his own life

at the age of seventy-two when breaking a bone in a minor accident seemed to convince him of impending physical decline. Love for a dead spouse also led to suicide. Portia, the daughter of Cato and the wife of Caesar's assassin, Brutus, took her own life after her husband's suicide upon his defeat by Caesar's heir, Octavian, in 42 B.C.E. Ancients also took their lives in the belief that their deaths could advance a cause, and we will look at such an act in the death of Samson. Indeed, we will examine ancient thought on such acts of self-destruction among the Greeks, the Romans, the Hebrews of the Old Testament, and early Christians.

Historians date Hellenic, or classical Greek, civilization from about 800 B.C.E., when growing commercial wealth and the development of an efficient writing system promoted the economic and intellectual flowering of Greek city-states on the Greek mainland, the islands of the Aegean, Asia Minor (modern Turkey), and the shores of the Black Sea. The epics of Homer helped to shape early Hellenic culture, with the heroes providing role models for young Greeks and the tales of the gods forming the basis for early belief in a cluster of deities, presided over by Zeus, inhabiting the heights of Mount Olympus. These religious beliefs of the Greeks had little of the creedal structure of modern religion, but emphasized instead the duty of citizens of an independent city-state (as most Greeks were) to live in accord with the community. For the early Greeks, as for most Mediterranean peoples of that period, death simply represented the spirit's journey to a shadowy realm of the dead.

The greatest accomplishment of Hellenic intellectuals was to begin to transcend this traditional Greek religion—which explained events in this life in terms of divine action—and to apply reason to their understanding of natural phenomena and human events. As they replaced myth with reason, the Greeks first attempted to explain the physical world around them. The Cosmologists, thinkers concerned with the origins, structure, and operation of the universe, including Thales (ca 624–548 B.C.E..), Anaximander (ca 611–547 B.C.E.), and Pythagoras (ca 580–507 B.C.E.), sought natural explanations for the origins of the universe and advanced the concept that the physical world operates according to mathematical, scientific laws. Greek philosophers also evaluated human society, examining political and ethical problems through the use of reason. Socrates (ca 469–399 B.C.E.) and Plato (ca 429–347 B.C.E.), philosophers we will study in this chapter, in particular led the Greek inquiry into ethical problems.

A political event fundamentally transformed the Hellenic age, however. In 338 B.C.E. King Philip of Macedon (382–336 B.C.E.), a primitive state in northern Greece, conquered the city-states of Greece and ended their independence by subjecting them to the rule of his growing empire. Philip planned further military campaigns; these were carried out after his death by his son, Alexander the Great (356–323 B.C.E.). Alexander conquered Greece's historic enemy, the Persian Empire, and created an empire that stretched to the borders of India. Although Alexander's empire dissolved into several smaller monarchies after his death, his conquests began a new Hellenistic age. Greek became the language of administration and intellectual life in the eastern Mediterranean world, and contact with eastern ideas reshaped Hellenic thought. Hellenistic philosophy reflected a search for intellectual peace for the individual in a world far less democratic and secure than that of the independent city-states of the Hellenic age.

Epicurus (342–270 B.C.E.) began to teach philosophy in Athens in the late fourth century, creating Epicureanism, one of the great schools of Hellenistic philosophy. Seeking intellectual tranquillity in a much less secure age, Epicurus urged his followers to withdraw from public affairs and civic responsibilities, which had been central to the earlier period of city-states. He also taught his students to abandon pursuit of worldly success. The wise person, Epicurus taught, would seek spiritual tranquillity instead, and he taught his students not to fear even divine interruptions of that peace. He affirmed the gods' existence, but held that they played no role in human affairs. Adopting the thought of the Cosmologist Democritus (ca 460–370 B.C.E.), Epicurus taught that the physical world consisted of matter made up of atoms governed by mechanical principles and unaffected by divine action. Death released the atoms making up the human form to constitute new matter, and so the peace Epicurus sought to instill in his followers was very much one of this world.

Zeno, who, as we have seen, committed suicide, founded a second school of Hellenistic philosophy. He taught on the *stoa poecile* (the "painted porch") near the agora, or marketplace, of Athens. As a consequence, his ideas came to be called Stoicism. Stoics accepted the new realities of the Greek and, later, Roman worlds by emphasizing the universality of human society. As expressed by Zeno, "All men should regard themselves as members of one city and people, having one life and order as a herd feeding together on a common pasture."[2] Stoics believed that the universe inhabited by such a society received order from divine reason, or Logos. Animals followed this divine order by instinct, and inanimate objects necessarily adhered to the physical laws of the universe—for example, those governing the regular movements of the heavenly bodies. Humans, however, had free will and could choose to reject the divine plan. But Stoics taught that the virtuous person could achieve happiness only by living in harmony with the Logos, subjecting personal emotions to reason, and accepting life's trials as part of the overall plan of the universe.

While Epicureans withdrew from the world and Stoics sought to live in accord with the Logos, the Cynics, a third group of Hellenistic philosophers led by Diogenes of Sinope (ca 412–323 B.C.E.), rejected social

conventions. They urged their followers to give up material possessions and the complexities of human society and live lives of self-sufficiency and high personal ethics. Because material matters meant little to Cynics, they were prepared to commit suicide if anything blocked their quest for the virtuous life. Indeed, Diogenes reportedly said that the conduct of life required either reason or the noose.

Imperial expansion fundamentally shaped Roman civilization. Thus, in the fourth century B.C.E., the Romans came into contact with the Greek settlements in the south of their native Italy, and Roman equivalents of the Greek deities soon replaced traditional Roman religion, which was centered on the gods of home and family. In philosophy, the Romans similarly embraced Hellenistic Epicureanism and Stoicism. But, ultimately, the fundamental force reshaping Roman thought as the empire conquered the Mediterranean world was religious. Rome's world empire only increased the sense of alienation and personal insecurity that we identified in the Hellenistic age, and while educated Romans adopted Stoicism and other rational solutions to these problems, others often sought religious answers. Popular among such people were the mystery religions, so called because they involved secret rituals known only to initiates. These religions, whose attraction only grew as the Roman Empire weakened, offered their adherents spiritual immortality in an afterlife. But the greatest religious force transforming Rome was Christianity, whose roots

2. Quoted in D. Brendan Nagle, *The Ancient World: A Social and Cultural History* (Englewood Cliffs, N.J.: Prentice-Hall, 1979), p. 206.

[205]

we must seek in the Jewish experience beginning in the Middle East in the late second millennium B.C.E.

The founders of this religious tradition, the Hebrews, originated a faith that was unique in the ancient Middle East. By the late second millennium B.C.E., their Judaism was a monotheistic religion centered on the deity Yahweh, who demanded ethical behavior of his followers. In this ethical monotheism of the early Hebrews, Yahweh enforced his laws by divine intervention in this life. There was no belief in a last judgment, and afterlife beliefs were quite similar to those of the Greeks; the Jews' Sheol was a dark underworld of the dead.

By the first century B.C.E., new ideas were taking root among the Jews of Palestine, dividing them into four main sects. The Sadducees, often drawn from the elite of Jewish society, maintained traditional beliefs and ceremonies and the letter of ancient religious law dating back to the days of the lawgiver Moses. The Pharisees, quite possibly representing the majority of Jews in Palestine, challenged the Sadducees by their willingness to admit the law to interpretation and by their acceptance of the eastern idea of a life after death, with the possibility of spiritual salvation through resurrection. The Essenes, the third group within first-century Judaism, also accepted the idea of resurrection, but formed a monastic-style community near the Dead Sea where they awaited the imminent establishment of the Kingdom of God on earth. The fourth sect, the Zealots, refused to accept Roman conquest of their homeland and engaged in violent resistance, culminating in a Jewish revolt in Palestine in 66 C.E.

A widely held belief among first-century Jews in Palestine was that they would be delivered from foreign domination by a Messiah. Many Jews conceived of the Messiah as a military leader, but when a peaceful figure, Jesus of Nazareth (ca 4 B.C.E.–ca 29 C.E.), declared that he was the Messiah, many Jews saw him as fulfilling their expectation, and Jesus soon had a growing following. Grounded in Jewish monotheism, Jesus' teachings called on his followers to repent their sins in order to enter the Kingdom of God and thus achieve spiritual salvation in a life after death. But to conservative Jews like the Sadducees, Jesus was defying traditional religious law, and they turned him over to Roman authorities. In a difficult province of their empire, these officials certainly saw Jesus as an unsettling presence who counted Zealots among his closest followers, and they ordered his execution.

Jesus' followers proclaimed his resurrection three days after his death as fulfillment of his teachings, and the nature of his following shortly began to change. More and more Gentiles, or non-Jews, joined Jesus' original Jewish followers, as Saint Paul (ca 5–ca 67 C.E.) emphasized that adherence to traditional Jewish law, including dietary rules and circumcision, was not required for membership in the Christian community. In the Hellenized culture of the Middle East, Jesus increasingly was referred to as "Christ," from the Greek *Christos*, or "the Anointed," a translation of the

Hebrew word Messiah. Thus, a new faith, Christianity, quite distinct from Judaism, emerged and grew steadily because of its promise of other-worldly rewards in a society already seeking such spiritual comfort in the mystery religions. Soon the Christian community grew large enough to attract the attention of Roman authorities to a faith that seemed subversive in its nonviolence and refusal even superficially to conform to the Roman civic practice of venerating the emperor. Imperial authorities responded with sporadic, often brutal, persecutions of Christians, beginning in 64 C.E. But the continued growth of the new faith led first to its legalization under Emperor Constantine in 313 C.E. and finally to its elevation to the status of Rome's official religion by Emperor Theodosius I in 392 C.E.

As it achieved legitimacy, Christianity also defined its belief system in an atmosphere of theological controversy. Many theologians whose ideas came to be viewed by the Church as false doctrines, or heresies, sought to promote their ideas in the Christian community. Thus, the followers of Arius (250–326 C.E.), a Greek priest of Alexandria, denied the absolute divinity of Christ, who had declared that he was the son of God. Arians, who taught that Christ

was certainly no mere mortal but that neither was he God's equal, received the Church's condemnation at the Council of Nicaea in 325 C.E. Another heretical group was the Donatists, who rejected the idea, held by the majority of Christians, that the Church should be a universal, or catholic, church embracing all, sinners as well as those meriting salvation. Donatists believed that the Church should include only the elect. Other heresies also spread, but the work of a group of theologians remembered as Church Fathers eventually imposed doctrinal uniformity on the early Church.

Your goal in this chapter is to analyze the thought of these ancient peoples on three levels defined by the central questions of this chapter. The first is very specific to the issue of suicide: What does the author of each selection say about suicide? The second asks you to place these ideas in their intellectual context: How do each author's ideas on self-destruction represent his own thought system and the intellectual outlook of the society in which he lived? The third requires that you perform one of the essential tasks of the historian and examine change over an extended period of time: What change in attitudes toward self-destruction do you see over the extended time period covered by these selections?

SOURCES AND METHOD

This chapter offers us ancient primary sources that present certain analytical challenges. Again, we must

recognize that the absolute accuracy of these texts cannot be verified the way records of modern scholars' writings can be checked in their printed works or in recordings or transcripts of their lectures. Products of a pre-print age, the handwritten originals of most of these sources have long ago disappeared, and students must rely on texts based on ancient scribes' transcriptions of the originals, which may not always be entirely faithful to the authors' precise words. Furthermore, because much ancient writing has failed to survive, it is often difficult to determine whether a given work represents all that its author had to say on a subject.

We also will encounter again sources that are not actually the work of those to whom they are attributed. We can know the thought of Socrates, who wrote nothing, only through the work of his student Plato, and scholars still disagree as to which ideas in the latter's writings are his own and which are those of his teacher. Such considerations require some analysis for all our sources in this chapter.

Source 1 is the work of Plato, an Athenian philosopher who, in the course of his long career, wrote on just about all the philosophical problems that have occupied Western thinkers since his death. His surviving works include letters and a number of dialogues. The dialogues replicate in written form the teaching method of Socrates. Socrates particularly concerned himself with the search for the values by which he and his fellow Athenians might live lives of moral excellence. Socrates believed that these values were not imparted to humanity by a deity, but rather that the individual could discover them through rational inquiry, and he devised a mode of inquiry,

dialectics, to facilitate that search. As practiced by Socrates and his followers, dialectics represented a logical discussion, propelled by the teacher's questions to the student, that forced the student to clarify and justify his thought. Thus, in Source 1, from Plato's dialogue *The Phaedo*, questions are posed by Socrates.

Many scholars divide Plato's dialogues into two chief categories, according to the order in which they probably were written. They call the earlier dialogues, including *The Apology*, *The Meno*, and *The Gorgias*, "Socratic" because they seem to express chiefly the ideas of Socrates. The later dialogues, including *The Phaedo*, seem more nearly to express the ideas of Plato himself.

Plato divided knowledge into two realms. One of these was knowledge of the material world, which can be gathered through sensory perceptions. The other, higher realm of knowledge was that of absolute reality and perfect virtues, the realm of forms or ideas for Plato, which could be achieved only intellectually.

In Source 1, one of the most dramatic episodes of ancient literature, Plato describes the execution of Socrates. Plato's teacher had employed his dialectic method not only with his students, but with his fellow citizens as well, in the hope of leading them to more ethical lives. Indeed, he became the Athenians' "gadfly," and he made more than a few enemies. When Athens lost the Peloponnesian War with Sparta, many of those enemies led Athenians who were seeking an explanation for their defeat to charge Socrates with having had a role in the military disaster. Indeed, several of Socrates' former students had betrayed their city in the war, and his enemies charged him with having led the youth of Athens away from the traditional gods and thereby contributed to the Spartan victory.

As was customary in Athens, the trial of Socrates took place before a jury with wide-ranging powers; the jury not only judged guilt or innocence but also determined the sentence. Plato's accounts of the procedure in *The Apology* make it clear that Socrates could have escaped serious penalty by going into voluntary exile before trial or, perhaps after conviction, by admitting error and promising to stop teaching. But when the jury found him guilty and asked him to suggest a punishment, Socrates almost mockingly proposed what amounted to civic honors. Even though he subsequently suggested a fine, the jury clearly took offense at his remarks; more jurors voted for the penalty of death by taking poison (hemlock) than had voted for the verdict of guilty.

Socrates' behavior at his trial and his subsequent refusal to approve the efforts of his friends Simmias and Cebes, who arrived with money to finance an escape from confinement, suggest to many scholars a sort of death wish. These scholars propose that the philosopher's end represented not so much an execution as a suicide. Indeed, self-destruction figures prominently in *The Phaedo*, which opens on Socrates' execution day (which had been delayed by Athenian religious observances). So-crates spent that day surrounded by friends, and one of these, Cebes, asked Socrates, on behalf of the poet Evenus, why he had lately taken to writing poetry. Socrates replied that he had no wish to rival Evenus, but simply wrote in response to a dream demanding that he "make music"; he wrote only so as to leave no duty undone as he met his end. Our selection from *The Phaedo* opens in the midst of the discussion of poetry. In that selection, why does Socrates think that philosophers in particular should welcome death? How should death open to philosophers the realm of ideas or forms? Does Socrates suggest any divine limitation on an individual's right to self-destruction? What suggests to you that Socrates believed that a divine necessity now permitted his death and that he welcomed his end as a remedy for the problems of this life? What in the thought of Socrates strikes you as characteristic of a philosopher who was a free citizen of a democratic city-state? What about Plato's thought might suggest to you that he was less optimistic than his teacher about finding perfection in this life?

While important portions of Plato's work have survived for modern study, the work of some other ancient philosophers comes to us less directly. This is the case with both Epicurus (ca 341–270 B.C.E.), of whose vast writings only fragments have survived, and Epictetus (ca 50–ca 138 C.E.), whose thought survives only in writings of a disciple, Arrian, based on notes of Epictetus' words.

Much of what we know of the life and thought of Epicurus comes from *Lives of Eminent Philosophers* by Diogenes Laertius, an author about whom scholars know very little. He wrote this history of ancient philosophers in Greek, and the contents of the book suggest that he composed it early in the third century after the birth of Christ. *Lives of Eminent Philosophers* is a remarkable source for ancient history because Diogenes Laertius included many writings that subsequently were lost and, therefore, are available nowhere else. The author illustrated his accounts of philosophers' lives with quotations from their philosophical writings as well as from decrees, letters, wills, and epitaphs. Indeed, Source 2 opens with a letter from Epicurus and concludes with a brief portion of the maxims that he expected his students to memorize, all drawn from *Lives of Eminent Philosophers*.

In the excerpts from the works of Epicurus in Source 2, what aim in life does he urge on his followers? How are they to attain that goal? Why will death be "nothing" to Epicureans? How did his thought relate to self-destruction? Why did the Roman thinker Cicero (106–43 B.C.E.) write the following passage?

For my part I think that in life we should observe the rule which is followed at Greek banquets:—"Let him either drink," it runs, "or go!" And rightly; for either he should enjoy the pleasure of tippling along with the others or get away early, that a sober man may not be a victim to the violence of those who are heated with wine.

Thus by running away one can escape the assaults of fortune which one cannot face. This is the same advice as Epicurus gives.[3]

How does this quotation embody developments we have examined in the Hellenistic and Roman worlds?

Source 3 presents a selection from the *Discourses* of Epictetus recorded by Arrian (ca 95–175 C.E.), who was a cosmopolitan figure indeed. A Greek born in Asia Minor, he entered Roman service and combined success as a governor and general with scholarship. Writing in Greek, he was the author of several histories, including one of Alexander the Great, and as a student of philosophy, Arrian wrote the only record of the thought of his teacher, Epictetus.

Like Arrian a Greek born in Asia Minor, Epictetus was the son of a slave woman and was a slave himself for many years. Taken to Rome as a youth, he studied philosophy there; once freed, perhaps at his master's death, he taught first in the imperial capital and then at Nicopolis in Greece. The teaching of Epictetus reflected this former slave's love of freedom and placed him in the ranks of the foremost Stoics.

Stoicism proved particularly attractive to the Romans, many of whom believed that their empire represented the Stoic ideal of a universal human community. For Roman audiences, Epictetus called Logos "God" in Source 3. What evidence do you find of the philosopher's love of free-

3. Cicero, *Tusculan Disputations*, translated by J. E. King (Cambridge, Mass.: Harvard University Press, 1960), pp. 543–545.

dom? What is the concern of "the good and excellent man" in life? When may such a person terminate his life? What similarity do you find between these circumstances and those in which Plato found suicide justifiable? How does the thought of Epictetus perhaps reflect problems of the Roman world?

With Sources 4 through 9, we move from the classical tradition of Greece and Rome to the roots of the Judeo-Christian heritage in Palestine. Sources 4 through 8 are from the thirty-nine books of the Hebrew scriptures that Jews refer to as *Tanak* and that Christians call the Old Testament of the Bible. Written between the thirteenth and second centuries B.C.E., the Hebrew scriptures provide a remarkable record of the experience of the Jewish people before the birth of Christ, and we must examine their utility as a work of history.

The compilers of the Old Testament were not historians but religious thinkers concerned with Jewish faith, law, and literature, as well as history. The Old Testament thus is the foundation of the modern Jewish and Christian faiths. Students of history find the Old Testament an invaluable source, but they also find that this work of religious inspiration sometimes contains historical contradictions and occasional factual errors, and so scholars must verify biblical accounts of events against records in other sources. Nevertheless, the Old Testament, a collection of works by many authors, contains a consistent expression of values and belief and is our best source for understanding the religion of the Hebrews, and it is from

that perspective that we will consider Sources 4 through 8.

We draw Sources 4 through 8 from the Hebrew scriptures' books of Judges, 1 and 2 Samuel, and 1 Kings, books that recount the teachings and careers of the great Hebrew prophets and leaders. These books contain all the acts of self-destruction that are found in the Hebrew scriptures. Sources 4 and 5 come from the Book of Judges, which describes the period in Hebrew history between the deaths of Moses and Joshua—who had led their people out of captivity in Egypt and into the promised land of Canaan—and the advent of kings as rulers among the Hebrews. Source 4 is from the Book of Judges' account of political instability among the Hebrews as they evolved from nomadic tribesmen into a more settled people who needed nontribal, permanent institutions of government. In search of that government, they offered the crown to the prophet Gideon, who rejected the overture, proclaiming that God alone should rule. After Gideon's death, his son Abimelech slew all but one of his brothers and seized the crown his father had rejected. Established as king, Abimelech brutally put down rebellions against his authority and, as told in Source 4, engaged in an attack on the rebellious city of Thebez. How did Abimelech meet his end? Why may we consider this suicide? Beyond the statement that Abimelech's death represented divine retribution, do you find any textual condemnation of the death of Abimelech?

Source 5 also comes from the Book of Judges; it is part of the account of the mighty Samson, a judge, or leader, of the Hebrews. According to this account, Samson possessed extraordinary strength, which he used against the pagan Philistines, who were enemies of the Hebrews. Samson's long hair represented his vows of devotion to God, and when the woman Delilah learned of this, she cut his hair, depriving Samson of his strength. The Philistines then captured Samson, blinded him, and enslaved him. But his hair grew back, and with it his strength, a fact unnoticed by the Philistines when they put him on display in a temple to their god, Dagon. What does Source 5 show Samson doing in the temple? While this is an act of martyrdom, why must it also be considered a suicide? Understanding that among many ancient peoples, burial in the family tomb was an honor, what can you conclude about the Hebrews' perception of Samson's death?

In Source 6 we have an account of the first anointed king of the Hebrews, Saul. Selected as king by the great judge Samuel, Saul disobeyed God's commands, and Samuel designated David as the new and rightful king. Nevertheless, Saul retained the crown, fighting David in a civil war, while continuing to battle the historic enemies of the Hebrews, the Philistines. What action did Saul, facing defeat by the Philistines atop Mount Gilboa, take in Source 6? Why must you conclude that Saul's death was a suicide? What is the reaction of the Hebrews to Saul's death? How does the following response of David to the death of Saul and his son Jonathan reinforce your conclusion

about the Hebrews' reaction to Saul's self-destruction?

Thy glory, O Israel, is slain upon thy
  high places!
How are the mighty fallen!
. . . . .

Saul and Jonathan, beloved and
  lovely!
In life and death they were not
  divided;
They were swifter than eagles, they
  were stronger than lions.[4]

Saul's death allowed David to gain the crown, but David's rule did not go unchallenged. He faced a rebellion by his son Absalom and his former counselor, Ahithophel. The advice of Ahithophel was highly esteemed, for "in those days the counsel which Ahithophel gave was as if one consulted the oracle of God."[5] Nevertheless, Absalom rejected the strategy proposed by Ahithophel, "For the Lord had ordained to defeat the good counsel of Ahithophel, so that the Lord might bring evil on Absalom."[6] What does Source 7 indicate was Ahithophel's response to Absalom's humiliating him by ignoring his advice? What happened to Ahithophel's remains? What response does this indicate that Ahithophel's contemporaries had to his death?

4. 2 Samuel 1:19, 23, in *The Oxford Annotated Bible with the Apocrypha* (New York: Oxford University Press, 1965), p. 375.

5. 2 Samuel 16:23, in *The Oxford Annotated Bible*, p. 397.

6. 2 Samuel 17:14, in *The Oxford Annotated Bible*, p. 398.

After the death of King David's son and heir, Solomon, the Hebrew kingdom divided into Israel and Judah, and Source 8 recounts an event in Israel. Zimri, a powerful military leader, killed King Elah and seized the throne. Zimri's coup did not go unopposed, however, and the forces of the army commander, Omri, besieged the usurper in the city of Tirzah. What end overtook Zimri, according to Source 8? While the text certainly suggests that God's punishment was a factor in Zimri's death, did the author in any way condemn the act of suicide?

Source 9 also is a biblical selection, but it comes from the writings commonly known among Christians as the New Testament. These Christian scriptures consist of the twenty-seven books that recount the life of Jesus Christ and record his teachings and those of his followers. They are central to the belief of all Christians. Source 9 describes the death of one of the twelve apostles of Jesus, Judas Iscariot. For thirty silver coins, Judas had betrayed Jesus' location to priests of the Temple in Jerusalem who opposed his teachings. Christ was arrested and executed by crucifixion, a mode of punishment commonly employed by the Roman authorities. Source 9 describes the suicide of Judas. Why, according to this account, did Judas take his own life? Is there any textual condemnation of this act of self-destruction? What response to suicide seems common to both Hebrew and Christian texts?

Source 10 is the work of Josephus, one of the greatest ancient historians. Josephus (37–ca 100 C.E.) was a com-

plex individual, and we require an understanding of his background in order to interpret his writings. A Jew born in Jerusalem, his early studies led Josephus to join the Pharisees. When Palestine erupted in a Jewish rebellion against Roman rule in 66 C.E., the scholarly Josephus took an active role, commanding rebel forces in Galilee. Roman legions eventually crushed the rebellion, and Josephus won the favor of their commander, Titus Flavius Vespasian; he even added "Flavius" to his own name. Vespasian went on to become emperor of Rome, and Josephus Flavius enjoyed imperial patronage in the capital. There he wrote in Greek several important histories, including *Jewish Antiquities*, a history of the Jews from Adam and Eve to the first century C.E., and *The Jewish War*, a history of the Jewish rebellion against Roman rule in Palestine.

Scholars detect many influences on Josephus that we must identify before reading his work. Certainly he was a devout Jewish Pharisee whose work represented an apology of sorts for his people's rebellion. At the same time, Josephus was a Roman citizen who had been thoroughly imbued with the Greco-Roman culture of the first century C.E. And we must not forget that Josephus enjoyed an imperial pension, which might have affected his portrayal of events in his histories.

Source 10 presents perhaps the most famous event in the Jewish rebellion, the last stand of the Zealots at the mountain fortress of Masada in 73 C.E. Faced with inevitable defeat, what step did the Zealots' leader,

Eleazar, urge upon them? How did the garrison respond? How many persons perished, according to Josephus? How does he portray this mass suicide? How does this portrayal replicate reactions to suicide in other ancient sources?

Our final source, Source 11, is the work of Saint Augustine (354–430 C.E.), one of the greatest early Church Fathers. Saint Augustine lived in turbulent times, when the Roman Empire in the West was in marked decline and heretical ideas challenged Christian doctrine. Raised as a Christian in his native North Africa, Augustine abandoned that faith during a rather dissolute period as a young man and adopted the Manichaean heresy, an eastern belief system founded upon the idea that the world was a battleground between the forces of good and evil deities. Eventually, in Milan, Italy, Augustine encountered the eloquent preaching of another Church Father, Saint Ambrose, bishop of Milan, which helped to win him back to Christianity.

Augustine returned to North Africa, became bishop of Hippo, and produced a large body of writings that helped to define Christian doctrine and to defend it against the numerous heresies of the day. *The City of God Against the Pagans*, excerpted in Source 11, is the most important of these. Saint Augustine wrote it in response to the sack of Rome by the Visigoths in 410. Non-Christians blamed this disaster on the Christianity that had won over much of the empire in the fourth century C.E. They saw the event as the revenge of the old gods that had

been abandoned by many Romans and as the result of Christians' refusal to perform military service. Saint Augustine denied such charges and reasoned that, while imperial Rome was the greatest city that humanity could realize, the true object of the Christian life should be attainment to the heavenly City of God. In short, the rise and fall of empires was unimportant compared to the individual's spiritual journey to heavenly salvation.

Saint Augustine also used *The City of God* to further his mission of defending Christian doctrine. An issue that particularly concerned him was how his contemporaries, Christians and heretics alike, fulfilled Christ's injunction in Mark 8:34–35: "If any man would come after me, let him deny himself and take up his cross and follow me. For whoever would save his life will lose it; and whoever loses his life for my sake and the gospel's will save it."[7] Early Christians sometimes actually sought martyrdom at the hands of Roman officers assigned to enforce the superficial rites of official veneration of the emperor. Such suicidal self-sacrifice especially occurred among Donatists.

This enthusiastic martyrdom caused several early Christian thinkers to distinguish between true martyrdom and suicide. Saint Augustine takes up this theme in Source 11 as part of his discussion of the plunder of Rome in 410, when a number of women committed suicide rather than suffer sexual assault by the Visigothic attackers. How does Saint Augustine

---

7. *The Oxford Annotated Bible*, p. 1225.

view suicide? How does Saint Augustine's interpretation of the deaths of Samson and Judas differ from the accounts in Sources 5 and 9? In what circumstances would Saint Augustine permit suicide? What religious change did these conditions reflect? What new approach to suicide did Saint Augustine introduce?

Using this background on ancient philosophy and theology, now examine the evidence. As you read each source, you should seek answers for the central questions of this chapter. What does the author of each selection say about suicide? How do each author's ideas on self-destruction represent his own thought system and the intellectual outlook of the society in which he lived? What change in attitude toward self-destruction do you observe over the extended time period covered by these selections?

THE EVIDENCE

Source 1 from Plato with English Translation, *vol. 1,* Euthyphro, Apology, Crito, Phaedo, Phaedrus, *translated by Harold North Fowler (Cambridge, Mass.: Harvard University Press, 1953), pp. 213–233, 399–403.*

1. Plato, *The Phaedo*

"So tell Evenus that, Cebes, and bid him farewell, and tell him, if he is wise, to come after me as quickly as he can. I, it seems, am going to-day; for that is the order of the Athenians."

And Simmias said, "What a message that is, Socrates, for Evenus! I have met him often, and from what I have seen of him, I should say that he will not take your advice in the least if he can help it."

"Why so?" said he. "Is not Evenus a philosopher?"

"I think so," said Simmias.

"Then Evenus will take my advice, and so will every man who has any worthy interest in philosophy. Perhaps, however, he will not take his own life, for they[8] say that is not permitted." And as he spoke he put his feet down on the ground and remained sitting in this way through the rest of the conversation.

Then Cebes asked him: "What do you mean by this, Socrates, that it is not permitted to take one's life, but that the philosopher would desire to follow after the dying?" . . .

---

8. **they:** Socrates refers here to the Pythagorean philosophers, including Philolaus, who opposed suicide. Pythagoreans believed that the soul was imprisoned in the body as punishment for sins in an earlier life. Thus, self-destruction was akin to a prison escape and was unacceptable to them.

"Why in the world do they say that it is not permitted to kill oneself, Socrates? I heard Philolaus, when he was living in our city, say the same thing you just said, and I have heard it from others, too, that one must not do this; but I never heard anyone say anything definite about it."

"You must have courage," said he, "and perhaps you might hear something. But perhaps it will seem strange to you that this alone of all laws is without exception, and it never happens to mankind, as in other matters, that only at some times and for some persons it is better to die than to live; and it will perhaps seem strange to you that these human beings for whom it is better to die cannot without impiety do good to themselves, but must wait for some other benefactor."

"And Cebes, smiling gently, said, "Gawd knows it doos," speaking in his own dialect.

"It would seem unreasonable, if put in this way," said Socrates, "but perhaps there is some reason in it. Now the doctrine that is taught in secret about this matter, that we men are in a kind of prison and must not set ourselves free or run away, seems to me to be weighty and not easy to understand. But this at least, Cebes, I do believe is sound, that the gods are our guardians and that we men are one of the chattels of the gods. Do you not believe this?"

"Yes," said Cebes, "I do."

"Well, then," said he, "if one of your chattels should kill itself when you had not indicated that you wished it to die, would you be angry with it and punish it if you could?"

"Certainly," he replied.

"Then perhaps from this point of view it is not unreasonable to say that a man must not kill himself until god sends some necessity upon him, such as has now come upon me."

"That," said Cebes, "seems sensible. But what you said just now, Socrates, that philosophers ought to be ready and willing to die, that seems strange if we were right just now in saying that god is our guardian and we are his possessions. For it is not reasonable that the wisest men should not be troubled when they leave that service in which the gods, who are the best overseers in the world, are watching over them. A wise man certainly does not think that when he is free he can take better care of himself than they do. A foolish man might perhaps think so, that he ought to run away from his master, and he would not consider that he must not run away from a good master, but ought to stay with him as long as possible; and so he might thoughtlessly run away; but a man of sense would wish to be always with one who is better than himself. And yet, Socrates, if we look at it in this way, the contrary of what we just said seems natural; for the wise ought to be troubled at dying and the foolish to rejoice." . . .

. . . "I wish now to explain to you, my judges, the reason why I think a man who has really spent his life in philosophy is naturally of good courage when

[216]

he is to die, and has strong hopes that when he is dead he will attain the greatest blessings in that other land. So I will try to tell you, Simmias, and Cebes, how this would be.

"Other people are likely not to be aware that those who pursue philosophy aright study nothing but dying and being dead. Now if this is true, it would be absurd to be eager for nothing but this all their lives, and then to be troubled when that came for which they had all along been eagerly practising."

And Simmias laughed and said, "By Zeus, Socrates, I don't feel much like laughing just now, but you made me laugh. For I think the multitude, if they heard what you just said about the philosophers, would say you were quite right, and our people at home would agree entirely with you that philosophers desire death, and they would add that they know very well that the philosophers deserve it."

"And they would be speaking the truth, Simmias, except in the matter of knowing very well. For they do not know in what way the real philosophers desire death, nor in what way they deserve death, nor what kind of a death it is. Let us then," said he, "speak with one another, paying no further attention to them. Do we think there is such a thing as death?"

"Certainly," replied Simmias.

"We believe, do we not, that death is the separation of the soul from the body, and that the state of being dead is the state in which the body is separated from the soul and exists alone by itself and the soul is separated from the body and exists alone by itself? Is death anything other than this?" "No, it is this," said he.

"Now, my friend, see if you agree with me; for, if you do, I think we shall get more light on our subject. Do you think a philosopher would be likely to care much about the so-called pleasures, such as eating and drinking?"

"By no means, Socrates," said Simmias.

"How about the pleasures of love?"

"Certainly not."

"Well, do you think such a man would think much of the other cares of the body—I mean such as the possession of fine clothes and shoes and the other personal adornments? Do you think he would care about them or despise them, except so far as it is necessary to have them?"

"I think the true philosopher would despise them," he replied.

"Altogether, then, you think that such a man would not devote himself to the body, but would, so far as he was able, turn away from the body and concern himself with the soul?"

"Yes."

"To begin with, then, it is clear that in such matters the philosopher, more than other men, separates the soul from communion with the body?"

"It is." . . .

"Now, how about the acquirement of pure knowledge? Is the body a hindrance or not, if it is made to share in the search for wisdom? What I mean is this: Have the sight and hearing of men any truth in them, or is it true, as the poets are always telling us, that we neither hear nor see anything accurately? And yet if these two physical senses are not accurate or exact, the rest are not likely to be, for they are inferior to these. Do you not think so?"

"Certainly I do," he replied.

"Then," said he, "when does the soul attain to truth? For when it tries to consider anything in company with the body, it is evidently deceived by it."

"True."

"In thought, then, if at all, something of the realities becomes clear to it?"

"Yes."

"But it thinks best when none of these things troubles it, neither hearing nor sight, nor pain nor any pleasure, but it is, so far as possible, alone by itself, and takes leave of the body, and avoiding, so far as it can, all association or contact with the body, reaches out toward the reality."

"That is true."

"In this matter also, then, the soul of the philosopher greatly despises the body and avoids it and strives to be alone by itself?"

"Evidently."

"Now how about such things as this, Simmias? Do we think there is such a thing as absolute justice or not?"

"We certainly think there is."

"And absolute beauty and goodness."

"Of course."

"Well, did you ever see anything of that kind with your eyes?"

"Certainly not," said he.

"Or did you ever reach them with any of the bodily senses? I am speaking of all such things, as size, health, strength, and in short the essence or underlying quality of everything. Is their true nature contemplated by means of the body? Is it not rather the case that he who prepares himself most carefully to understand the true essence of each thing that he examines would come nearest to the knowledge of it?"

"Certainly."

"Would not that man do this most perfectly who approaches each thing, so far as possible, with the reason alone, not introducing sight into his reasoning nor dragging in any of the other senses along with his thinking, but who employs pure, absolute reason in his attempt to search out the pure, absolute essence of things, and who removes himself, so far as possible, from eyes and ears, and, in a word, from his whole body, because he feels that its companionship disturbs the soul and hinders it from attaining truth and wisdom? Is not this the man, Simmias, if anyone, to attain to the knowledge of reality?"

"That is true as true can be, Socrates," said Simmias.

"Then," said he, "all this must cause good lovers of wisdom to think and say one to the other something like this: 'There seems to be a short cut which leads

[218]

us and our argument to the conclusion in our search that so long as we have the body, and the soul is contaminated by such an evil, we shall never attain completely what we desire, that is, the truth. "For, if pure knowledge is impossible while the body is with us, one of two thing[s] must follow, either it cannot be acquired at all or only when we are dead; for then the soul will be by itself apart from the body, but not before. And while we live, we shall, I think, be nearest to knowledge when we avoid, so far as possible, intercourse and communion with the body, except what is absolutely necessary, and are not filled with its nature, but keep ourselves pure from it until God himself sets us free. And in this way, freeing ourselves from the foolishness of the body and being pure, we shall, I think, be with the pure and shall know of ourselves all that is pure—and that is, perhaps, the truth. For it cannot be that the impure attain the pure.' Such words as these, I think, Simmias, all who are rightly lovers of knowledge must say to each other and such must be their thoughts. Do you not agree?"

"Most assuredly, Socrates."

"Then," said Socrates, "if this is true, my friend, I have great hopes that when I reach the place to which I am going, I shall there, if anywhere, attain fully to that which has been my chief object in my past life, so that the journey which is now imposed upon me is begun with good hope; and the like hope exists for every man who thinks that his mind has been purified and made ready." . . .

Thereupon Crito nodded to the boy who was standing near. The boy went out and stayed a long time, then came back with the man who was to administer the poison, which he brought with him in a cup ready for use. And when Socrates saw him, he said: "Well, my good man, you know about these things; what must I do?" "Nothing," he replied, "except drink the poison and walk about till your legs feel heavy; then lie down, and the poison will take effect of itself."

At the same time he held out the cup to Socrates. He took it, and very gently, Echecrates, without trembling or changing colour or expression, but looking up at the man with wide open eyes, as was his custom, said: "What do you say about pouring a libation[9] to some deity from this cup? May I, or not?" "Socrates," said he, "we prepare only as much as we think is enough." "I understand," said Socrates; "but I may and must pray to the gods that my departure hence be a fortunate one; so I offer this prayer, and may it be granted." With these words he raised the cup to his lips and very cheerfully and quietly drained it. Up to that time most of us had been able to restrain our tears fairly well, but when we watched him drinking and saw that he had drunk the poison, we could do so no longer. . . . He walked about and, when he said his legs were heavy, lay down on his back, for such was the advice of the attendant. The man who had administered the poison laid his hands on

9. **libation:** the ritual pouring out of wine or holy oil as an offering to a deity.

him and after a while examined his feet and legs, then pinched his foot hard and asked if he felt it. He said "No"; then after that, his thighs; and passing upwards in this way he showed us that he was growing cold and rigid. And again he touched him and said that when it reached his heart, he would be gone. The chill had now reached the region about the groin, and uncovering his face, which had been covered, he said—and these were his last words— "Crito, we owe a cock to Aesculapius.[10] Pay it and do not neglect it." "That," said Crito, "shall be done; but see if you have anything else to say." To this question he made no reply, but after a little while he moved; the attendant uncovered him; his eyes were fixed. And Crito when he saw it, closed his mouth and eyes.

Such was the end, Echecrates, of our friend, who was, as we may say, of all those of his time whom we have known, the best and wisest and most righteous man.

Source 2 from Diogenes Laertius, Lives of Eminent Philosophers, *vol. 2, translated by Robert Drew Hicks (New York: G. P. Putnam's Sons, 1925), pp. 651–653, 657, 665.*

2. Epicurus on the Meaning of Death

[*From a letter*]

"Accustom thyself to believe that death is nothing to us, for good and evil imply sentience,[11] and death is the privation of all sentience; therefore a right understanding that death is nothing to us makes the mortality of life enjoyable, not by adding to life an illimitable time, but by taking away the yearning after immortality. For life has no terrors for him who has thoroughly apprehended that there are no terrors for him in ceasing to live. Foolish, therefore, is the man who says that he fears death, not because it will pain when it comes, but because it pains in the prospect. Whatsoever causes no annoyance when it is present, causes only a groundless pain in the expectation. Death, therefore, the most awful of evils, is nothing to us, seeing that, when we are, death is not come, and, when death is come, we are not. It is nothing, then, either to the living or to the dead, for with the living it is not and the dead exist no longer. But in the world, at one time men shun death as the greatest of all evils, and at another time choose it as a respite from the evils in life. The wise man does not deprecate life nor does he fear the cessation of life. The thought of life is no offence to him, nor is the cessation of life regarded as an evil. And even as men

10. **Aesculapius:** sometimes also rendered "Asclepius," this was the chief god of healing. It was common in the ancient world to offer animal sacrifices to deities as part of prayerful entreaties or as offerings of thanks.

11. **sentience:** the capacity for feeling or sensation.

choose of food not merely and simply the larger portion, but the more pleasant, so the wise seek to enjoy the time which is most pleasant and not merely that which is longest. . . .

"When we say, then, that pleasure is the end and aim, we do not mean the pleasures of the prodigal or the pleasures of sensuality, as we are understood to do by some through ignorance, prejudice, or wilful misrepresentation. By pleasure we mean the absence of pain in the body and of trouble in the soul. It is not an unbroken succession of drinking-bouts and of revelry, not sexual love, not the enjoyment of the fish and other delicacies of a luxurious table, which produce a pleasant life; it is sober reasoning, searching out the grounds of every choice and avoidance, and banishing those beliefs through which the greatest tumults take possession of the soul. Of all this the beginning and the greatest good is prudence. Wherefore prudence is a more precious thing even than philosophy; from it spring all the other virtues, for it teaches that we cannot lead a life of pleasure which is not also a life of prudence, honour, and justice; nor lead a life of prudence, honour, and justice, which is not also a life of pleasure. For the virtues have grown into one with a pleasant life, and a pleasant life is inseparable from them. . . ."

[*From the maxims*]

Death is nothing to us; for the body, when it has been resolved into its elements, has no feeling, and that which has no feeling is nothing to us.

Source 3 from Epictetus, The Discourses as Reported by Arrian, the Manual, and Fragments, *vol. 2, translated by W(illiam) A(bbott) Oldfather (New York: G. P. Putnam's Sons, 1926), pp. 215–217.*

3. Epictetus on Ending Life

For this reason the good and excellent man, bearing in mind who he is, and whence he has come, and by whom he was created, centres his attention on this and this only, how he may fill his place in an orderly fashion, and with due obedience to God. "Is it Thy will that I should still remain? I will remain as a free man, as a noble man, as Thou didst wish it; for Thou hast made me free from hindrance in what was mine own. And now hast Thou no further need of me? Be it well with Thee. I have been waiting here until now because of Thee and of none other, and now I obey Thee and depart." "How do you depart?" "Again, as Thou didst wish it, as a free man, as Thy servant, as one who has perceived Thy commands and Thy prohibitions. But so long as I continue to live in Thy service, what manner of man wouldst Thou have me be? An official or a private citizen, a senator or one of the common people, a soldier or a general, a teacher or the head of a household? Whatsoever station and post

Thou assign me, I will die ten thousand times, as Socrates says, or ever I abandon it.[12] And where wouldst Thou have me be? In Rome, or in Athens, or in Thebes, or in Gyara? Only remember me there. If Thou sendest me to a place where men have no means of living in accordance with nature, I shall depart this life, not in disobedience to Thee, but as though Thou wert sounding for me the recall. I do not abandon Thee—far be that from me! but I perceive that Thou hast no need of me. Yet if there be vouchsafed a means of living in accordance with nature, I will seek no other place than that in which I am, or other men than those who are now my associates."

Sources 4 through 9 from the Revised Standard Version of the Bible, *pp. 307–308; p. 316; p. 373; p. 399; p. 441; p. 1209.*

4. The Death of Abimelech
(Judges 9:50–56)

Then Abim'elech went to Thebez, and encamped against Thebez, and took it. But there was a strong tower within the city, and all the people of the city fled to it, all the men and women, and shut themselves in; and they went to the roof of the tower. And Abim'elech came to the tower, and fought against it, and drew near to the door of the tower to burn it with fire. And a certain woman threw an upper millstone upon Abim'elech's head, and crushed his skull. Then he called hastily to the young man his armor-bearer, and said to him, "Draw your sword and kill me, lest men say of me, 'A woman killed him.' " And his young man thrust him through, and he died. And when the men of Israel saw that Abim'elech was dead, they departed every man to his home. Thus God requited the crime of Abim'elech, which he committed against his father in killing his seventy brothers.

5. The Death of Samson
(Judges 16:23–31)

Now the lords of the Philistines gathered to offer a great sacrifice to Dagon their god, and to rejoice; for they said, "Our god has given Samson our enemy into our hand." And when the people saw him, they praised their god; for they said, "Our god has given our enemy into our hand, the ravager of our country, who has slain many of us." And when their hearts were merry, they said, "Call Samson, that he may make sport for us." So they called Samson out of the

---

12. This is a paraphrase of the words of Socrates in Plato's dialogue *The Apology*, which recounts the philosopher's defense at his trial.

[222]

prison, and he made sport before them. They made him stand between the pillars; and Samson said to the lad who held him by the hand, "Let me feel the pillars on which the house rests, that I may lean against them." Now the house was full of men and women; all the lords of the Philistines were there, and on the roof there were about three thousand men and women, who looked on while Samson made sport.

Then Samson called to the Lord and said, "O Lord God, remember me, I pray thee, and strengthen me, I pray thee, only this once, O God, that I may be avenged upon the Philistines for one of my two eyes." And Samson grasped the two middle pillars upon which the house rested, and he leaned his weight upon them, his right hand on the one and his left hand on the other. And Samson said, "Let me die with the Philistines." Then he bowed with all his might; and the house fell upon the lords and upon all the people that were in it. So the dead whom he slew at his death were more than those whom he had slain during his life. Then his brothers and all his family came down and took him and brought him up and buried him between Zorah and Esh'ta-ol in the tomb of Mano'ah his father. He had judged Israel twenty years.

6. The Deaths of Saul and His Armor-Bearer (1 Samuel 31:1–13)

Now the Philistines fought against Israel; and the men of Israel fled before the Philistines, and fell slain on Mount Gilbo'a. And the Philistines overtook Saul and his sons; and the Philistines slew Jonathan and Abin'adab and Mal'chishu'a, the sons of Saul. The battle pressed hard upon Saul, and the archers found him; and he was badly wounded by the archers. Then Saul said to his armor-bearer, "Draw your sword, and thrust me through with it, lest these uncircumcised come and thrust me through, and make sport of me." But his armor-bearer would not; for he feared greatly. Therefore Saul took his own sword, and fell upon it. And when his armor-bearer saw that Saul was dead, he also fell upon his sword, and died with him. Thus Saul died, and his three sons, and his armor-bearer, and all his men, on the same day together. And when the men of Israel who were on the other side of the valley and those beyond the Jordan saw that the men of Israel had fled and that Saul and his sons were dead, they forsook their cities and fled; and the Philistines came and dwelt in them.

On the morrow, when the Philistines came to strip the slain, they found Saul and his three sons fallen on Mount Gilbo'a. And they cut off his head, and stripped off his armor, and sent messengers throughout the land of the Philistines, to carry the good news to their idols and to the people. They put his armor in the temple of Ash'taroth; and they fastened his body to the wall of Beth-shan. But when the inhabitants of Ja'besh-gil'ead heard what the

Philistines had done to Saul, all the valiant men arose, and went all night, and took the body of Saul and the bodies of his sons from the wall of Beth-shan; and they came to Jabesh and burnt them there. And they took their bones and buried them under the tamarisk tree in Jabesh, and fasted seven days.

7. The Death of Ahithophel
(2 Samuel 17:23)

When Ahith'ophel saw that his counsel was not followed, he saddled his ass, and went off home to his own city. And he set his house in order, and hanged himself; and he died, and was buried in the tomb of his father.

8. The Death of Zimri
(1 Kings 16:18–19)

And when Zimri saw that the city was taken, he went into the citadel of the king's house, and burned the king's house over him with fire, and died, because of his sins which he committed, doing evil in the sight of the Lord, walking in the way of Jerobo'am,[13] and for his sin which he committed, making Israel to sin.

9. The Death of Judas
(Matthew 27:1–8)

When morning came, all the chief priests and the elders of the people took counsel against Jesus to put him to death; and they bound him and led him away and delivered him to Pilate the governor.

When Judas, his betrayer, saw that he was condemned, he repented and brought back the thirty pieces of silver to the chief priests and the elders, saying, "I have sinned in betraying innocent blood." They said, "What is that to us? See to it yourself." And throwing down the pieces of silver in the temple, he departed; and he went and hanged himself. But the chief priests, taking the pieces of silver, said, "It is not lawful to put them into the treasury, since they are blood money." So they took counsel, and bought with them the potter's field, to bury strangers in. Therefore that field has been called the Field of Blood to this day.

13. **Jeroboam:** a traitor and idolater in the Old Testament who led an unsuccessful revolt of the north of the Hebrew state against King David's son, Solomon. He later led a successful rebellion against Solomon's son, King Rehoboam, and established an independent state in which he encouraged the worship of idols, not Yahweh.

Source 10 from Josephus with English Translation, *vol. 3,* The Jewish War, *Books IV–VII, translated by Henry St. John Thackeray (New York: G. P. Putnam's Sons, 1928), pp. 595–603, 613–619.*

10. Josephus on Mass Suicide at Masada, 73 C.E.

However, neither did Eleazar himself contemplate flight, nor did he intend to permit any other to do so. Seeing the wall consuming in the flames, unable to devise any further means of deliverance or gallant endeavour, and setting before his eyes what the Romans, if victorious, would inflict on them, their children and their wives, he deliberated on the death of all. And, judging, as matters stood, this course the best, he assembled the most doughty of his comrades and incited them to the deed by such words as these:

"Long since, my brave men, we determined neither to serve the Romans nor any other save God, for He alone is man's true and righteous Lord; and now the time is come which bids us verify that resolution by our actions. At this crisis let us not disgrace ourselves; we who in the past refused to submit even to a slavery involving no peril, let us not now, along with slavery, deliberately accept the irreparable penalties awaiting us if we are to fall alive into Roman hands. For as we were the first of all to revolt, so are we the last in arms against them. Moreover, I believe that it is God who has granted us this favour, that we have it in our power to die nobly and in freedom—a privilege denied to others who have met with unexpected defeat. Our fate at break of day is certain capture, but there is still the free choice of a noble death with those we hold most dear. For our enemies, fervently though they pray to take us alive, we can no more prevent this than we can now hope to defeat them in battle. . . .

. . . Let our wives thus die undishonoured, our children unacquainted with slavery; and, when they are gone, let us render a generous service to each other, preserving our liberty as a noble winding-sheet. But first let us destroy our chattels and the fortress by fire; for the Romans, well I know, will be grieved to lose at once our persons and the lucre. Our provisions only let us spare; for they will testify, when we are dead, that it was not want which subdued us, but that, in keeping with our initial resolve, we preferred death to slavery."

Thus spoke Eleazar; but his words did not touch the hearts of all hearers alike. Some, indeed, were eager to respond and all but filled with delight at the thought of a death so noble,[14] but others, softer-hearted, were moved with compassion for their wives and families, and doubtless also by the vivid

14. Scholars disagree about the precise translation of the original Greek text at this point. Some render "filled with delight at the thought of a death so noble" as "filled with pleasure supposing such a death to be noble." The latter translation significantly modifies the meaning of Josephus.

[225]

prospect of their own end, and their tears as they looked upon one another revealed their unwillingness of heart. Eleazar, seeing them flinching and their courage breaking down in face of so vast a scheme, feared that their whimpers and tears might unman even those who had listened to his speech with fortitude. Far, therefore, from slackening in his exhortation, he roused himself and, fired with mighty fervour, essayed a higher flight of oratory on the immortality of the soul. Indignantly protesting and with eyes intently fixed on those in tears, he exclaimed:

"Deeply, indeed, was I deceived in thinking that I should have brave men as associates in our struggles for freedom—men determined to live with honour or to die. But you, it seems, were no better than the common herd in valour or in courage, you who are afraid even of that death that will deliver you from the direst ills, when in such a cause you ought neither to hesitate an instant nor wait for a counsellor. For from of old, since the first dawn of intelligence, we have been continually taught by those precepts, ancestral and divine—confirmed by the deeds and noble spirit of our forefathers—that life, not death, is man's misfortune. For it is death which gives liberty to the soul and permits it to depart to its own pure abode, there to be free from all calamity; but so long as it is imprisoned in a mortal body and tainted with all its miseries, it is, in sober truth, dead, for association with what is mortal ill befits that which is divine. . . .

. . . Unenslaved by the foe let us die, as free men with our children and wives let us quit this life together! This our laws enjoin, this our wives and children implore of us. The need for this is of God's sending, the reverse of this is the Romans' desire, and their fear is lest a single one of us should die before capture. Haste we then to leave them, instead of their hoped-for enjoyment at securing us, amazement at our death and admiration of our fortitude."

He would have pursued his exhortation but was cut short by his hearers, who, overpowered by some uncontrollable impulse, were all in haste to do the deed. Like men possessed they went their way, each eager to outstrip his neighbour and deeming it a signal proof of courage and sound judgement not to be seen among the last: so ardent the passion that had seized them to slaughter their wives, their little ones and themselves. . . . They had died in the belief that they had left not a soul of them alive to fall into Roman hands; but an old woman and another, a relative of Eleazar, superior in sagacity and training to most of her sex, with five children, escaped by concealing themselves in the subterranean aqueducts, while the rest were absorbed in the slaughter. The victims numbered nine hundred and sixty, including women and children; and the tragedy occurred on the fifteenth of the month Xanthicus.[15]

The Romans, expecting further opposition, were by daybreak under arms and, having with gangways formed bridges of approach from the earthworks,

15. May 2, 73 C.E.

advanced to the assault. Seeing none of the enemy but on all sides an awful solitude, and flames within and silence, they were at a loss to conjecture what had happened. At length, as if for a signal to shoot, they shouted, to call forth haply any of those within. The shout was heard by the women-folk, who, emerging from the caverns, informed the Romans how matters stood, one of the two lucidly reporting both the speech and how the deed was done. But it was with difficulty that they listened to her, incredulous of such amazing fortitude; meanwhile they endeavoured to extinguish the flames and soon cutting a passage through them entered the palace. Here encountering the mass of slain, instead of exulting as over enemies, they admired the nobility of their resolve and the contempt of death displayed by so many in carrying it, unwavering, into execution.

Source 11 from Saint Augustine, Volume 1, *Loeb Classical Library Volume L411, translated by George E. McCracken (Cambridge, Mass.: Harvard University Press, 1957), pp. 77–79, 91– 101, 109–113. Reprinted by permission of the publishers and the Trustees of the Loeb Classical Library. The Loeb Classical Library ® is a registered trademark of the President and Fellows of Harvard College.*

11. Saint Augustine, *The City of God*, Book I

XVII ON SUICIDE CAUSED BY FEAR OF PUNISHMENT OR DISGRACE.

For if it is not right on individual authority to slay even a guilty man for whose killing no law has granted permission, certainly a suicide is also a homicide, and he is guilty, when he kills himself, in proportion to his innocence of the deed for which he thought he ought to die. If we rightly execrate Judas' deed, and truth pronounces that when he hanged himself, he increased rather than expiated the crime of that accursed betrayal, since by despairing of God's mercy, though he was at death repentant, he left himself no place for a saving repentance, how much more should the man who has no guilt in him to be punished by such means refrain from killing himself!

When Judas killed himself, he killed an accursed man, and he ended his life guilty not only of Christ's death but also of his own, because, though he was killed to atone for his crime, the killing itself was another crime of his. Why, then, should a man who has done no evil do evil to himself, and in doing away with himself do away with an innocent man so as not to suffer from the crime of another, and perpetrate upon himself a sin of his own, so that another's may not be perpetrated on him?

[227]

XX THAT THERE IS NO AUTHORITY THAT ALLOWS CHRISTIANS IN ANY CASE THE RIGHT TO DIE OF THEIR OWN WILL.

Not for nothing is it that in the holy canonical books no divinely inspired order or permission can be found authorizing us to inflict death upon ourselves, neither in order to acquire immortality nor in order to avert or divert some evil. For we must certainly understand the commandment as forbidding this when it says: "Thou shalt not kill,"[16] particularly since it does not add "thy neighbour," as it does when it forbids false witnessing. . . .

On this basis some try to extend this commandment even to wild and domestic animals and maintain that it is wrong to kill any of them. Why not then extend it also to plants and to anything fixed and fed by roots in the earth? For things of this kind, though they have no feeling, are said to live, and therefore can also die, and hence, when violence is exercised, be slain. Thus the Apostle, when he speaks of seeds of this sort, says: "That which thou sowest is not quickened except it die,"[17] and we find in a psalm, "He killed their vines with hail."[18] Do we from this conclude, when we hear "Thou shalt not kill," that it is wrong to pull up a shrub? Are we so completely deranged that we assent to the Manichaean error?

Hence, putting aside these ravings, if when we read, "Thou shalt not kill," we do not understand this phrase to apply to bushes, because they have no sensation, nor to the unreasoning animals that fly, swim, walk or crawl, because they are not partners with us in the faculty of reason, the privilege not being given them to share it in common with us—and therefore by the altogether righteous ordinance of the Creator both their life and death are a matter subordinate to our needs—the remaining possibility is to understand this commandment, "Thou shalt not kill," as meaning man alone, that is, "neither another nor thyself," for in fact he who kills himself kills what is no other than a man.

XXI WHAT CASES OF HOMICIDE ARE EXCEPTED FROM THE CHARGE OF MURDER?

This very same divine law, to be sure, made certain exceptions to the rule that it is not lawful to kill a human being. The exceptions include only such persons

16. Exodus 20:16. Saint Augustine makes frequent biblical references in his text.
17. 1 Corinthians 15:36.
18. Psalms 78:46.

as God commands to be put to death, either by an enacted law or by special decree applicable to a single person at the given time—but note that the man who is bound to this service under orders, as a sword is bound to be the tool of him who employs it, is not himself the slayer, and consequently there is no breach of this commandment, which says, "Thou shalt not kill," in the case of those who by God's authorization have waged wars, or, who, representing in their person the power of the state, have put criminals to death in accordance with God's law, being vested, that is, with the imperial prerogative of altogether righteous reason. Abraham too not only was not blamed for cruelty, but was even praised for piety, because he resolved to slay his son, not with criminal motives but in obedience to God. And it is properly a question whether we should regard it as equivalent to a command of God when Jephthah slew his daughter who ran to meet him after he had vowed to sacrifice to God the first victim that met him as he returned victorious from battle.[19] Nor is Samson acquitted of guilt on any other plea, inasmuch as he crushed himself by the collapse of the house along with his enemies, than the plea that the Spirit who through him had been working miracles,[20] had secretly ordered this. With these exceptions then, those slain either by application of a just law or by command of God, the very fount of justice, whoever kills a human being, either himself or no matter who, falls within the meshes of the charge of murder.

XXII WHETHER SUICIDE IS EVER A SIGN OF GREATNESS OF MIND.

Those who have laid violent hands upon themselves are perhaps to be admired for the greatness of their souls, but not to be praised for the soundness of their wisdom. If, however, you take reason more carefully into account, you will not really call it greatness of soul which brings anyone to suicide because he or she lacks strength to bear whatever hardships or sins of others may occur. For the mind is rather detected in weakness, if it cannot bear whether it be the harsh enslavement of its own body, or the stupid opinion of the mob; and a mind might better be called greater that can endure instead of fleeing from a distressful life, and that can in the light of pure conscience despise the judgement of men, especially that of the mob, which as a rule is wrapped in a fog of error.

Therefore, if suicide can be thought to be a great-souled act, this quality of greatness of soul was possessed by that Theombrotus[21] of whom they say that,

19. Judges 11:29–40.
20. Judges 16:28–30.
21. **Theombrotus:** a philosopher of Ambracia, Greece.

when he had read Plato's book containing a discussion of the immortality of the soul,[22] he hurled himself headlong from a wall and so departed from this life to that which he thought a better. He was not urged to this act by any calamity of fortune or accusation, false or true, that he had not strength to bear and so made away with himself. Nay, his sole motive for seeking death and breaking the sweet bonds of this life was his greatness of soul. Nevertheless, this Plato himself whom he had read could have borne witness that he acted greatly rather than well, for assuredly Plato would have made this act the first step and the most important step he took himself, and might well have pronounced in favour of it too, had he not, with that intellect by which he saw the soul's immortality, reached the conclusion that suicide should not be committed, nay more, should be forbidden.

Yet in fact many have killed themselves to prevent falling into the hands of the enemy. We are not now asking whether this was done but whether it should have been done. Sound reasoning, naturally, is to be preferred even to precedents, but there are precedents for that matter not discordant with reason—such, be it noted, as are precedents the more worthy of imitation as they are more outstanding in piety. No case of suicide occurred among patriarchs, among prophets, among apostles, seeing that the Lord Christ himself, when he advised them, if they suffered persecution, to flee from city to city,[23] might then have advised them to lay hands upon themselves to avoid falling into the hands of their persecutors. Furthermore, granted that he gave no command or advice to His disciples to employ this means of departing from life, though he promised that he would prepare everlasting mansions for them when they departed, then, no matter what precedents are brought forward by heathen that know not God, it is obvious that suicide is unlawful for those who worship the one true God.

XXVI WHAT EXPLANATION WE SHOULD ADOPT TO ACCOUNT FOR THE SAINTS' DOING CERTAIN THINGS THAT THEY ARE KNOWN TO HAVE DONE WHICH IT IS NOT LAWFUL TO DO.

But, they say, in time of persecution certain saintly women, to avoid the pursuers of their chastity, cast themselves into a river that would ravish and drown them, and in that way they died and their memorial shrines are frequented by great numbers who venerate them as martyrs in the Catholic Church.

22. Plato's dialogue *The Phaedo*.
23. Matthew 10:5-15.

With regard to these women I dare not give any rash judgement. I do not know whether the divine authority has counselled the church by some trustworthy testimonies to honour their memory in this, and it may be so. For what if the women acted as they did, not by human misconception, but by divine command, and they did not go astray in their act, but were obedient? Compare the case of Samson, where it would be sin to hold any other view. When God, moreover, gives a command and makes it clear without ambiguity that he gives it, who can summon obedience to judgement? Who can draw up a brief against religious deference to God? . . .

. . . Let anyone, therefore, who is told that he has no right to kill himself, do the deed if he is so ordered by him whose orders must not be slighted. There is just one proviso: he must be sure that his divine command is not made precarious by any doubt. It is through the ear that we take note of men's thoughts; we do not arrogate to ourselves any right to judge such as are kept secret. No one "knows what goes on in a man except the spirit of the man that is in him."[24]

This we say, this we declare, this we by all means endorse: that no man ought to inflict on himself a voluntary death, thinking to escape temporary ills, lest he find himself among ills that are unending; that no one ought to do so because of another's sins, lest by the very act he bring into being a sin that is his own, when he would not have been polluted by another's; that no one ought to do so on account of any past sins, inasmuch as he needs this life the more to make possible their healing by repentance; that no one ought to do so thinking to satisfy his hunger for the better life for which we hope after death, inasmuch as the better life after death does not accept those who are guilty of their own death.

QUESTIONS TO CONSIDER

The evidence in this chapter all deals with the central issue of suicide, but it comes from sources originating over an extraordinarily long period, about a millennium and one-half of the ancient period. Our objective in spanning such a period is to examine the continuities and changes in ancient thought on the subject of self-destruction by asking you to address three progressively more probing central questions based on the sources.

The first question asks that you consider each of the selections individually by identifying every author's thought on the suicide that was common in much of the ancient world. How do all of the authors, except Saint Augustine, implicitly or more directly accept suicide as justifiable? What sort of ethical considerations does the act raise for each author? What limitations, if any, does each place on self-destruction?

The second question requires that you place each of the sources in the intellectual context within which

24. 1 Corinthians 2:11.

[231]

its author wrote. You must consider the religious beliefs and philosophical outlook of each period represented in the sources: the Hellenic and Hellenistic ages, the Roman Empire, Old and New Testament Palestine, and the early Christian era. How did the ideas of the vari-ous thinkers reflect the religious and philosophical orientations of their respective ages?

The third question asks that you examine the evolution of ancient ideas on suicide over an extended period of time. What basic continuities on this subject do you note in ancient thought? At what point did ancient thought on suicide change? What aspects of Christian doctrine and the controversies surrounding

this faith in the third and fourth centuries C.E. promoted the viewpoint advanced by Saint Augustine? On what basis did he deny that the acts of self-destruction in the Bible were true suicides? Why might you assume that Saint Augustine's theology heavily influenced Western attitudes toward suicide in the Christian era that emerged from the decline and fall of the Roman Empire?

As you consider your answers to these questions, you should better comprehend the ancients' views on suicide, but even more importantly, you should understand the philosophical and theological foundations for those ideas.

EPILOGUE

Very few ancient thinkers unconditionally condemned the act of self-destruction, although as we have seen, Socrates noted one such group, the Pythagoreans. [We must add that Neoplatonists like Plotinus (205–270) also condemned suicide. They held that since one's standing in the afterlife rested on the state of one's soul at death, suicide was inadmissible because the possibility of moral improvement existed as long as life endured.] Thus, Saint Augustine's general condemnation of suicide reflected a distinct break with the past. Indeed, his dictum that suicide was murder, reaffirmed by later theologians, including Saint Thomas Aquinas (1225–1274), shaped the religious and legal response of

the Christian West to the act of self-destruction into the twenty-first century.[25]

Religiously, Saint Augustine's condemnation of all forms of suicide, perhaps reinforced by primitive suicide taboos among the Germanic tribes overwhelming late ancient Rome, became part of canon law. That law always relieved persons of

---

25. Indeed, the very word *suicide* did not exist in Western languages prior to the early seventeenth century, and some variation of the phrase "murder of oneself" described the act of self-destruction in most European tongues. The word *suicide* seems first to have appeared in a work of the Englishman Sir Thomas Browne, *Religio medici*, published in 1642. The use of the term slowly gained ground in English usage, and in the eighteenth century it found its way into French, Italian, Portuguese, and Spanish lexicons. Literally translated from its Latin roots as "to strike oneself mortally," the word itself is highly significant because it eschews the more condemnatory term *murder*.

diminished psychological capacity from the spiritual consequence of suicide. But for suicides of apparently sound mind, the act of self-destruction incurred severe spiritual penalties. Theologians believed suicides by such individuals represented despair and thus rejection of the Christian message, perhaps reflecting Satanic possession. Thus at the Council of Braga in 563, the Roman Catholic Church denied religious burial to these persons, a practice many Protestant groups perpetuated after the Reformation of the sixteenth century.

Legally, most medieval and early modern Western states reflected canon law by adopting statutes recognizing suicide as a form of murder. Thus, persons taking their own lives might incur worldly as well as spiritual penalties if a postmortem judicial proceeding determined that they had, indeed, ended their own lives while in a sound mental state. Worldly penalties typically included two elements. The first was financial in nature. Under laws dating from at least as early as the thirteenth century in England and France, the state confiscated the property of the successful suicide. In the second form of punishment, the authorities desecrated the corpse of the suicide in ceremonies that included the spiritual penalty of denied burial. Thus, in Catholic France prior to the Revolution, judicial authorities dragged suicides' corpses through the streets, frequently displayed the remains to the public, and disposed of the bodies without burial rites, often as refuse. In England, after the Reformation, the authorities buried suicides' remains without religious sacraments at crossroads. Because of popular fears that the spirits of suicides might return to the world of the living, the authorities often drove stakes through the bodies and into the ground to prevent the return of the deceased from their graves. Other Western countries engaged in similar practices that long endured, and attempted suicide was a capital offense in many legal codes for centuries.

Only in the late seventeenth and eighteenth centuries, in a process that historians have called a "secularization of suicide,"[26] did many Western thinkers begin to view the act of self-destruction as a social, psychological, or medical problem rather than the moral and theological issue defined by Saint Augustine. Nevertheless, the law long reflected this earlier attitude, and the act of suicide persistently excited basic religious and philosophical controversies. Suicide remained a crime in France until 1791, and the last English crossroads burial occurred in 1823. Attempted suicide continued to be a crime in England until 1961, and until that same year, those of sound mind who took their own lives might be denied burial rites by the Church of England. Attempted suicide remains a criminal offense in a small number of American states today.

26. This terminology was introduced by the work of Michael MacDonald and Terence Murphy, *Sleepless Souls: Suicide in Early Modern England* (Oxford: Oxford University Press, 1990).

CHAPTER TEN

SLAVE LAW IN ROMAN AND

GERMANIC SOCIETY

In all the cultures of the ancient Mediterranean, some people were slaves, owned as property by other people. In Mesopotamia and Egypt, people became slaves in a variety of ways, and the earliest law codes, such as that of Hammurabi (ca 1780 B.C.E.), include provisions regarding slavery. Many slaves were war captives, brought into the area from outside along with other types of booty. Some were criminals, for whom slavery was the punishment for a crime. Some had been sold into slavery by their parents or had sold themselves into slavery in times of economic hardship. Others became slaves to repay debts, a condition that was often temporary. In these cultures, slaves performed a variety of tasks, from farming to highly skilled professional and administrative work, but the proportion of slaves in the population was not very great and most work was carried out by free persons.

Thus, historians describe Mesopotamia and Egypt as slave-using but not slave societies.

By contrast, republican Rome was truly a slave society, in which a significant proportion of the population were slaves—perhaps one-quarter or one-third by the second century B.C.E.—and in which slaves did much of the productive labor. The military conquests of Rome during the second and first centuries B.C.E. provided many new war captives and also increased the wealth of Rome's elite, who invested in huge agricultural estates (termed *latifundia*). These estates were too large to be worked by single peasant families—who were often migrating to the cities in any case—and so an increasing share of agricultural production was carried on by large labor gangs of slaves under the supervision of overseers, who might themselves be slaves. The owners of both the land and the slaves were often absentee, living in Rome or another urban center rather than out on the latifundia themselves. This system of agricultural slavery continued into the Roman Empire, although the influx of new slaves lessened somewhat as military expansion slowed and laws were passed prohibiting the enslavement of subjects of the Empire. In addition, urban slaves who worked as household servants, artisans, teachers, gladiators, or shopkeepers continued to be very common.

The Germanic tribes that gradually migrated into the Roman Empire beginning in the second century were also slave-owning cultures, although the relative number of slaves among them was probably less than that in Rome. When they conquered Roman lands, they generally took a proportion of the slaves and the land for themselves, leaving the rest to the existing Roman proprietors. However, the breakdown in communication and political control that accompanied the disintegration of the Roman Empire in the West made it increasingly difficult for absentee owners to control their estates and to ship their products safely to distant markets. Thus, like many other aspects of life during this period, slavery became increasingly localized and less economically significant than it had been earlier in these areas, although it did not disappear.

Slavery in both Roman and Germanic societies was based not on racial distinctions but on notions of personal freedom that could be very complex. At the heart of this complexity was the issue that a slave was both a person, able to engage in relationships with other persons and to act on his or her own, and a thing, owned by another person. Law codes developed by both Romans and Germans had to balance these two aspects of being a slave, as well as regulate other matters concerning slaves and slavery. They had to establish and protect the boundaries between slave and free, but also establish ways in which those boundaries could be crossed, as slavery was not necessarily a permanent status. Your task in this chapter will be to investigate Roman and Germanic laws regarding slavery during the period 400 to 1000, in order to answer the following questions: How were legal distinctions between slave and free established, structured, and maintained, and how could they be overcome? What similarities and differences are there in Roman and Germanic laws regarding slavery?

SOURCES AND METHOD

When historians investigate legal developments, they often use law codes in conjunction with court records and other documents to examine the actual workings of the law, or to contrast legal theory with reality. For the period we are investigating in this chapter, sources describing actual legal practice in central and western Europe are virtually nonexistent, and so our focus will be strictly on the law codes. (Other sources regarding slavery in the Roman Empire do exist, such as economic treatises, histories of slave revolts, and philosophical discussions of slavery, but there are no parallel sources for early Germanic societies.) We must thus keep in mind that everything we read is essentially legal theory, describing what is supposed to happen rather than what actually does happen. Law codes are not written in a vacuum, however. They reflect not only the ideals of the legal and political authorities who were their authors, but also these authorities' assumptions about what people—in this case slaves, their owners, and people who came into contact with slaves and their owners—might actually do. In some cases laws also explicitly describe actual conduct, generally as a preamble to a prohibition of this conduct, or a succession of laws implies actual conduct, as prohibitions are made more specific or penalties are made more stringent.

It is important in this chapter, then, to keep in mind the limitations of using law codes as a source, and it is also important to recognize that the law codes we will be using come from two cultures that had very different notions concerning the origin, function, and purpose of law. Roman law began during the republican period as a set of rules governing the private lives of citizens, and was later expanded to include the handling of disputes between Romans and non-Romans and between foreigners under Roman jurisdiction. The first written codification, the Twelve Tables, was made in the middle of the fifth century B.C.E. and posted publicly, giving at least those Romans who could read direct access to it. Legal interpreters called *praetors*

and *judges* called judices made decisions based on explicit statutes and also on their own notions of what would be fair and equitable, which gave them a great deal of flexibility. Praetors generally followed the laws set by their predecessors, announcing publicly at the beginning of their terms of office that they would do this, but they also added to the body of law as new issues arose. Thus Roman law was adaptable to new conditions, with jurists in the Empire regarding their work as building on that of earlier centuries rather than negating it. Ultimately all those living within the boundaries of the Roman Empire were regarded as subject to the same law, the *ius gentium*, or "law of peoples."

Roman law regarding slavery—like all Roman law—for most of the republican and imperial periods was a mixture of senatorial statutes, edicts of elected officials, opinions of learned jurists, imperial decrees, and rulings by lesser officials. Under Emperor Theodosius II (r. 408–450), an attempt was made to compile some of the actual imperial decrees, and the resultant Theodosian Code promulgated in 435–438 contained all of the imperial laws issued since the time of the emperor Constantine (r. 311–337) that were still in effect, including those on slavery. Theodosius ruled the eastern half of the Roman Empire (which later came to be called the Byzantine Empire), but his laws were promulgated for both the eastern and western halves. The Theodosian Code was expanded under the direction of the Byzantine Emperor Justinian (r. 527–565), with older and newer laws and the opinions of jurists added. Justinian's Code, promulgated in 529–533 and officially termed the *Corpus Juris Civilis*, became the basis of Byzantine legal procedure for nearly a millennium.

In contrast to Roman written statutory law, Germanic law remained a body of traditions handed down orally for almost a thousand years after the first codification of Roman law. Like all systems of customary law around the world, it was regarded as binding because it represented the immemorial customs of a specific tribe. The ultimate authority in this legal system was not an abstract body of laws or a group of legal interpreters, but the king, whose chief legal function was to "speak the law"—that is, to decide cases based on existing oral tradition; neither the king nor anyone else could (at least in theory) make new laws. This body of custom was regarded as the inalienable possession of all members of a tribe, no matter where they happened to be, and was thus attached to persons rather than to geographic areas the way Roman (and today's) statutory law codes were.

At roughly the same time that codifications of Roman law were promulgated by the emperors Theodosius and Justinian, Germanic kings in western Europe supported the initial written codifications of what had been oral customary law. These codes usually bore the name of the tribe, such as the Lombard Law, the Burgundian Law, or the Salic Law (the law of the Salian Franks). On the continent of Europe, such law codes were written down in Latin, often by Roman jurists employed by Germanic kings, so that they sometimes included Roman legal tradition as well as Germanic customs, particularly in southern Europe, where Roman culture was strongest. In northern Europe and in England—where the laws were initially written in the West Saxon dialect that became Old English—Roman influences were weaker, making the codes of these areas, such as those of the Frisians and the Anglo-Saxons, more purely customary in origin.

When the Germanic tribes came into the Empire, these two notions of the law—statutory and geographic versus customary and personal—came into direct conflict. The problem was solved initially by letting Romans be judged according to written Roman law while non-Romans were judged by their own oral customs. As the Germanic kingdoms became more firmly established, their rulers saw the merits of a written code, but two legal systems—one for Romans and one for Germanic people—often existed side by side for centuries in these areas. Only in cases that involved a conflict between a Roman and a German was the former expected to follow the new Germanic code. As noted above, however, Roman principles did shape these Germanic codes to some degree. Though the initial codifications claimed to be simply the recording of long-standing customs, in reality the laws often modified customs that no longer fit the needs of the Germanic peoples as they became more settled and adopted some aspects of the more sophisticated

Roman culture. Later kings were also not hesitant to make new laws when situations demanded it and to state explicitly that this is what they were doing. Thus Germanic codes gradually evolved from records of tribal customs based on moral sanctions and notions of a common tradition into collections of royal statutes based on the political authority of kings. They remained more closely linked to the ruler than Roman law and never included the opinions of legal commentators the way Justinian's Code did, but, like Roman law, they were eventually tied to a geographic area rather than to a group of people.

There were thus significant differences between Roman and Germanic societies in the function and complexity of law, but the legal codes of all these societies included provisions regarding slavery. The sources for this chapter come from seven different law codes, two from Roman tradition—the Theodosian Code and Justinian's Code—and five from Germanic tradition—Burgundian, Salic, Lombard, Alemannic, and Anglo-Saxon. Many of these law codes exist in multiple manuscript versions, with the earliest extant version often dating from centuries after the code was first compiled. This provides much fuel for scholarly disagreement about exactly when they were drawn up, exactly which sections date from the initial codification and which from later revisions, and exactly how certain sections are supposed to read. (Scholars can often trace the path manuscripts followed by noting which errors were recopied by subsequent scribes; often this does not help in determining which versions are more "authentic," however.) For this chapter, we have used the version of these codes most widely accepted by recent scholarship, but you should be aware that any edition or translation of texts like these from manuscript cultures involves a decision on the part of the editor as to which version to use.

To explore the legal definitions of and boundaries between slavery and freedom, we will be examining four basic issues in this chapter: (A) How could a person become a slave, or a slave become free? (B) How were slaves valued, in comparison to other things a person might own, and what limits were placed on the treatment of slaves by their owners? (C) How were personal relationships between slave and free regulated? (D) How were slaves differentiated from free persons in terms of criminal actions committed by them or against them? To assist you in working through the issues in this chapter, provisions in the laws have been grouped according to these four topics rather than being presented in the order in which they appear in the codes. (In many of these codes, particularly the Germanic ones, laws are arranged completely haphazardly in any case, so that the order makes no difference.) Thus, as you are taking notes on the sources, it would be a good idea to draw up a chart for each issue. Other than this, your basic method in this chapter is careful reading.

Source 1 includes selections from the Theodosian Code. According to the selections in Source 1A, what are some of the ways in which one could become a slave in the late Roman

Empire? What are some ways in which slaves could become free? According to 1B, what would happen to a master who beat his slaves? According to 1C, what would happen to a woman who had sexual relations with or married one of her slaves? To a man who had sexual relations with one of his slaves? To a decurion (a man who was a member of a local municipal council) who did so? According to 1D, what would happen to rebellious slaves?

Source 2 contains selections from Justinian's Code, which was itself divided into three parts: the *Codex*, actual imperial legislation, including much that was contained in the Theodosian Code; the *Digest*, the opinions of various jurists from throughout the history of Rome; and the *Institutes*, an officially prescribed course for first-year law students, in which some of the opinions found in the *Digest* are repeated. The legal opinions included in the *Digest* sometimes refer to specific imperial statutes, and sometimes simply describe what the commentator saw as Roman tradition in regard to legal categories or procedures. Like legal opinions today, however, the judgments of these jurists shaped the handling of cases, for later judges and lawyers looked to earlier precedents and opinions when making their decisions. They are thus much more important than the opinion of a private person on an issue would be, and all the selections included here come from the *Digest*. According to Source 2A, what were some of the ways in which one could become a slave or become free? Would becoming free remove all obligations a slave had toward his master? According to 2C, did slaves have family relationships? According to 2D, what would happen to someone who killed a slave? To slaves whose master was killed while they were within earshot? To runaway slaves and those who protected them?

Putting the information from Sources 1 and 2 together, you can begin to develop an idea about the legal status of slaves in the later Roman Empire. What are some of the ways one could cross from slave to free? From free to slave? Is this a hard boundary, as the writers of the *Digest* imply in 2A, or are there intermediate steps? How do restrictions on slave/free sexual relationships help to maintain the boundaries? Why do you think there are gender differences in such restrictions? In what ways do the laws in 1D and 2D regard the slave as a thing? In what ways as a person?

Sources 3 through 7 are selections from Germanic law codes, which were often written down under the reign of one king and then expanded under his successors. Compared with Roman law, Germanic codes were extremely short and consist solely of statements of law, with no juristic opinions such as those contained in the *Digest*. They thus offer a less full picture of slave life than does Roman law, but slaves are mentioned in many of their clauses. In Germanic society, murder, injuries, or insults to honor had resulted in feuds between individuals and families, but by the time the law codes were written down, a system of monetary compensatory payments—called *wergeld* in the case of murder or *composition* in the case of lesser injuries—was being devised as a substitute. These compensatory payments were set according to the severity of the loss or injury, and also according to the social status of the perpetrator and the victim.

Source 3 comes from one of the earliest Germanic law codes, the Law of Gundobad, drawn up for his Burgundian subjects by King Gundobad (r. 474–516), who ruled the Burgundian kingdom in what is now southeastern France. (Following the principle that customary law applied to persons and not territories, Gundobad also drew up a separate code for his Roman subjects, the *Lex Romana Burgundionem*, at about the same time.) According to the laws in Source 3A, what were some of the ways in which one could become a slave or be freed if one were a slave? According to 3C, what were the penalties for rape of freewomen and slaves? For women who willingly had sexual relations with slaves? According to 3D, what was the relative value of slaves as compared to that of free persons and freedmen (former slaves), at least in regard to their teeth and female honor?

Source 4 comes from the Germanic tribe known as the Franks, who conquered the Burgundian kingdom in 534. The original Frankish code, the *Pactus Legis Salicae*, was issued by King Clovis in about 510 and was amended and revised by many of his successors. (Like all Germanic codes, it did not apply to everyone living under Frankish overlordship; Burgundians living within the Frankish kingdom continued to be judged by

Burgundian law for centuries after the conquest.) It includes no laws on how one becomes a slave or is released from slavery, but it does include sections on sexual relations with slaves, and on slaves who steal or run away. According to the laws in Source 4C, in the first group, what would happen to a freeman or freewoman who marries or has sexual intercourse with a slave? To a slave who marries or has sexual intercourse with a free person or another slave? According to 4D, how were the slave's owners' rights balanced against those of the person from whom the slave stole? How were those who encouraged slaves to run away to be punished? How does this punishment compare with that set for slaves who steal?

Source 5 contains selections from the Lombard Laws, written down between 643 and 755 under the direction of various Lombard kings, including King Rothair (issued in 643), King Luitprand (issued 713–735), and King Aistulf (issued 750–755). The Lombards invaded Italy in 568, after the Franks, Burgundians, and other tribes had already established successor kingdoms in parts of the old Roman Empire, and established a kingdom in central and northern Italy that lasted until 774, when it was conquered by the Frankish ruler Charlemagne. Like Burgundian law, Lombard law remained in force for Lombards within Frankish territory for centuries—in fact, until the city-states of Italy began to adopt Roman legal principles and the *Corpus Juris Civilis* in the twelfth century. Lombard law was more comprehensive than the Burgundian and Frankish codes, and included provisions regarding all of the issues we are investigating in this chapter. According to the laws in Source 5A, what were some of the ways in which a person could become a slave in Lombard society? How could a slave be freed? According to 5B, what was the relative value of slaves as compared to horses? According to 5C, how were marriages between slaves, freed persons, and free people to be handled? According to 5D, how were fugitive slaves and slaves who revolted to be handled?

Source 6 comes from the Germanic tribe known as the Alamans, who settled in what is now southern Germany and Switzerland in the third century C.E. and wrote their law codes between 613 and 713. Like other Germanic codes, Alamannic law set compensatory payments for various injuries and actions, and also used slavery as a punishment for certain crimes. According to Source 6A, what was one of the ways in which people could become slaves? According to 6B, were there limits on a master's treatment of slaves? According to 6C, what would happen to a freewoman who married a slave? According to 6D, what were the relative values placed on men and women from the three basic social groups, free persons, freedpersons, and slaves? How was the rape of slaves to be compensated?

Source 7, the final source for this chapter, contains provisions from Anglo-Saxon law codes from the various kingdoms of England, dating from the sixth through the tenth centuries. These codes were written in Old English, not in Latin, and show no signs of Roman influence, although many of their provisions are similar to those we have seen in other Germanic codes. According to Source 7A, laws issued by Edward the Elder (dated between 901 and 925), what was one way in which a person could become a slave? According to 7B, from the laws of Ine (688–695), what were some of the limitations on a master's treatment of his slaves? According to 7D, laws of Aethelbert of Kent (565–604) and Alfred (890–899), what was the punishment for rape of a slave? How did this differ depending on the status of the slave and the perpetrator?

You now need to put together the Germanic material in the same way that you did the Roman. How could people in Germanic society move from free people to slaves? From slaves to free people? Are there intermediate steps between these two, and how do the rights of these people differ from those of free people and slaves? What are the consequences of various types of slave/free sexual relationships? Are there hierarchies of status and value among slaves? On what are these based? Do the laws regarding crimes against slaves and crimes committed by slaves tend to view slaves as things or as persons?

THE EVIDENCE

Source 1 from Clyde Pharr, editor, The Theodosian Code (Princeton, N.J.: Princeton University Press, 1952), Sections 3.3.1; 4.6.7; 5.6.3; 5.9.1; 7.13.16; 7.18.4; 9.12.1–2; 9.9.1–3, 6; 10.10.33; 14.18.1. Copyright © 1952 by Princeton University Press. Reprinted by permission of Princeton University Press.

1. Theodosian Code

A. Slave to Free/Free to Slave

[3.3.1] All those persons whom the piteous fortune of their parents has consigned to slavery while their parents thereby were seeking sustenance shall be restored to their original status of free birth. Certainly no person shall demand repayment of the purchase price, if he has been compensated by the slavery of a freeborn person for a space of time that is not too short.

INTERPRETATION: If a father, forced by need, should sell any freeborn child whatsoever, the child cannot remain in perpetual slavery, but if he has made compensation by his slavery, he shall be restored to his freeborn status without even the repayment of the purchase price.

[4.6.7] We sanction that the name of natural children shall be placed upon those who have been begotten and brought into this world as the result of a lawful union without an honorable performance of the marriage ceremony. But it is established that children born from the womb of a slave woman are slaves, according to the law . . . [I]f natural children have been born from a slave woman and have not been manumitted by their master, they are reckoned among the slaves belonging to his inheritance.

[5.6.3] We have subjected the Scyrae, a barbarian nation, to Our power after We had routed a very great force of Chuni, with whom they had allied themselves. Therefore We grant to all persons the opportunity to supply their own fields with men of the aforesaid race.

[5.9.1] If any person should take up a boy or a girl child that has been cast out of its home with the knowledge and consent of its father or owner, and if he should rear this child to strength with his own sustenance, he shall have the right to keep the said child under the same status as he wished it to have when he took charge of it, that is, as his child or as a slave, whichever he should prefer.

[14.18.1] If there should be any persons who adopt the profession of mendicancy[1] and who are induced to seek their livelihood at public expense, each of them shall be examined. The soundness of body and the vigor of years of each one of them shall be investigated. In the case of those who are able, the necessity shall be placed upon them that the zealous and diligent informer shall

---

1. **mendicancy:** begging.

obtain the ownership of those beggars who are held bound by their servile status, and such informer shall be supported by the right to the perpetual colonate[2] of those beggars who are attended by only the liberty of their birth rights, provided that the informer should betray and prove such sloth.

[7.13.16] In the matter of defense against hostile attacks,[3] We order that consideration be given not only to the legal status of soldiers, but also to their physical strength. Although We believe that freeborn persons are aroused by love of country, We exhort slaves[4] also, by the authority of this edict, that as soon as possible they shall offer themselves for the labors of war, and if they receive their arms as men fit for military service, they shall obtain the reward of freedom, and they shall also receive two solidi each for travel money. Especially, of course, do We urge this service upon the slaves of those persons who are retained in the armed imperial service, and likewise upon the slaves of federated allies and of conquered peoples, since it is evident that they are making war also along with their masters.

[7.18.4] [In the case of deserters,] if a slave should surrender such deserter, he shall be given freedom. If a freeborn person of moderate status should surrender such deserter, he shall gain immunity.[5]

B. Value and Treatment of Slaves

[9.12.1–2] If a master should beat a slave with light rods or lashes or if he should cast him into chains for the purpose of custody, he shall not endure any fear of criminal charges if the slave should die, for We abolish all consideration of time limitations and legal interpretation.[6] The master shall not, indeed, use his own right immoderately, but he shall be guilty of homicide if he should kill the slave voluntarily by a blow of a club or of a stone, at any rate if he should use a weapon and inflict a lethal wound or should order the slave to be hanged by a noose, or if he should command by a shameful order that he be thrown from a high place or should administer the virus of a poison or should lacerate his body by public punishments,[7] that is, by cutting through his sides with the claws of wild beasts[8] or by applying fire and burning his body, or if with the savagery of monstrous barbarians he should force bodies and limbs weakening and flowing with dark blood, mingled with gore, to surrender their life almost in the midst of tortures.

2. **colonate:** forced labor on farms.

3. At this time the Roman Empire was gradually crumbling from the attacks of the barbarians.

4. In violation of long-established Roman custom.

5. From compulsory public services, including taxes.

6. The references seem to be to preceding laws, which specified distinctions depending on whether a slave died immediately or after a period of time, and which contained various technicalities.

7. Types of punishment that were inflicted for certain public crimes.

8. Implements of torture, actually made of metal.

Whenever such chance attends the beating of slaves by their masters that the slaves die, the masters shall be free from blame if by the correction of very evil deeds they wished to obtain better conduct on the part of their household slaves. . . .

INTERPRETATION: If a slave should die while his master is punishing a fault, the master shall not be held on the charge of homicide, because he is guilty of homicide only if he is convicted of having intended to kill the slave. For disciplinary correction is not reckoned as a crime.

C. Slave/Free Relations

[9.9.1–6] If any woman is discovered to have a clandestine love affair with her slave, she shall be subject to the capital sentence, and the rascally slave shall be delivered to the flames. All persons shall have the right to bring an accusation of this public crime; office staffs shall have the right to report it; even a slave shall have permission to lodge information, and freedom shall be granted to him if the crime is proved, although punishment threatens him if he makes a false accusation. 1. If a woman has been so married[9] before the issuance of this law, she shall be separated from such an association, shall be deprived not only of her home but also of participation in the life of the province, and shall mourn the absence of her exiled lover. 2. The children also whom she bears from this union shall be stripped of all the insignia of rank. They shall remain in bare freedom, and neither through themselves nor through the interposition of another person shall they receive anything under any title of a will from the property of the woman. 3. Moreover, the inheritance of the woman, in case of intestacy, shall be granted either to her children, if she has legitimate ones, or to the nearest kinsmen and cognates, or to the person whom the rule of law admits, so that whatever of their own property her former lover and the children conceived from him appear by any chance to have had shall be joined to the property of the woman and may be vindicated by the aforesaid successors. . . .

6. For after the issuance of this law We punish by death those persons who commit this crime. But those who have been separated in accordance with this law and secretly come together again and renew the forbidden union and who are convicted by the evidence of slaves or that of the office of the special investigator or also by the information of nearest kinsmen shall sustain a similar penalty.

INTERPRETATION: If any freeborn woman should join herself secretly to her own slave, she shall suffer capital punishment. A slave also who should be convicted of adultery with his mistress shall be burned by fire. Whoever wishes shall have it in his power to bring accusation of a crime of this kind.

9. A loose use of the word marriage, as slaves could not enter legally recognized marriages (*conubia*) because those were contracts available only to free persons. Instead they were joined in less formal unions termed *contubernia*.

Even slaves or maidservants, if they should bring an accusation of this crime, shall be heard, on this condition, however, that they shall obtain their freedom if they prove their accusation; that if they falsify, they shall be punished. The inheritance of a woman who defiles herself with such a crime shall be granted either to her children, if they were conceived from her husband, or to those near kinsmen who succeed according to law.

[12.1.6] Although it appears unworthy for men, even though not endowed with any high rank, to descend to sordid marriages with slave women, nevertheless this practice is not prohibited by law; but a legal marriage cannot exist with servile persons, and from a slave union of this kind, slaves are born. We command, therefore, that decurions shall not be led by their lust to take refuge in the bosom of the most powerful houses. For if a decurion should be secretly united with any slave woman belonging to another man and if the overseers and procurators should not be aware of this, We order that the woman shall be cast into the mines through sentence of the judge, and the decurion himself shall be deported to an island; his movable property and his urban slaves shall be confiscated; his landed estates and rustic slaves shall be delivered to the municipality of which he had been a decurion, if he had been freed from paternal power and has no children or parents, or even close kinsmen, who may be called to his inheritance, according to the order of the law. But if the overseers or procurators of the place in which the disgraceful act was committed were aware of it and were unwilling to divulge this crime of which they were aware, they shall be cast into the mines. But if the master permitted such offense to be committed or afterwards learned of the deed and concealed it, and if indeed, it was perpetrated on his farm, the farm with the slaves and flocks and all other things which are used in rural cultivation shall be [confiscated].

D. Criminal Actions
by/toward Slaves

[10.10.33] The lawful distinction between slavery and freedom shall stand firm. We sanction the rights of masters by the restitution of their slaves, who shall not rebel with impunity.

Source 2 from S. P. Scott, translator, Corpus Juris Civilis: The Civil Law *(Cincinnati, Ohio: The Central Trust, 1932), Sections 1.5.4–5; 9.2.2; 11.4.1; 29.5.1; 37.14.1, 19; 38.10.10; 40.1.5.*

2. Selections from the *Digest* of Justinian's Code

A. Slave to Free/Free to Slave

[1.5.4] Liberty is the natural power of doing whatever anyone wishes to do unless he is prevented in some way, by force or by law.

(1) Slavery is an institution of the Law of Nations by means of which anyone may subject one man to the control of another, contrary to nature.

(2) Slaves are so called for the reason that military commanders were accustomed to sell their captives, and in this manner to preserve them, instead of putting them to death.

(3) They are styled *mancipia*, because they are taken by the hands [*manus*] of their enemies.

[1.5.5] One condition is common to all slaves; but of persons who are free some are born such, and others are manumitted.

(1) Slaves are brought under our ownership either by the Civil Law or by that of Nations. This is done by the Civil Law where anyone who is over twenty years of age permits himself to be sold for the sake of sharing in his own price. Slaves become our property by the Law of Nations when they are either taken from the enemy, or are born of our female slaves.

(2) Persons are born free who are born from a free mother, and it is sufficient for her to have been free at the time when her child was born, even though she may have been a slave when she conceived; and, on the other hand, if she was free when she conceived, and was a slave when she brought forth, it has been established that her child is born free, nor does it make any difference whether she conceived in a lawful marriage or through promiscuous intercourse; because the misfortune of the mother should not be a source of injury to her unborn child.

(3) Hence the following question arose, where a female slave who was pregnant, has been manumitted, and is afterwards again made a slave, or, after having been expelled from the city, should bring forth a child, whether that child should be free or a slave? It was very properly established that it was born free; and that it is sufficient for a child who is unborn that its mother should have been free during the intermediate time.

[40.1.5] If a slave should allege that he was purchased with his own money, he can appear in court against his master, whose good faith he impugns, and complain that he has not been manumitted by him; but he must do this at Rome, before the Urban Prefect, or in the provinces before the Governor, in accordance with the Sacred Constitutions of the Divine Brothers; under the penalty, however, of being condemned to the mines, if he should attempt this and not prove his case; unless his master prefers that he be restored to him, and then it should be decided that he will not be liable to a more severe penalty.

(1) Where, however, a slave is ordered to be free after having rendered his accounts, an arbiter between the slave and his master, that is to say, the heir, shall be appointed for the purpose of having the accounts rendered in his presence.

[37.14.1] Governors should hear the complaints of patrons against their freedmen, and their cases should be tried without delay; for if a freedman is ungrateful, he should not go unpunished. Where, however, the freedman fails in the duty which he owes to his patron, his patroness, or their children, he should only be punished lightly, with a warning that a more severe penalty will be imposed if he again gives cause for complaint, and then be dismissed. But if he is guilty of insult or abuse of his patrons, he should be sent into temporary exile. If he offers them personal violence, he must be sentenced to the mines.

[37.14.19] A freedman is ungrateful when he does not show proper respect for his patron, or refuses to manage his property, or undertake the guardianship of his children.

C. Slave/Free Relations

[38.10.10] We make use of this term, that is to say, cognates, even with reference to slaves. Therefore, we speak of the parents, the children, and the brothers of slaves; but cognation is not recognized by servile laws.

D. Criminal Actions by/toward
Slaves

[11.4.1] He who conceals a fugitive slave is a thief.

(1) The Senate decreed that fugitive slaves shall not be admitted on land or be protected by the superintendents or agents of the possessors of the same, and prescribed a fine. But, if anyone should, within twenty days, restore fugitive slaves to their owners, or bring them before magistrates, what they had previously done will be pardoned; but it was afterwards stated in the

same Decree of the Senate that immunity is granted to anyone who restores fugitive slaves to their masters, or produces them before a magistrate within the prescribed time, when they are found on his premises. . . .

(4) And the magistrates are very properly notified to detain them carefully in custody to prevent their escape. . . .

(7) Careful custody permits the use of irons.

[9.2.2] It is provided by the first section of the *Lex Aquilia* that, "Where anyone unlawfully kills a male or female slave belonging to another, or a quadruped included in the class of cattle, let him be required to pay a sum equal to the greatest value that the same was worth during the past year."

[29.5.1] As no household can be safe unless slaves are compelled, under peril of their lives, to protect their masters, not only from persons belonging to his family, but also from strangers, certain decrees of the Senate were enacted with reference to putting to public torture all the slaves belonging to a household in case of the violent death of their master . . . , for the reason that slaves are punished whenever they do not assist their master against anyone who is guilty of violence towards him, when they are able to do so. . . . Whenever slaves can afford assistance to their master, they should not prefer their own safety to his. Moreover, a female slave who is in the same room with her mistress can give her assistance, if not with her body, certainly by crying out, so that those who are in the house or the neighbors can hear her; and this is evident even if she should allege that the murderer threatened her with death if she cried out. She ought, therefore, to undergo capital punishment, to prevent other slaves from thinking that they should consult their own safety when their master is in danger.

Source 3 from Katherine Fischer Drew, translator, The Burgundian Code *(Philadelphia: University of Pennsylvania Press, 1972), Sections 26, 30, 33, 35, 88, Constitutiones Extravagantes 21.9. Copyright © 1972 University of Pennsylvania Press. Reprinted by permission of the University of Pennsylvania Press.*

3. Selections from The Burgundian Code

A. Slave to Free/Free to Slave

[Constitutiones Extravagantes, 21.9] If anyone shall buy another's slave from the Franks, let him prove with suitable witnesses how much and what sort of price he paid and when witnesses have been sworn in, they shall make oath in the following manner: "We saw him pay the price in our presence, and he who purchased the slave did not do so through any fraud or connivance with the enemy." And if suitable witnesses shall give oaths in this manner, let him receive back only the price which he paid; and let him not seek back the cost of support and let him return the slave without delay to his former owner.

[88] Since the title of emancipation takes precedence over the law of possession, great care must be exercised in such matters. And therefore it should be observed, that if anyone wishes to manumit a slave, he may do so by giving him his liberty through a legally competent document; or if anyone wishes to give freedom to a bondservant without a written document, let the manumission thus conferred be confirmed with the witness of not less than five or seven native freemen, because it is not fitting to present a smaller number of witnesses than is required when the manumission is in written form.

C. Slave/Free Relations

[30] OF WOMEN VIOLATED.

1. Whenever native freeman does violence to a maidservant, and force can be proved, let him pay twelve solidi to him to whom the maidservant belongs.

2. If a slave does this, let him receive a hundred fifty blows.

[35] OF THE PUNISHMENT OF SLAVES WHO COMMIT A CRIMINAL ASSAULT ON FREEBORN WOMEN.

1. If any slave does violence to a native freewoman, and if she complains and is clearly able to prove this, let the slave be killed for the crime committed.

2. If indeed a native free girl unites voluntarily with a slave, we order both to be killed.

3. But if the relatives of the girl do not wish to punish their own relative, let the girl be deprived of her free status and delivered into servitude to the king.

D. Criminal Actions
by/toward Slaves

[26] OF KNOCKING OUT TEETH.

1. If anyone by chance strikes out the teeth of a Burgundian of the highest class, or of a Roman noble, let him be compelled to pay fifteen solidi.

2. For middle-class freeborn people, either Burgundian or Roman, if a tooth is knocked out, let composition[10] be made in the sum of ten solidi.

3. For persons of the lowest class, five solidi.

4. If a slave voluntarily strikes out the tooth of a native freeman, let him be condemned to have a hand cut off; if the loss which has been set forth above has been committed by accident, let him pay the price for the tooth according to the status of the person.

5. If any native freeman strikes out the tooth of a freedman, let him pay him three solidi. If he strikes out the tooth of another's slave, let him pay two solidi to him to whom the slave belongs.

[33] OF INJURIES WHICH ARE SUFFERED BY WOMEN.

1. If any native freewoman has her hair cut off and is humiliated without cause (when innocent) by any native freeman in her home or on the road, and this can be proved with witnesses, let the doer of the deed pay her twelve solidi, and let the amount of the fine be twelve solidi.

2. If this was done to a freedwoman, let him pay her six solidi.

3. If this was done to a maidservant, let him pay her three solidi, and let the amount of the fine be three solidi.

4. If this injury (shame, disgrace) is inflicted by a slave on a native freewoman, let him receive two hundred blows; if a freedwoman, let him receive a hundred blows; if a maidservant, let him receive seventy-five blows.

5. If indeed the woman whose injury we have ordered to be punished in this manner commits fornication voluntarily (i.e., if she yields), let nothing be sought for the injury suffered.

10. **composition:** restitution.

Source 4 from Katherine Fischer Drew, translator, The Laws of the Salian Franks *(Philadelphia: University of Pennsylvania Press, 1991), Sections 25, 39, 40, 98. Copyright © 1991 University of Pennsylvania Press. Reprinted by permission of the University of Pennsylvania Press.*

4. Selections from Salic Law

C. Slave/Free Relations

[25] ON HAVING INTERCOURSE WITH SLAVE GIRLS OR BOYS

1. The freeman who has intercourse with someone else's slave girl, and it is proved against him . . . , shall be liable to pay six hundred denarii (i.e., fifteen solid[i]) to the slave girl's lord.

2. The man who has intercourse with a slave girl belonging to the king and it is proved against him . . . , shall be liable to pay twelve hundred denarii (i.e., thirty solidi).

3. The freeman who publicly joins himself with (i.e., marries) another man's slave girl, shall remain with her in servitude.

4. And likewise the free woman who takes someone else's slave in marriage shall remain in servitude.

5. If a slave has intercourse with the slave girl of another lord and the girl dies as a result of this crime, the slave himself shall pay two hundred forty denarii (i.e., six solidi) to the girl's lord or he shall be castrated; the slave's lord shall pay the value of the girl to her lord.

6. If the slave girl has not died . . . , the slave shall receive three hundred lashes or, to spare his back, he shall pay one hundred twenty denarii (i.e., three solidi) to the girl's lord.

7. If a slave joins another man's slave girl to himself in marriage without the consent of her lord . . . , he shall be lashed or clear himself by paying one hundred twenty denarii (i.e., three solidi) to the girl's lord.

[98] CONCERNING THE WOMAN WHO JOINS HERSELF TO HER SLAVE

1. If a woman joins herself in marriage with her own slave, the fisc[11] shall acquire all her possessions and she herself will be outlawed.

2. If one of her relatives kills her, nothing may be required from that relative or the fisc for her death. The slave shall be placed in the most severe torture, that is, he shall be placed on the wheel. And if one of the relatives of the woman gives her either food or shelter, he shall be liable to pay fifteen solidi.

D. Criminal Actions by/toward Slaves

[40] CONCERNING THE SLAVE ACCUSED OF THEFT

1. In the case where a slave is accused of theft, if [it is a case where] a freeman would pay six hundred denarii (i.e., fifteen solidi) in composition, the slave stretched on a rack shall receive one hundred twenty blows of the lash.

2. If he [the slave] confesses before torture and it is agreeable to the slave's lord, he may pay one hundred twenty denarii (i.e., three solidi) for his back [i.e., to avoid the lashes]; and the slave's lord shall return the value of the property stolen to its owner. . . .

4. . . . If indeed he [the slave] confessed in the earlier torture, i.e., before the one hundred twenty lashes were completed, let him [the slave] be castrated or pay two hundred forty denarii (i.e., six solidi); the lord should restore the value of the property stolen to its owner.

5. If he [the slave] is guilty of a crime for which a freeman or a Frank would be liable to pay eight thousand denarii (i.e., two hundred solidi), let the slave compound fifteen solidi (i.e., six hundred denarii). If indeed the slave is guilty of a more serious offense—one for which a freeman would be liable to pay eighteen hundred denarii (i.e., forty-five solidi)—and the slave confessed during torture, he shall be subjected to capital punishment. . . .

11. If indeed it is a female slave accused of an offense for which a male slave would be castrated, then she should be liable to pay two hundred forty denarii (i.e., six solidi)—if it is agreeable for her lord to pay this—or she should be subjected to two hundred forty lashes.

11. **fisc:** king's treasury.

[39] ON THOSE WHO INSTIGATE
SLAVES TO RUN AWAY

1. If a man entices away the bondsmen of another man and this is proved against him . . . , he shall be liable to pay six hundred denarii (i.e., fifteen solidi) [in addition to return of the bondsmen plus a payment for the time their labor was lost].

Source 5 from Katherine Fischer Drew, translator, The Lombard Laws *(Philadelphia: University of Pennsylvania Press, 1973), Sections Rothair 156, 217, 221, 222, 267, 280, 333, 334; Luitprand 55, 63, 80, 140, 152. Copyright © 1973 University of Pennsylvania Press. Reprinted by permission of the University of Pennsylvania Press.*

5. Selections from
Lombard Laws

A. Slave to Free/Free to Slave

[Rothair 156] In the case of a natural son who is born to another man's woman slave, if the father purchases him and gives him his freedom by the formal procedure . . . , he shall remain free. But if the father does not free him, the natural son shall be a slave to him to whom the mother slave belongs.

[Luitprand 63] He who renders false testimony against anyone else, or sets his hand knowingly to a false charter, and this fraud becomes evident, shall pay his wergeld as composition, half to the king and half to him whose case it is. If the guilty party does not have enough to pay the composition, a public official ought to hand him over as a slave to him who was injured, and he [the offender] shall serve him as a slave.

[Luitprand 80] In connection with thieves, each judge shall make a prison underground in his district. When a thief has been found, he shall pay composition for his theft, and then the judge shall seize him and put him in prison for two or three years, and afterwards shall set him free.

If the thief is such a person that he does not have enough to pay the composition for theft, the judge ought to hand him over to the man who suffered the theft, and that one may do with him as he pleases.

If afterwards the thief is taken again in theft, he [the judge] shall shave . . . and beat him for punishment as befits a thief, and shall put a brand on his forehead and face. If the thief does not correct himself and if after such punishment he has again been taken in theft, then the judge shall sell him outside the province, and the judge shall have his sale price provided, nevertheless, that it be a proved case for the judge ought not to sell the man without certain proof.

[Luitprand 152] If the man who is prodigal or ruined, or who has sold or dissipated his substance, or for other reasons does not have that with which to pay composition, commits theft or adultery or a breach of the peace . . . or injures another man and the composition for this is twenty solidi or more, then a public representative ought to hand him over as a slave to the man who suffered such illegal acts.

[Luitprand 55] If anyone makes his slave folkfree and legally independent . . . or sets him free from himself in any manner by giving him into the hand of the king or by leading him before the altar of a church, and if afterwards that freedman [continues] to serve at the will of his patron, the freedman ought at frequent intervals to make clear his liberty to the judge and to his neighbors and [remind them] of the manner in which he was freed.

Afterward the patron or his heirs may at no time bring complaints against him who was freed by saying that because [he continues to serve] he ought still to obey, for it was only on account of the goodness of his lord that the former slave continued to serve his commands of his own free will. He shall remain permanently free.

[Luitprand 140] If a freeman has a man and woman slave, or aldius and aldia,[12] who are married, and, inspired by hatred of the human race, he has intercourse with that woman whose husband is the slave or with the aldia whose husband is the aldius, he has committed adultery and we decree that he shall lose that slave or aldius with whose wife he committed adultery and the woman as well. They shall go free where they wish and shall be as much folkfree . . . as if they had been released by the formal procedure for alienation . . . —for it is not pleasing to God that any man should have intercourse with the wife of another.

B. Value and Treatment of Slaves

[Rothair 333] On mares in foal. He who strikes a mare in foal and causes a miscarriage shall pay one solidus as composition. If the mare dies, he shall pay as above for it and its young.

[Rothair 334] On pregnant woman slaves. He who strikes a woman slave large with child and causes a miscarriage shall pay three solidi as composition. If, moreover, she dies from the blow, he shall pay composition for her and likewise for the child who died in her womb.

C. Slave/Free Relations

[Rothair 217] On the aldia who marries a slave. The aldia or freedwoman who enters another man's house to a husband and marries a slave shall lose her liberty. But if the husband's lord neglects to reduce her to servitude, then

12. **aldius** and **aldia:** freedman and freedwoman.

[254]

when her husband dies she may go forth together with her children and all the property which she brought with her when she came to her husband. But she shall have no more than this as an indication of her mistake in marrying a slave.

[Rothair 221] The slave who dares to marry a free woman or girl shall lose his life. With regard to the woman who consented to a slave, her relatives have the right to kill her or to sell her outside the country and to do what they wish with her property. And if her relatives delay in doing this, then the king's gastald or schultheis[13] shall lead her to the king's court and place her there in the women's apartments among the female slaves.

[Rothair 222] On marrying one's own woman slave. If any man wishes to marry his own woman slave, he may do so. Nevertheless he ought to free her, that is, make her worthy born . . . , and he ought to do it legally by the proper formal procedure. . . . She shall then be known as a free and legal wife and her children may become the legal heirs of their father.

D. Criminal Actions
by/toward Slaves

[Rothair 267] The boatman who knowingly transports fugitive bondsmen, and it is proved, shall search for them and return them together with any properties taken with them to their proper owner. If the fugitives have gone elsewhere and cannot be found, then the value of those bondsmen together with the sworn value of the property which they carried with them shall be paid by that ferryman who knowingly transported the fugitives. In addition, the ferryman shall pay twenty solidi as composition to the king's fisc.

[Rothair 280] On seditious acts committed by field slaves. If, for any reason, rustics[14] . . . associate together for plotting or committing seditious acts such as, when a lord is trying to take a bondsman or animal from his slave's house, blocking the way or taking the bondsman or animal, then he who was at the head of these rustics shall either be killed or redeem his life by the payment of a composition equal to that amount at which he is valued. And each of those who participated in this evil sedition shall pay twelve solidi as composition, half to the king and half to him who bore the injury or before whom he presumed to place himself. And if that one who was trying to take his property endures blows or suffers violence from these rustics, composition for such blows or violence shall be paid to him just as is stated above, and the rustics shall suffer such punishment as is noted above for this presumption. If one of the rustics is killed no payment shall be required because he who killed him did it while defending himself and in protecting his own property.

13. **gastald** and **schultheis:** royal officials.
14. **rustics:** field slaves.

Source 6 from Theodore John Rivers, translator, Laws of the Alamans and Bavarians *(Philadelphia: University of Pennsylvania Press, 1977), Alamannic Law, Sections 17, 18, 37, 39, 75. Copyright © 1977 University of Pennsylvania Press. Reprinted by permission of the author.*

6. Laws of the Alamans

A. Slave to Free/Free to Slave

[39] We prohibit incestuous marriages. Accordingly, it is not permitted to have as wife a mother-in-law, daughter-in-law, step-daughter, step-mother, brother's daughter, sister's daughter, brother's wife, or wife's sister. Brother's children and sister's children are under no pretext to be joined together. If anyone acts against this, let them [the married pair] be separated by the judges in that place, and let them lose all their property, which the public treasury shall acquire. If there are lesser persons who pollute themselves through an illicit union, let them lose their freedom; let them be added to the public slaves.

B. Value and Treatment of Slaves

[37] 1. Let no one sell slaves . . . outside the province, whether among pagans or Christians, unless it is done by the order of the duke.

C. Slave/Free Relations

[17] 1. Concerning maidservants.[15] If a freewoman was manumitted by a charter or in a church, and after this she married a slave, let her remain permanently a maidservant of the church.

2. If, however, a free Alamannic woman marries a church slave and refuses the servile work of a maidservant, let her depart. If, however, she gives birth to sons or daughters there, let them remain slaves and maidservants permanently, and let them not have the right of departure.

D. Criminal Actions
by/toward Slaves

[18] 1. Concerning waylayers . . . , [if a man blocks the way of a freeman], let him pay six solidi.

2. If it is a freedman [who is blocked] , let the perpetrator pay four solidi.

---

15. **maidservants:** here, female slaves.

3. If it is a slave, three solidi.

4. If he does this to a free Alamannic woman, let him compensate with twelve solidi.

5. If it is a freedwoman, let him compensate with eight solidi.

6. If it is a maidservant, let him pay four solidi.

7. If a man seizes her hair, [let him compensate similarly].

[75] 1. If anyone lies with another's chambermaid against her will, let him compensate with six solidi.

2. And if anyone lies with the first maid of the textile workshop against her will, let him compensate with six solidi.

3. If anyone lies with other maids of the textile workshop against their will, let him compensate with three solidi.

Source 7 from F. L. Attenborough, editor, Laws of the Earliest English Kings, *Laws of Edward the Elder, Section 6; Laws of Ine, Section 3. Laws of Aethelbert, Sections 10, 11, 16; Laws of Alfred, Section 25.*

7. Laws of Anglo-Saxon Kings

A. Slave to Free/Free to Slave

[Edward the Elder 6] If any man, through [being found guilty of] an accusation of stealing, forfeits his freedom and gives up his person to his lord, and his kinsmen forsake him, and he knows no one who will make legal amends for him, he shall do such servile labour as may be required, and his kinsmen shall have no right to his wergeld [if he is slain] .

B. Value and Treatment of Slaves

[Ine 3] If a slave works on Sunday by his lord's command, he shall become free, and the lord shall pay a fine of 30 shillings.

§1. If, however, the slave works without the cognisance of his master, he shall undergo the lash or pay the fine in lieu thereof.

§2. If, however, a freeman works on that day, except by his lord's command, he shall be reduced to slavery, or [pay a fine of] 60 shillings. A priest shall pay a double fine.

D. Criminal Actions
by/toward Slaves

[Aethelbert 10] If a man lies with a maiden belonging to the king, he shall pay 50 shillings compensation.

[Aethelbert 11] If she is a grinding slave, he shall pay 25 shillings compensation. [If she is of the] third [class], [he shall pay] 12 shillings compensation.

[Aethelbert 16] If a man lies with a commoner's serving maid, he shall pay 6 shillings compensation; [if he lies] with a slave of the second class, [he shall pay] 50 sceattas[16] [compensation]; if with one of the third class, 30 sceattas.

[Alfred 25] If anyone rapes the slave of a commoner, he shall pay 5 shillings to the commoner, and a fine of 60 shillings.[17]

§1. If a slave rapes a slave, castration shall be required as compensation.

QUESTIONS TO CONSIDER

The central questions for this chapter ask you to do two things: investigate the boundaries between slave and free in various law codes, and then compare these issues in Roman and Germanic cultures. Your answers to the second question are based, of course, on your answers to the first, and the Sources and Method section suggests some of the questions you might ask yourself about slave law in each of these two cultures.

In addition to these, in the Roman codes, what role does military conquest play in the determination of slave and free? Does conquest simply provide slaves, or does it also offer them opportunities? What limitations were placed on a male owner's treatment of his slaves? On a female owner's treatment of her slaves? What obligations does—or could— the status of freedman or freed-woman entail? Do these obligations make this status appear closer to that of a slave or that of a free person? How are family relationships among slaves regarded legally? The provision in Justinian's Code (Source 2D) that slaves who did not prevent a master's being killed were to be killed themselves may seem very harsh. Why do you think this was part of Roman slave law? What other provisions strike you as especially harsh, and why might these have been enacted? Given the role of slavery in the Roman economy, why were there such strong provisions about runaway slaves? Other than the restrictions on those who aided runaways, what laws discuss actions by those who were neither owners nor slaves? How might these have shaped general attitudes toward slavery and slaves?

Turning now to the Germanic codes, what are the hierarchies you

16. 20 sceattas = one shilling.
17. The 60 shillings went to the king's treasury.

find among slaves based on? Given the nature of Germanic society, in which tribes often moved around a great deal, why do you think there was so much concern about not taking slaves away to other areas, even if it was their owners who were taking them? Historians often point out the importance of personal honor in Germanic societies. Do you find evidence of this? Do slaves have honor? Do any of their actions affect the honor of others in ways that the actions of free people do not? A close examination of the laws indicates that the only nonpunishable sexual relation between slave and free was a man marrying his own slave among the Lombards, mentioned in Source 5C. Why do you think this was allowed? What must a man do before he does this, and why do you think this was important?

You are now ready to investigate some comparative questions: In what ways do the different notions of the law in Roman and Germanic cultures—territorial versus personal, statutory versus traditional—emerge in laws regarding slavery? When comparing Germanic culture to Roman, historians often point to the relative propensity to interpersonal violence and the importance of the family among the Germans. Do the laws regarding slavery from these

two cultures provide evidence of these factors? What evidence do you see of the different economic structures in the two cultures, i.e., of the greater complexity of the Roman economic system?

Comparing two cultures involves exploring continuities along with contrasts. One of the issues in slave systems was how to punish slaves without harming their owners. How do the laws handle this? Do you see much difference between Roman and Germanic cultures in this? How do the laws handle the issue that slaves do not own property? How are the actions and obligations of freed slaves toward their former masters handled in both cultures? Why do you think it was important in both cultures to have an intermediate status between slave and free? Do you see much difference with regard to laws concerning sexual relations between slaves and free in the two cultures? Why might there have been continuity in this?

After putting all of this material together, you are now ready to answer the central questions for this chapter: How were legal distinctions between slave and free established, structured, and maintained, and how could they be overcome? What similarities and differences are there in Roman and Germanic law regarding slavery?

EPILOGUE

During the Renaissance, scholars and thinkers began to divide the history of Europe into three stages, ancient, medieval, and modern, a division that has persisted until today. They viewed the end of the Roman Empire as a dramatic break in history, and saw the Germanic successor states as sharply different from Rome. This view is increasingly being modified today as historians point to a number of continuities between late ancient and early medieval society.

As you have discovered in this chapter, the slave system was one of those continuities, for slavery did not disappear from the European scene with the fall of Rome, nor did the spread of Christianity lead to an end of slavery. (Christianity did not oppose slavery on moral grounds, although it did praise those who chose to free their slaves and pushed for slaves being allowed to marry in legally binding ceremonies.) Gradually, however, more people came to occupy the intermediate stage between slave and free that you have seen in these laws, which became known as serfdom. Serfdom was a legal condition in which people were personally free—not owned by another individual as slaves were—but were bound to the land, unable to move and owing labor obligations to their lord. For former slaves, serfdom was a step up; for others, however, it was a step down, for the bulk of the serfs in Europe probably came from families that had originally been free peasants, but had traded their labor and freedom to move in return for protection. In any case, serfdom did not immediately replace slavery; both continued side by side for centuries, and the laws you have seen here regarding slaves often shaped later laws regarding serfs. Law codes alone, of course, cannot tell us about relative numbers of slaves or serfs, and they sometimes hide major changes. The transformation of slave to serf was so gradual that it occa-sioned little comment in the codes, which had, as we have seen, long included discussion of intermediate stages between slave and free and of hierarchies among slaves.

The laws you have seen here also had great influence beyond Europe. As you have discovered, Germanic law did not break sharply with Roman on many issues regarding slavery, indicating that Justinian's Code probably influenced some early medieval Germanic codes. Justinian's Code was also rediscovered in western Europe in the eleventh century, and became the basis of legal education at the law schools that were established in southern Europe in the twelfth century. It influenced national and local codes in this era of expanding states and growing cities, and ultimately all of the legal systems of western Europe except for that of England became based on Roman law. When Portugal and Spain set up slave systems extending into the New World, Roman law was the basis of many provisions regarding slavery. Thus, two of the New World's most heavily slave societies—the French Caribbean and Brazil—based their systems on Roman law.

The other slave societies in the New World—the British Caribbean and the southern United States before the Civil War—did not base their laws as directly on those of Rome, but their laws did grow out of Germanic codes such as those you have seen here. Though these systems were different from the Roman and Germanic systems in that slavery came to be based on race, many of the laws—those concerning owners' freedom to treat slaves as they wished, sexual relations between slave and free, punishment of those who aided runaway slaves—were remarkably similar. Once slavery came to be racially based, however, the permeable boundary between slave and free that you have traced in this chapter, with slavery not necessarily being a permanent status, became much harder to cross. Poverty, begging, theft, debt, capture in war, false testimony, or incest did not make a white person a slave, nor did turning in deserters, marriage to an owner, or—except in rare instances—military service make a black person free.

CHAPTER ELEVEN

THE TRANSFORMATION OF CHRISTIANITY

The Christian religion began as a minority sect within Judaism in an outlying region of the vast Roman Empire. During the reign of the emperor Nero, Roman officials initiated campaigns of persecution against Christians, especially when unrest broke out in the empire. Christians were blamed for not honoring the traditional gods, thus provoking the gods' displeasure and leading to turmoil and crisis. Persecution of this group did not have the desired effect, however. The courage of Christians facing death convinced many people throughout the Roman Empire that Christianity offered something unique. The first three centuries after the death of Christ saw a gradual but steady growth in the number of Christians, particularly in urban areas. Christians began to organize support networks for new converts, providing them not only with spiritual guidance but also with

food and shelter if they needed it, which further increased the attractiveness of the new religion.

Some new and highly educated Christians began to expand the original teachings into a more complex philosophical and theological system, which made Christianity more appealing and acceptable to those educated in Greek philosophy. Officials within the church gradually asserted their authority over beliefs and practices. Christianity found adherents at all social levels, especially among upper-class women; gradually even Roman government officials converted. Though it is very difficult to determine exact numbers, scholars estimate that by 300 C.E. perhaps as many as 20 percent of the inhabitants of the Roman Empire were Christian, even though the religion was still officially prohibited.

If we skip ahead another three hundred years, however, we find not simply further growth but a complete transformation. By 600 Christianity was the only legal religion in the

Roman Empire (which by this time consisted only of the eastern half of the original Roman Empire), and it was the official religion in all the kingdoms that had replaced the Roman Empire in the West. Missionary efforts had also reached far beyond the borders of the old Roman Empire, so that Ireland and parts of Germany were also Christian. The next few centuries would extend the religion even further as eastern Europe, Scandinavia, and Russia gradually became Christianized.

Not only did the Christian religion expand in numbers of converts during this period of late antiquity and the early Middle Ages, it also grew in economic strength and political power. In many parts of Europe, the Church came to own about a quarter of all land, gradually acquiring property through gifts and bequests from individuals and rulers alike. *Bishops*, the regional Church officials, became advisers to rulers and also rulers of territory themselves. The increased power of the Church was most dramatically evident in western Eur-

ope, where, after the collapse of the Roman Empire, Church leaders often took over many of the functions of the secular government. As it grew in power, the western Church also became more centralized as the Bishop of Rome began to claim authority over all other bishops and, eventually, authority over all secular rulers as well. By 600, and even more so by several centuries later, Christianity was western Europe's most powerful political, cultural, and economic institution—an institution centralized under the authority of one man, the Bishop of Rome, who had taken the title *pope*, a word derived from the Latin word *papa*, which means "father."

The Church's preeminent position during the Middle Ages was not an outcome that could have been predicted during the first decades of Christianity, and probably not even in the year 300. How was Christianity transformed from an outlawed minority sect to the most powerful religious and secular institution in all of Europe?

SOURCES AND METHOD

In studying the earliest history of any religious movement, including Christianity, the primary problem is a lack of sources. In addition, those sources that exist were written not to record historical facts but to win converts and bolster the faith of believers.

The problem is somewhat different for the later period we are investigating here. Many more primary sources

are available, but almost all were written by Christians, most of whom were members of the clergy. This is particularly true in western Europe, where all schools, the only places one could learn to read and write, were run by the Church. Secular rulers and Church officials often hired writers to compose chronicles and biographies, but because of their training these writers always felt it important to stress events of religious significance. The subject of the biography as well

[263]

often wanted emphasis laid on his or her piety and Christian devotion.

Many of the sources from late antiquity and the early Middle Ages have an even stronger religious purpose, for they are biographies of those individuals whom the Church judged to be saints and were written to provide other Christians with models of behavior. Though they are not fiction, these works often mold the events of the real person's life to fit the model expected of a saint and always include *miracles*—acts of God unexplainable by the laws of nature—for these happenings were a requirement for sainthood. Once we understand their limitations, however, these saints' lives, called *hagiography*, can provide a great deal of information about missionaries and Church leaders and about how the Church developed. Because stories about saints were repeated orally by missionaries and preachers, they also explain how people who could not read were introduced to Christianity.

This chapter's sources were thus written by people who were not simply recording human actions but trying to show the hand of God at work in the establishment of the Christian religion. Just those human actions, however, are what interest us as historians, so we must make distinctions between the real and the miraculous when we use these sources. To answer the questions posed in this chapter, your first task will be to extract specific information about human actions from the documents. You may want to make a list of the factors you see as important in explaining the rapid and widespread growth of Christianity. What types of

people played a significant role in building this religion? What tactics did they use? What institutions did the Church create to help build up its power? What ideas were developed to help justify the changes?

The first three sources are all from biographies of rulers or histories written by members of the clergy. The first is from the life of the Roman emperor Constantine, written shortly after his death in 337 by his friend and adviser Bishop Eusebius. Constantine, searching for ways to build up the power of Rome, thought that new gods might provide one answer. How does Eusebius describe Constantine's conversion to Christianity? What role did the existing Christian clergy play? (Eusebius does not call them priests but simply "those who were acquainted with the mysteries of His doctrines.") Source 2, describing the conversion of King Clovis of the Franks in 496, is taken from the *History of the Franks* by Bishop Gregory of Tours, who lived in the sixth century. What inspired Clovis to convert? What role did the bishop play in his conversion? Source 3, from the *History of the English Church and People* written in the eighth century by the English scholar and monk Bede, also describes a royal conversion. What role did the pope (*pontiff*) play in the events described? What reservations did King Ethelbert have about accepting Christianity? What ultimately persuaded him to convert?

Before you continue, compare the three conversion accounts. What role did the miraculous play in each? What kinds of clergy were important? What influence did the ruler's wife exert? What aspects of Christianity attracted the rulers? What actions did the rulers take after converting to Christianity?

Sources 4 and 5 provide additional information about imperial or royal actions. Selection 4 presents two extracts from the law code of the Roman emperor Theodosius II, who ruled from 408 to 450. Constantine had legalized Christianity after his conversion; how did Theodosius further transform the status of Christianity? How did he propose to enforce his proclamation? Source 5, a selection from the thirteenth-century sagas of the Norse kings written by an unknown author, describes events that occurred much later than those presented in the preceding documents, because Christianity was slow in reaching the remote parts of northern Europe. King Olaf's actions were quite similar to those of Theodosius, however, and followed a pattern set by earlier rulers. How did Olaf convince his subjects to convert? How did he and Theodosius justify violent actions or the use of force in the name of religion? How would you compare their actions with those of King Ethelbert from Source 3?

From the five sources you have read so far, what types of people have you included in your list of important players in the development of Christianity? What types of tactics? How would you describe the relationship between the rulers and the Church? How would you compare the roles of the ruler and his subjects in these sources; that is, was conversion always imposed from the top down? What sorts of activities did the clergy participate in? How were these activities important in the growth of the Church?

Several of the sources you have read so far have referred to the pope; the next five documents discuss the papacy directly. Source 6 comes from a sermon by Pope Leo in 446 that states his reasons for believing that the pope should have supreme control over the church. On what foundation does Leo base papal authority? Source 7 provides another perspective on this issue, namely, that of the emperor. This is an edict from the emperor Valentinian III in 445. What bases does Valentinian see for papal power? Why does he think it important for the Church that only one individual hold power? Why does he feel this is important for the empire as well? What role does he envision for the emperor in enforcing papal authority? Source 8, an excerpt from a letter by Pope Gelasius to the emperor during the late fifth century, provides an example of how the popes' conception of their own authority had developed by the fifth century. How does Gelasius describe the relationship between the pope's power and that of the secular ruler? What would you expect the emperor's reaction to have been? How would you compare the relationship between pope and emperor described here with that described by Valentinian in the previous document?

Papal authority may have been based on theoretical statements, but it grew out of direct papal actions. Sources 9 and 10 give two versions of the same historical event, the meeting between Pope Leo I and Attila the Hun in 452. The ninth selection was written by Prosper, a Christian chronicler, about three years after the meeting took place; the tenth, by a later unknown author. How would this meeting have helped build up papal authority? Why might the later author have expanded the account in the way that he did? Reading these documents about the papacy has doubtless prompted you to add entries to your list of individuals and institutions. What ideas did the popes choose to emphasize as they gained power?

The sources you have read so far have primarily viewed the expansion of Christianity from the perspective of emperors, kings, and popes. They have, however, described the actions of individual missionaries and Church officials, and the last three sources describe several of these men in detail. All are taken from saints' lives that were written shortly after the death of each saint by one of his followers. Source 11 comes from the life of St. Bonitus, a seventh-century bishop of Auvergne in France; Source 12 from the life of St. Boniface, an eighth-century English missionary to the Germans; and Source 13 from the life of St. Sturmi, one of Boniface's converts and disciples. Because miracles were an essential prerequisite for sainthood, all three selections describe miraculous events, but they also provide other clues about why these men were successful missionaries and Church leaders. As you read Source 11, note those aspects of Bonitus's background that might help explain his high Church position. What was his family like? What kind of education did he receive? What sorts of relationships did he develop with political rulers? How would these factors have helped in building up the power of a bishop? As you read Source 12, note those people

whom Boniface selected to work with him as he prepared to cut down the oak of Thor. Why would he choose not to perform this act alone?

At first glance, the last source might appear to contradict some of what you have read so far. Unlike Bonitus, Sturmi did not become a Church official but went deeper and deeper into the forests of Germany. In this retreat he was following a pattern begun many centuries earlier by Christians who already were questioning the growing worldliness of their religion. During the reign of Constantine, some Christian thinkers wondered whether the Church could be powerful and holy at the same time and whether it should have close relations with secular powers. Many of these believers rejected the official Church and moved out into the deserts of Egypt to live what they regarded was the true Christian life of prayer, meditation, and devotion, sharply criticizing the wealthy bishops who built elaborate churches and wore luxurious robes of office. These "desert fathers" (and mothers) often tried to live as hermits, but as their reputations for holiness grew they attracted disciples. Soon whole communities sprang up in the desert, communities that came to be called *monasteries,* supporting themselves by their own labor and generally forbidding marriage and private property to their members.

Initially a reaction against the organized and institutional church, the monasteries became increasingly popular and, as the monastic movement spread to Europe, they too became institutionalized. Elaborate codes of rules were laid down regulating the running of monasteries and the lives of their occupants. Though their original founders were opposed to the Church's extreme wealth, many monasteries prospered themselves as people gave them land or money in return for those spiritual services, such as prayers for the soul, offered by monks and nuns. The bishops and the pope alike realized that the monks, who were often very devoted and consequently held in high regard for their piety and moral life, made effective missionaries for the Christian religion. Monks, as you have read in the third selection on Augustine, were sent out by the pope to gain converts and were able to bring large areas under his religious jurisdiction.

The life of St. Sturmi provides some evidence about how this process hap-pened. What were Sturmi's original aims? What sort of life did the monks lead at first? How did Boniface change things? What kind of relationship developed between the monastery and the secular rulers?

Careful reading of the sources has given you a great deal of information about the development of Christianity as a religion and a secular power during this period. Reviewing your list of people, tactics, and institutions, which of these factors appear most important to the sheer growth in numbers of Christians? Which to the growth of church power? How did Christian ideology and teachings change as the Church developed into a powerful institution?

THE EVIDENCE

Source 1 from R. Schaff and H. Wace, editors, The Library of the Nicene and Post-Nicene Fathers, *vol. 1 (New York: The Christian Literature Society. 1890), pp. 489-491.*

1. The Conversion of Constantine, early 4th century

Being convinced, however, that he [Constantine] needed some more powerful aid than his military forces could afford him,[1] on account of the wicked and magical enchantments which were so diligently practiced by the tyrant [Maxentius], he sought Divine assistance, deeming the possession of arms and a numerous soldiery of secondary importance, but believing the cooperating power of Deity invincible and not to be shaken. He considered, therefore, on what God he might rely for protection and assistance . . .

Accordingly he called on Him with earnest prayer and supplications that he would reveal to him who He was, and stretch forth His right hand to help him in his present difficulties. And while he was thus praying with fervent entreaty, a most marvelous sign appeared to him from heaven, the account of

---

1. In 312 C.E. Constantine, who ruled Gaul and Britain, was about to invade Italy and try to gain the throne of the Western Roman Empire by defeating Maxentius, who ruled Rome.

which it might have been hard to believe had it been related to any other person. But since the victorious emperor himself long afterwards declared it to the writer of this history, when he was honored with his acquaintance and society, and confirmed his statement by an oath, who could hesitate to accredit the relation, especially since the testimony of after-time has established its truth? He said that about noon, when the day was already beginning to decline, he saw with his own eyes the trophy of a cross of light in the heavens, above the sun, and bearing the inscription, CONQUER BY THIS. At this sight he himself was struck with amazement, and his whole army also, which followed him on this expedition, and witnessed the miracle.

He said, moreover, that he doubted within himself what the import of this apparition could be. And while he continued to ponder and reason on its meaning, night suddenly came on; then in his sleep the Christ of God appeared to him with the same sign which he had seen in the heavens, and commanded him to make a likeness of that sign which he had seen in the heavens, and to use it as a safeguard in all engagements with his enemies.

At the dawn of day he arose, and communicated the marvel to his friends: and then, calling together the workers in gold and precious stones, he sat in the midst of them and described to them the figure of the sign he had seen, bidding them represent it in gold and precious stones. And this representation I myself have had an opportunity of seeing. . . .

The emperor constantly made use of this sign of salvation as a safeguard against every adverse and hostile power, and commanded that others similar to it should be carried at the head of all his armies.

These things were done shortly afterwards. But at the time above specified, being struck with amazement at the extraordinary vision, and resolving to worship no other God save Him who had appeared to him, he sent for those who were acquainted with the mysteries of His doctrines, and enquired who that God was, and what was intended by the sign of the vision he had seen.

They affirmed that He was God, the only begotten Son of the one and only God: that the sign which had appeared was the symbol of immortality, and the trophy of that victory over death which He had gained in time past when sojourning on earth. They taught him also the causes of His advent, and explained to him the true account of His incarnation. Thus he was instructed in these matters, and was impressed with wonder at the divine manifestation which had been presented to his sight. Comparing, therefore, the heavenly vision with the interpretation given, he found his judgment confirmed; and, in the persuasion that the knowledge of these things had been imparted to him by Divine teaching, he determined thenceforth to devote himself to the reading of the inspired writings.

Source 2 from Roland H. Bainton, The Medieval Church *(Princeton: D. VanNostrand, 1962), pp. 99–101.*

2. The Conversion of Clovis, 496

The queen [Clotilde] never ceased to entreat the king [Clovis] to recognize the true God and give up idols, but nothing could move him to believe these things until he was engaged in a war with the Alemanni[2] in which he was compelled by constraint to confess what he had refused to do voluntarily. It came to pass that his army was in danger of being wiped out. Thereupon, lifting his eyes to heaven, with compunction of heart and moved to tears, he cried, "Jesus Christ, who art according to Clotilde the Son of the living God, who art said to give aid to those in trouble and victory to those who hope in Thee . . . I beseech Thee . . . if Thou wilt give me victory over mine enemies I will believe in Thee and be baptized in Thy name. I have called upon my gods and they are far removed from helping me. Hence I believe they are powerless, since they do not succour their followers. I now call upon Thee. Only save me from mine enemies." When he had thus spoken the Alemanni turned their backs and took to flight. . . . Clovis returning related to the queen how he had won the victory by calling upon the name of Christ. Then the queen with haste secretly summoned Remigius, the bishop of Rheims, that he should instruct the king in the word of salvation. He then began privately to tell his majesty that he should believe in the true God, the maker of heaven and earth and should give up idols. The king said, "Willingly, holy father, but there is one difficulty. My people will not give up their gods. But I will go and speak to them according to your word." But before he had opened his mouth all the people cried, "Pious king, we reject the mortal gods and are ready to follow the immortal God, whom Remigius preaches." Then the bishop with great joy gave orders to prepare the fount. The church was resplendent with banners, flickering candles and the scent of wax and incense, so that those present believed that they partook of the savor of heaven. The king asked that he be baptized by the pontiff. Like a new Constantine Clovis ascended to the laver,[3] putting off his former leprosy. As he went down into the water the bishop said, "Bow thy neck. Adore what you have burned. Burn what you have adored." Now the holy bishop Remigius, a man of consummate learning and of great sanctity, may fitly be compared to the holy Sylvester *[who baptized Constantine]*.

2. **Alemanni**: one of the German tribes.
3. **laver**: baptismal font.

[269]

Source 3 from Bede, A History of the English Church and People, *translated by Leo Sherley-Price (Baltimore: Penguin, 1955.), pp. 66, 68–71.*

3. The Conversion of King
Ethelbert, 597

In the year of our Lord 582, Maurice, fifty-fourth in succession from Augustus, became Emperor, and ruled for twenty-one years. In the tenth year of his reign, Gregory, an eminent scholar and administrator, was elected Pontiff of the apostolic Roman see,[4] and ruled it for thirteen years, six months, and ten days. In the fourteenth year of this Emperor, and about the one hundred and fiftieth year after the coming of the English to Britain, Gregory was inspired by God to send his servant Augustine with several other God-fearing monks to preach the word of God to the English nation. . . .

At this time the most powerful king there was Ethelbert, who reigned in Kent and whose domains extended northwards to the river Humber, which forms the boundary between the north and south Angles. To the east of Kent lies the large island of Thanet, which by English reckoning is six hundred hides[5] in extent; it is separated from the mainland by a waterway about three furlongs[6] broad called the Wantsum, which joins the sea at either end and is fordable only in two places. It was here that God's servant Augustine landed with companions, who are said to have been forty in number. At the direction of blessed Pope Gregory, they had brought interpreters from among the Franks, and they sent these to Ethelbert, saying that they came from Rome bearing very glad news, which infallibly assured all who would receive it of eternal joy in heaven and an everlasting kingdom with the living and true God. On receiving this message, the king ordered them to remain in the island where they had landed, and gave directions that they were to be provided with all necessaries until he should decide what action to take. For he had already heard of the Christian religion, having a Christian wife of the Frankish royal house named Bertha, whom he had received from her parents on condition that she should have freedom to hold and practice her faith unhindered with Bishop Liudhard, whom they had sent as her helper in the faith.

After some days, the king came to the island and, sitting down in the open air, summoned Augustine and his companions to an audience. But he took precautions that they should not approach him in a house; for he held an ancient superstition that, if they were practisers of magical arts, they might have opportunity to deceive and master him. But the monks were endowed with power from God, not from the Devil, and approached the king carrying a silver cross as their standard and the likeness of our Lord and Saviour painted on a board. First of all they offered prayer to God, singing a litany for the

4. **see**: official seat of authority of a bishop or the pope.
5. **hide**: approximately 125 square miles.
6. **furlong**: one-eighth of a mile.

eternal salvation both of themselves and of those to whom and for whose sake they had come. And when, at the king's command, they had sat down and preached the word of life to the king and his court, the king said: "Your words and promises are fair indeed; but they are new and uncertain, and I cannot accept them and abandon the age-old beliefs that I have held together with the whole English nation. But since you have travelled far, and I can see that you are sincere in your desire to impart to us what you believe to be true and excellent, we will not harm you. We will receive you hospitably and take care to supply you with all that you need; nor will we forbid you to preach and win any people you can to your religion." The king then granted them a dwelling in the city of Canterbury, which was the chief city of all his realm, and in accordance with his promise he allowed them provisions and did not withdraw their freedom to preach. Tradition says that as they approached the city, bearing the holy cross and the likeness of our great King and Lord Jesus Christ as was their custom, they sang in unison this litany: "We pray Thee, O Lord, in all Thy mercy, that Thy wrath and anger may be turned away from this city and from Thy holy house, for we are sinners. Alleluia."

As soon as they had occupied the house given to them they began to emulate the life of the apostles and the primitive Church. They were constantly at prayer; they fasted and kept vigils; they preached the word of life to whomsoever they could. They regarded worldly things as of little importance, and accepted only the necessities of life from those they taught. They practised what they preached, and were willing to endure any hardship, and even to die for the truth which they proclaimed. Before long a number of heathen, admiring the simplicity of their holy lives and the comfort of their heavenly message, believed and were baptized. On the east side of the city stood an old church, built in honour of Saint Martin during the Roman occupation of Britain, where the Christian queen of whom I have spoken went to pray. Here they first assembled to sing the psalms, to pray, to say Mass, to preach, and to baptize, until the king's own conversion to the Faith gave them greater freedom to preach and to build and restore churches everywhere.

At length the king himself, among others, edified by the pure lives of these holy men and their gladdening promises, the truth of which they confirmed by many miracles, believed and was baptized. Thenceforward great numbers gathered each day to hear the word of God, forsaking their heathen rites and entering the unity of Christ's holy Church as believers. While the king was pleased at their faith and conversion, it is said that he would not compel anyone to accept Christianity; for he had learned from his instructors and guides to salvation that the service of Christ must be accepted freely and not under compulsion. Nevertheless, he showed greater favour to believers, because they were fellow-citizens of the kingdom of heaven. And it was not long before he granted his teachers in his capital of Canterbury a place of residence appropriate to their station, and gave them possessions of various kinds to supply their wants.

[271]

Source 4 from Henry Bettenson, editor and translator, Documents of the Christian Church *(London; Oxford, 1963), p. 22 (first part); James Harvey Robinson, editor and translator,* Readings in European History, *vol. 1 (Boston: Ginn, 1904), p. 26 (second part).*

4. From the Theodosian Code,
438

It is our [Theodosius's] desire that all the various nations which are subject to our Clemency and Moderation, should continue in the profession of that religion which was delivered to the Romans by the divine Apostle Peter, as it hath been preserved by faithful tradition; and which is now professed by the Pontiff Damasus and by Peter, Bishop of Alexandria, a man of apostolic holiness. According to the apostolic teaching and the docrine of the Gospel, let us believe the one deity of the Father, the Son and the Holy Spirit, in equal majesty and in a holy Trinity. We authorize the followers of this law to assume the title of Catholic Christians; but as for the others, since, in our judgement, they are foolish madmen, we decree that they shall be branded with the ignominious name of heretics, and shall not presume to give to their conventicles the name of churches. They will suffer in the first place the chastisement of the divine condemnation, and in the second the punishment which our authority, in accordance with the will of Heaven, shall decide to inflict.

We command that their [the heretics'] books, which contain the substance of their criminal teachings, be sought out with the utmost care and burnt with fire under the eyes of the magistrates. Should any one perchance be convicted of concealing, through deceit or othrwise, and of failing to produce, any work of this kind, let him know that as the possessor of harmful books written with criminal intent he shall suffer capital punishment.

Source 5 from Samuel Laing, translator. Heimskringla or the Sagas of the Norse Kings *(London: J. C. Nimmo, 1889), pp. 150–151.*

5. Conversion of Scandinavia,
996–997

When Harald Gormson, king of Denmark, had adopted Christianity, he sent a message over all his kingdom that all people should be baptized. . . . In Viken many were baptized *[but subsequently lapsed].* But now (996) that Olaf Trygveson was king of Norway, he remained long during the summer in Viken *[and summoning his relatives he declared that he would]* either bring it to this that all Norway should be Christian or die. . . . King Olaf immediately made it known to the public that he recommended Christianity to all the people in his kingdom, which message was well received and approved of by those who had before given him their promise; and these being the most powerful among the people assembled, the others followed their example, and all the inhabitants of the east part of Viken allowed themselves to be baptized. The king then went to the north part of Viken, and invited every man to accept Christianity; and those who opposed him he punished severely, killing some, mutilating others, and driving some into banishment. . . . During that summer (996) and the following winter (997) all Viken was made Christian.

Source 6 from James Harvey Robinson, editor and translator, Readings in European History, *vol. 1 (Boston: Ginn, 1904), pp. 69–71.*

6. Sermon by Pope Leo, 446

A single person, Peter, is appointed from the whole world as a leader in the calling of all peoples, and is placed above all the other apostles and the fathers of the Church. Although there are many priests among the people of God, and many pastors, Peter should of right rule all of those whom Christ himself rules in the first instance. Great and marvelous, my dear brethren, is the participation in its own power which it has pleased the Divine Excellency to grant to this man. And such powers as it granted to other leaders in common with Peter were granted only through Peter. Our Lord, indeed, asked all the apostles what men said of him, but so long as it was left to all to reply, so long was the hesitation of human ignorance clearly displayed. But when the opinion of the apostles was asked, he who was first in apostolic dignity was the first to reply; who when he had answered, "Thou art the Christ, the Son of the living God," Jesus said to him, "Blessed art thou, Simon Bar-jonah: for flesh and blood hath not revealed it unto thee, but my Father which is in heaven";[7]—that is to say, thou art blessed for this reason, for my father has taught thee, neither has mere earthly opinion misled thee, but thou art instructed by a heavenly inspiration. . . . I am the foundation than which none other can be established; yet thou too art a rock *[petra]* because thou art made firm by my strength, so that those things which I have in virtue of my power thou shalt have in common with me by participation. "And upon this rock I will build my church; and the gates of hell shall not prevail against it." . . .

And he said to the blessed Peter, "I will give unto thee the keys of the kingdom of heaven: and whatsoever thou shalt bind on earth shall be bound in heaven: and whatsoever thou shalt loose on earth shall be loosed in heaven." The right to this power passed also to the other apostles, and the provisions of this ordinance went forth to all the leaders of the Church. Still it was not in vain that what was made known to all was especially recommended to one.

7. Matthew xvi. 16–17.

For this power was entrusted expressly to Peter, since Peter was placed as a model before all the rulers of the Church. Peter's prerogative remains and everywhere his judgment goes forth in equity. For never is severity too great nor forgiveness too lax where nothing is bound nor loosed except the blessed Peter bind or loose it.

Just before his passion,[8] which was about to shake the apostles' constancy, the Lord said to Simon, "Simon, Simon, behold, Satan asked to have you, that he might sift you as wheat: but I made supplication for thee, that thy faith fail not: and do thou, when once thou hast turned again, stablish thy brethren,"[9] that you should not enter into temptation. The danger of the temptation to yield to fear was common to all the apostles and all alike needed the aid of divine protection, since the devil desired to confound and ruin them all. Yet the Lord took special care of Peter and prayed especially that Peter might have faith, as if the state of the others would be more secure if the mind of their chief was not overcome. In Peter, therefore, the strength of all was confirmed and the aid of divine grace so ordered that the strength which was granted to Peter by Christ was in turn transmitted through Peter to the apostles.

Since, therefore, beloved brethren, we[10] behold this protection divinely appointed to us, we may properly and justly rejoice in the merits and dignity of our leader, sending up thanks to our eternal King and Redeemer, our Lord Jesus Christ, for giving such power to him whom he made the head of the whole Church: so that if anything, even in our own days, is rightly done by us and rightly ordained, it should be properly attributed to the influence and guidance of him to whom it was said: "When once thou hast turned again, stablish thy brethren." To whom, moreover, his Lord, after his resurrection, when Peter had three times professed his eternal love, said mystically three times, "Feed my sheep."[11] Like a faithful shepherd, he has beyond a doubt fulfilled his Lord's command, confirming us by his exhortations, and never ceasing to pray for us that we be not overcome by any temptation.

Source 7 from Henry Bettenson, editor and translator, Documents of the Christian Church, *2d edition (London: Oxford, 1963), pp. 22-23. Reprinted by permission of Oxford University Press.*

7. Edict of Emperor Valentinian III, 445

We are convinced that the only defence for us and for our Empire is in the favour of the God of heaven: and in order to deserve this favour it is our first

8. **passion**: crudfixion and death.

9. Luke xxii. 31-32.

10. Popes, like emperors, refer to themselves as "we."

11. John xxi. 15 *sqq.*

care to support the Christian faith and its venerable religion. Therefore, inasmuch as the pre-eminence of the Apostolic See is assured by the merit of S. Peter, the first of the bishops, by the leading position of the city of Rome and also by the authority of the holy Synod,[12] let not presumption strive to attempt anything contrary to the authority of that See. For the peace of the churches will only then be everywhere preserved when the whole body acknowledge its ruler. Hitherto this has been observed without violation; but Hilary, Bishop of Aries,[13] as we have learnt from the report of that venerable man Leo, the pope of Rome, has with contumacious presumption ventured upon certain unlawful proceedings; and thus an abominable confusion has invaded the church beyond the Alps. . . . By such presumptuous acts confidence in the Empire, and respect for our rule is destroyed. Therefore in the first place we put down so great a crime: and, beyond that, in order that no disturbance, however slight, may arise among the churches, and the discipline of religion may not appear to be impaired in any case whatever, we decree, by a perpetual edict, that nothing shall be attempted by the Gallican[14] bishops, or by those of any other province, contrary to the ancient custom, without the authority of the venerable pope of the Eternal City. But whatsoever the authority of the Apostolic See has enacted, or shall enact, let that be held as law for all. So that if any bishop summoned before the pope of Rome shall neglect to attend, let him be compelled to appear by the governor of the province.

Source 8 from Roland H. Bainton, The Medieval Church *(Princeton: D. VanNostrand, 1962), p. 108.*

8. Letter of Pope Gelasius to the Emperor, late 5th century

There are indeed two [*powers*] most august Emperor, by which chiefly this world is ruled, the sacred authority of the pontiffs and the royal power. Of the two the priesthood has the greater weight to the degree that it must render an account for kings themselves in matters divine. Know then, most clement son, that although you preside with dignity in human affairs, as to the divine you are to submit your neck to those from whom you look for salvation and from whom you receive the celestial sacraments. You are to be subject rather than to rule in the religious sphere and bow to the judgment of the priests rather than

12. **synod**: meetings of the Church bishops.

13. Hilary had presided at a synod that deposed Chelidonius, Bishop of Besançon. Chelidonius refused to resign, was excommunicated, went to Rome, and appealed to Leo, who admitted him to communion. Hilary went to Rome to protest. But Leo acquitted Chelidonius, ordered his reinstatement, and deprived Hilary of the primacy he had exercised in the Gallican church.

14. **Gallican**: French.

seek to bend them to your will. For, if in the area of public discipline the priests recognize your authority as derived from above and obey your laws, lest in purely secular matters they should appear to resist, how much more willingly should you obey them who are charged with the administration of the venerable mysteries? . . . And if it is proper that the hearts of the faithful should be submitted to priests in general, by how much more should obedience be rendered to him who presides over that see which the Highest Divinity desired to be preeminent above all priests [*i.e., the see of Rome*]?

Sources 9 and 10 from James Harvey Robinson, editor and translator, Readings in European History, *vol. 1 (Boston: Ginn, 1904), pp. 49–50; pp. 50–51.*

9. Prosper's Account of the Meeting Between Pope Leo and Attila the Hun, 455

Now Attila, having once more collected his forces which had been scattered in Gaul [at the battle of Chalons], took his way through Pannonia into Italy. . . . To the emperor and the senate and Roman people none of all the proposed plans to oppose the enemy seemed so practicable as to send legates[15] to the most savage king and beg for peace. Our most blessed Pope Leo—trusting in the help of God, who never fails the righteous in their trials—undertook the task, accompanied by Avienus, a man of consular rank, and the prefect Trygetius. And the outcome was what his faith had foreseen; for when the king had received the embassy, he was so impressed by the presence of the high priest that he ordered his army to give up warfare and, after he had promised peace, he departed beyond the Danube.

10. Anonymous Account of the Meeting Between Pope Leo and Attila the Hun, 6th century

Attila, the leader of the Huns, who was called the scourge of God, came into Italy, inflamed with fury, after he had laid waste with most savage frenzy Thrace and Illyricum, Macedonia and Moesia, Achaia and Greece, Pannonia and Germany. He was utterly cruel in inflicting torture, greedy in plundering, insolent in abuse. . . . He destroyed Aquileia from the foundations and razed to the ground those regal cities, Pavia and Milan; he laid waste many other towns,[16] and was rushing down upon Rome.

15. **legate**: representative.

16. This is an exaggeration. Attila does not seem to have destroyed the buildings, even in Milan and Pavia.

Then Leo had compassion on the calamity of Italy and Rome, and with one of the consuls and a large part of the Roman senate he went to meet Attila. The old man of harmless simplicity, venerable in his gray hair and his majestic garb, ready of his own will to give himself entirely for the defense of his flock, went forth to meet the tyrant who was destroying all things. He met Attila, it is said, in the neighborhood of the river Mincio, and he spoke to the grim monarch, saying: "The senate and the people of Rome, once conquerors of the world, now indeed vanquished, come before thee as suppliants. We pray for mercy and deliverance. O Attila, thou king of kings, thou couldst have no greater glory than to see suppliant at thy feet this people before whom once all peoples and kings lay suppliant. Thou hast subdued, O Attila, the whole circle of the lands which it was granted to the Romans, victors over all peoples, to conquer. Now we pray that thou, who hast conquered others, shouldst conquer thyself. The people have felt thy scourge; now as suppliants they would feel thy mercy."

As Leo said these things Attila stood looking upon his venerable garb and aspect, silent, as if thinking deeply. And lo, suddenly there were seen the apostles Peter and Paul, clad like bishops, standing by Leo, the one on the right hand, the other on the left. They held swords stretched out over his head, and threatened Attila with death if he did not obey the pope's command. Wherefore Attila was appeased by Leo's intercession—he who had raged as one mad. He straightway promised a lasting peace and withdrew beyond the Danube.

Source 11 from Carrolly Erickson, The Records of Medieval Europe *(Garden City, New York: Anchor, 1971), pp. 98–100. Copyright © 1971 by Carrolly Erickson. Used by permission of Doubleday, a division of Random House, Inc.*

11. Life of St. Bonitus, 7th century

Here Begins the Life of Saint Bonitus, Bishop and Confessor

The illustrous Bonitus was descended from Arvernian lineage. His father was called Theodatus, his mother Syagria; they were at least of senatorial rank, and from noble stock. Bonitus, then, before he was born, was held to have received a significant presage of devotion [*salutatio*] from a certain holy priest named Frigio. When this priest came to the paternal household he was received by Bonitus's mother-to-be with great joy, and when she, as was customary, asked for his blessing, she is said to have heard this reply given as a devotion: "Thou holy to God and venerable lord", he said, "give me your blessing." When the mother had grasped the meaning of what he had said, and silently weighing it, was pondering it in her heart, nonetheless inquiring of the servant of God, she spoke saying: "What is this you say, father?" . . .

[277]

And he said: "I did not ask a blessing, as you think, from you, but from him who is in your womb, since I perceive him to be a most high priest, chosen by God." And she, praying, said: "I ask, O father, that that which you have spoken shall, through your prayers, come to pass."

Afterwards, when the child had become a boy and was settled with his parents in the forenamed city, he was trained in the rudiments of grammar, instructed in the Theodosian decrees, and excelling in related studies also, he was examined by his instructors, and advanced. When he was of the age of puberty, his father being dead, with God as his guide he went to the royal palace and put himself in the hands of Sigebert, a minister of the king. Because Sigebert had grown very fond of him, he was chosen to be the royal cup-bearer. Not long after this, he gained the office of master of requests, accepting the ring from the king's own hand; he fulfilled it so nobly that he gained the affections of the prince and all the nobles, all the duties having been handed over to him by the ministers of the palace. For he had, to be sure, bodily beauty, but was more beautiful in the mind and in the strength of his chastity.

Soon after this, he gratefully accepted a great honor from the prince. Then the prince died, and, his son being dead, his great-grandson succeeded him. So pleasing was Bonitus in his sight that he chose him to be prefect of Marseille, the first province, but he insisted to the suitors brought before him that he would rather be considered a priest than a judge. . . .

[*Bonitus is raised to the episcopacy by the king.*]

Having thus accepted the bishopric, he considered himself to have accepted not an honor, but a burden, and he augmented the labor of his daily obligations by his fasts and vigils, which he kept throughout the night, and by silent reading in private, most especially during the Lenten season; in all, he was so zealous that you would think him not only most worthy of the priesthood, but worthy to live the monastic life as well. He bore two- and three-day fasts; indeed, we know him to have fasted for as many as four days. . . .

Now I shall relate how the Lord worked miracles by his virtue. When the day of the Lord's resurrection dawned, the brothers begged him to perform the solemnities of the mass for them. But, when, as was his custom, he washed his hands at the altar . . . a certain incapacitated brother named Auderamnus came and asked for the *levita*,[17] so that he might drink water from the priestly hands.

Having done so, he was restored to his former health, and immediately overjoyed, sat down to table with the brothers.

And another brother in the same monastery named Natholenum, when he took some of the water, was, according to many, relieved of a fever by its virtue [alone]. These things which are related above were told us by the venerable father Adelfius. . . .

17. **levita**: a small vessel used in priestly ablutions.

When the man of God, returning from Rome, came into the city of Chiusi in Tuscany, a certain blind woman begged his servants to give her the water in which he had washed his hands as a remedy to bathe her eyes. Although they were anxious to fulfil her request, the man of God, having washed his hands, ordered that the water be poured on the ground, as was his custom, so that they were able to steal hardly a drop of it; and giving it to the woman, they said: "Go and keep vigil tonight with this water in the basilica of the blessed Peter, which is in this city, and in the morning touch it to your eyes, as you have asked, according to your faith; we believe it will bring deliverance to you." The woman did as they said, and having fulfilled all, her eyesight restored, she beheld the light which she had sought with all her heart's desire. . . .

Now at that time nothing remained to him that he could give away as alms, and so as the gospel says he was naked, and did not even have two tunics to put on, and following the example of the blessed apostle Peter he had no gold or silver; but, restored by his divine virtues, he expended the treasure of health, which is more precious. Behold what the word of truth has said in the gospel: "He who hath forsaken all for my name's sake, shall receive a hundredfold, and shall inherit everlasting life. He receives a hundredfold who is established in the holiness and grace of God."[18] As blessed Paul said: "Our conversation is in heaven."[19] . . . Just so the blessed priest, who left much behind in this world, neither sought nor deserved anything earthly afterwards; but he received a hundredfold, since he shone with the grace of perfection, and now possesses eternal life with the saints in glory.

Then returning after this to Loudun, he remained there for four years, and continuing until the end, with God's aid, to do the good he had always done, he closed his days.

Here Ends the Life of Saint Bonitus, Bishop and Confessor.

Sources 12 and 13 from James Harvey Robinson, editor and translator, Readings in European History, *vol. 1 (Boston: Ginn, 1904), pp. 106–107; pp. 107–111.*

12. From the Life of St. Boniface, 8th century

Many of the people of Hesse were converted [by Boniface] to the Catholic faith and confirmed by the grace of the spirit: and they received the laying on of hands. But some there were, not yet strong of soul, who refused to accept wholly the teachings of the true faith. Some men sacrificed secretly, some even openly, to trees and springs. Some secretly practiced divining, soothsaying,

18. Mark 10, 29–30.
19. Phil. 3, 20.

and incantations, and some openly. But others, who were of sounder mind, cast aside all heathen profanation and did none of these things; and it was with the advice and consent of these men that Boniface sought to fell a certain tree of great size, at Geismar, and called, in the ancient speech of the region, the oak of Jove [i.e., Thor].

The man of God was surrounded by the servants of God. When he would cut down the tree, behold a great throng of pagans who were there cursed him bitterly among themselves because he was the enemy of their gods. And when he had cut into the trunk a little way, a breeze sent by God stirred overhead, and suddenly the branching top of the tree was broken off, and the oak in all its huge bulk fell to the ground. And it was broken into four parts, as if by the divine will, so that the trunk was divided into four huge sections without any effort of the brethren who stood by. When the pagans who had cursed did see this, they left off cursing and, believing, blessed God. Then the most holy priest took counsel with the brethen: and he built from the wood of the tree an oratory,[20] and dedicated it to the holy apostle Peter.

13. From the Life of St. Sturmi, 8th century

For almost three years he [Sturmi] fulfilled the duties of the priesthood, preaching and baptizing among the people. Then by the inspiration of God the purpose came into his soul to chasten himself by the straiter life and the hardships of the wilderness. He sought counsel thereupon from Boniface— his master in the spirit—who, when he understood Sturmi, knew that this purpose was inspired of God and rejoiced that God had designed to lead him by his grace. He gave Sturmi two companions, and when he had prayed and blessed them all he said: "Go forth into that solitude which is called Bochonia[21] and seek a place meet[22] for the servants of God to dwell in. For God is able to prepare for his servants a place in the wilderness."

And so those three went forth into the wilderness and entered into places solitary and rough, and saw almost nothing but heaven and earth and great trees; and they prayed Christ fervently that he would direct their feet in the path of peace. On the third day they came to the place which even to this day is called Hersfeld,[23] and when they had seen and explored the region round about, they asked Christ that the place might be blest to the dwellers therein. On the very spot where the monastery now stands they built poor huts of the

20. **oratory**: a small chapel.
21. **Bochonia**: central Germany.
22. **meet**: suitable.
23. **Hersfeld**: in central Germany.

bark of trees. There they tarried many days, serving God with holy fasts and watching and prayer. . . .

[*Boniface advised Sturmi to go farther and search for a more secluded place. He did and found a place that appeared right.*]

When he had come thither straightway the holy man Sturmi was filled with exceeding great joy, for he knew that through the merits and prayers of the holy bishop Boniface the place had been revealed to him by God.

Then on the second day the man of God came again to Hersfeld and found his brethren there calling upon God with fervent prayers. He told them of the place he had found and bade them make ready to go thither with him. But Sturmi went straightway to the holy bishop Boniface to tell him how he had found a place for the brethren to dwell in. Together they rejoiced and gave God thanks and held sweet converse about the life and conversation of monks. Then did the bishop let Sturmi go back to his wilderness, while he went to the palace of Carloman, the king, to gain from him a grant of the place Sturmi had chosen.

When Boniface came before the king, he said to him: "We have found in the wilderness called Bochonia, beside the river named Fulda, a place meet for the servants of God to dwell in, where before us no man has dwelt. It is under your sway, and we do beg of your beneficence to give us this place, so that we may be enabled to serve God under your protection." . . . Then did the king before all the lords of his palace give over to the bishop the place he had asked for, saying, "This place which thou seekest on the bank of the river Fulda I give over whole and entire from my law to the law of God—from that place in all directions in a circle four thousand paces toward east and west and north and south, yet shall hold the region."

Then the king gave command that a charter be written to this end, and he sealed it with his own hand.

In the year of the incarnation of Christ 744, in the first month, the twelfth day of the month, while the brothers Carloman and Pippin were reigning over the Frankish people, did Sturmi arise, in the name of God, and with seven brethren he did go to the place where now the monastery stands. They prayed to the Lord Christ that he would ever protect and defend them by his power; and, serving God in sacred psalms and in fasts, vigils, and prayers by day and by night, they did busy themselves cutting down the forests and clearing the ground by their own labor so far as strength was given them.

When two months had passed by, and a multitude of men were gathered together, the reverend archbishop Boniface came unto them; and when he looked and saw the convenience and great resources of the place, he exulted in the Holy Spirit, giving thanks and praising Christ because he had deigned to bestow upon his servants such a lodge in the wilderness.

QUESTIONS TO CONSIDER

By now you have a good idea of some of the reasons for the growth and success of Christianity during late antiquity and the early Middle Ages, in particular the political and institutional factors involved. Reviewing your lists, how would you rank the factors you have identified in order of importance?

Your assessment of the development of Christianity is based on your extraction of the human element from documents that also pay great attention to the miraculous. This emphasis on human action is important in our understanding of historical change, but to understand how early medieval people viewed historical change we have to look at the miracles as well.

To gain some flavor of the medieval world-view, return to the documents and this time read them only for the "acts of God." What role did the miraculous play in the royal conversions? Why might some of the accounts, such as Constantine's, put more emphasis on miracles than others? Why would the author of the second account of Pope Leo's meeting with Attila add the miraculous details he does? What sorts of miracles are included in the saints' lives? Do these seem to stress the power of God or the special holiness of the individual saint? Why do the miracles link the saints with other saints or with biblical characters?

The accounts often flow very easily from historical to supernatural events. What does this tell you about ideas of the boundaries between the natural and the supernatural during this period? How might this world-view have been shaped by the level of general understanding of disease, astronomical occurrences, or other natural phenomena at the time?

Your description of the development of Christianity is probably quite different from the account that one of the authors in this chapter would have written. What might their list of shaping factors look like? How would they fit the factors you view as important into their story? How might their ranking of factors differ from yours? For example, you have read several different justifications for papal primacy—biblical, political, and miraculous. Which do you feel is most important? Which do you feel contemporary observers regarded as the most important?

We currently term "miraculous" only those events that defy logical explanation, such as a military victory over a powerful opponent by a smaller or poorly equipped force. Do you think these writers would have agreed? Or might they have viewed military advantage as simply further evidence of God's favor? Using these documents as evidence, how would you compare their views of history with modern ones?

EPILOGUE

The transformation of Christianity from a minority religious sect emphasizing the life and teachings of Jesus to the official religion of Europe was not universally regarded as positive by all Christians. We have already seen how the desert fathers and mothers attempted to separate themselves from the official Church, but the monastic movement they started itself became institutionalized and powerful in secular affairs.

Though this close relationship with the centralized Church was acceptable to many monks, others wanted to return to the original ideals of the movement, believing that worldly goods only corrupted the Church and that close relations between Church and state were not desirable. The entire Middle Ages witnessed calls for reform, for restoring what was perceived as the original message of Christianity. The institutional Church tolerated these protests as long as only a few people were involved; when such movements became large, however, the Church reacted by declaring them heresy and thus unacceptable. In some cases, the Church itself led military campaigns or crusades against these groups in the same way that earlier kings persecuted non-Christians once they became Christians themselves—and in the same way the Roman authorities once persecuted the Christian minority.

No single reform was effective in changing the basic structure of the Church that grew up in the early Middle Ages. From 330 on, Christianity would be closely connected with secular governments and would become a wealthy and powerful secular institution in its own right. The form adopted by the Roman church would even survive the theological change of the Protestant Reformation. Though Protestant areas broke with the papacy in Rome, they continued to set up state churches, magnificent buildings, and a hierarchy of officials with great power over many areas of life. Even today the close relationship between church and state begun by Constantine, Clovis, Ethelbert, and Olaf has not ended in Europe; western European countries still support official Christian churches by taxation, even though actual church attendance is low in comparison with the United States.